W9-BRK-195

Stirring the
Head, Heart,
and Soul

SECOND EDITION

Dedicated to my family—
they stir my heart and soul:
Ken, Kenny, Jodie, Kelly,
Patrick, Trevor, and Connor

Stirring the Head, Heart, and Soul

SECOND EDITION

Redefining Curriculum WITHDRAWN and Instruction

H. Lynn Erickson

71.95

For information:

Corwin Press, Inc.
A Sage Publications Company
2455 Teller Road
Thousand Oaks, California 91320
E-mail: order@corwinpress.com

Sage Publications Ltd.
6 Bonhill Street
London EC2A 4PU
United Kingdom

Sage Publications India Pvt. Ltd.
M-32 Market
Greater Kailash I
New Delhi 110 048 India

Printed in the United States of America

Library of Congress Cataloging-in-Publication Data

Erickson, H. Lynn.
    Stirring the head, heart, and soul: Redefining curriculum and instruction /
by H. Lynn Erickson — 2nd ed.
        p.   cm.
    Includes bibliographical references and index.
    ISBN 0-8039-6884-1 (cloth: alk. paper)
    ISBN 0-8039-6885-X (pbk.: alk. paper)
        1. Curriculum change—United States.   2. Curriculum-based assessment—
    United States.   3. Educational change—United States.   4. Educational tests and
    measurements—United States.   I. Title.
        LB1570 .E74   2000
        375′.000973—dc21   00-009940

This book is printed on acid-free paper.

01   02   03   04   05   06   07   7   6   5   4   3   2   1

Production Editor:	Denise Santoyo
Editorial Assistant:	Candice Crossetti
Typesetter/Designer:	Lynn Miyata
Indexer:	Teri Greenberg

Contents

Preface

Innovations launch in schools like fireworks in July. Some explode with a bang, like the "whole language" movement, and whiz back and forth trying to find their philosophical resting place. Some, like the 1970s "new math," shoot straight up and then nose-dive, leaving a trail of fading light. Some give a little "pop," hoping for attention, and some, like the President's Goals and National Standards, implode with a sonic boom as we run for cover from the fallout.

As an educator over the past 32 years, I helped to detonate some of the dazzling displays. Through these experiences, I gained a sense of when to tuck and when to toss from Innovation's door. Eager to aid learning, educators embrace innovation and fad with wholesale zealousness. We buy the program dogma with nary a question, disregarding the research that doesn't fit into the popular paradigm, instead of asking, "What works and is reasonable, and what is not?"

This book will discuss what is reasonable and workable in contemporary curriculum design and provide educators with a practical structure for deciding whether to tuck or toss from the dizzying display of the day. The overriding message throughout this book will be the need to design curriculum and instruction that will guide thinking and learning through the facts to the conceptual level of understanding—the level where knowledge transfers and thinking become integrated.

The standards movement, so prominent today, defines student standards as "what we want our students to know and be able to do by the time they graduate from high school." In districts across the United States, these standards deal with processes and skills, factual content knowledge, and conceptual understanding. Standards provide an anchor for aligning district curricula, but standards vary in their expectations and design. In some states, the design raises the intellectual standard for district curricula; in others, the state design actually impedes quality curricular programming and instruction.

National and state policymakers call for performance-based assessments using "benchmark indicators" of progress, at various grade levels, to ensure that students are attaining the identified process and content abilities. Benchmark indicators are examples of developmental performance, related to the student standards, which have been identified for various grade levels or grade groupings.

This book will examine the current state of curriculum and instruction and propose a curricular plan for achieving higher standards without sacrificing intellectual integrity. The proposed plan will focus on the following premises:

- ♦ Thinking teachers inspire thinking students. We need curriculum frameworks that encourage teachers to use facts and skills to develop deeper understanding of key concepts and principles of disciplines.

- ♦ When curriculum and instruction engage the personal intellect of the students (and teachers), they are more motivated and interested in the study, and students exhibit a greater degree of retention and understanding.

- ♦ Self-assessment is a powerful learning tool for both students and teachers.

- ♦ Curriculum that is relevant to issues surrounding the human condition and our world challenges the intellect and engages the spirit.

- ♦ *Concept-based curricula* are more effective than topic-based curricula, for the world of today and tomorrow, because they take teaching and learning to a higher level as students analyze, synthesize, and generalize from facts to deeper understanding.

- ♦ Concept-based, integrated curriculum provides depth to learning and a focus on relevant issues, problems, and ideas.

As you read the following chapters, you will evaluate the elements and impediments of the change process in learning organizations and look at the factors of time, training, and funding. You will design a vision for learning that links desired student outcomes with sound schooling practice. You will learn new approaches to the development of subject area and integrated curricula, explore the changing character of student assessment, and consider the integral role of technology as a thinking tool. Finally, you will consider what it takes to stir the head, heart, and soul and form a vision of "loving to learn." Students and teachers who love to learn create positive tension and energy that ripple through a room with enthusiasm, curiosity, and creativity. It is my hope that you will leave this book with that same creative tension and energy—loving to learn and eager to stir the head, heart, and soul.

About the Author

H. Lynn Erickson is an independent consultant assisting schools and districts around the country with curriculum design. From 1987 to 1994, she was Director of Curriculum for the Federal Way Public Schools in Federal Way, Washington. She is a recognized presenter at national conferences and is featured in the video, "Creating Concept-Based Curriculum for Deep Understanding" (produced by The Video Journal) as well in videos for the Association for Supervision and Curriculum Development. She is the author of *Concept-Based Curriculum and Instruction: Teaching Beyond the Facts* (1998).

She was born and raised in Fairbanks, Alaska, the daughter of a pioneering gold miner and a first-grade teacher. She graduated from the University of Alaska in 1968 and taught first, second, fourth, and fifth grades, as well as combination classes, while in California. She also served as a reading specialist before moving with her family to Missoula, Montana. At the University of Montana, she earned master's and doctorate degrees in Curriculum and Instruction and Advanced School Administration. She worked as the Curriculum Coordinator for Missoula's Public Schools before becoming an elementary principal for 6 years in Libby, Montana.

She has two grown children, Kelly and Kenneth; a daughter-in-law, Jodie Erickson; a son-in-law, Patrick Cameron; and two grandsons, Trevor and Conner Cameron. They stir her heart and soul. When she isn't traveling to school districts, she enjoys motorcycling and flying (as a passenger) with her life partner, Ken Erickson.

Making Change in a Changing World

THE STATE OF EDUCATIONAL CHANGE

Innovations and Restructuring

Everybody is doing it. Ask an elementary grade teacher in Anywhere, U.S.A., "What are the innovations in your school?" and the litany ensues: "multiple intelligences, *cooperative learning,* integrated curriculum, multiage, inclusion, portfolios, and so on." Secondary schools are joining many of the elementary grade movements and adding innovations of their own, from creative *block scheduling* to theme-based high schools.

The national impetus to restructure schools and improve education has brought us into the best and worst of times. The best of times:

♦ Engaging students in active and meaningful learning

♦ Articulating clearly in curriculum documents what students should know and be able to do in an increasingly complex world

♦ Helping students develop greater self-efficacy and self-esteem as they take more responsibility for learning

♦ Encouraging teachers to design learning experiences for students instead of relying solely on textbooks as the controller of what and how to teach

♦ Critically examining education at all levels in light of changing paradigms for teaching and learning

But the fast pace to incorporate new ways of doing business in schools has created some concerns among teachers:

"How do we know these innovations really make a difference in helping students achieve?"

"We have so many pieces going on in our school—sometimes it feels like an innovation jigsaw puzzle."

"We need a system to make sure we have a coherent, articulated, and coordinated plan for our school program."

"I have concerns about some of the different innovations. Some things just don't feel right."

"We need more time to think, dialogue, and plan in schools. These changes require ongoing development of people and programs."

"Will I still be able to meet state standards and assessments if I take the time to engage students with active learning through these innovations?"

PRESSURE GROUPS

Add to these concerns the conflicting messages from a society carrying multiple agendas and worldviews, and the job of educational change becomes highly complex. Five pressure groups are especially pronounced. It is important to understand their views and concerns if we are to effectively educate to meet the diverse needs of society.

Business and the World of Work

First, there is business and the world of work. The globalization of economics and trade, stimulated by advances in technology, transportation, and world democratization, has changed the traditional business models forever. Employers decry the quality of education in the United States and lament, "If only workers had the skills we need, our companies could be even more economically competitive in the global marketplace."

The Global Economy

The famed economist Lester Thurow (1993), in his provocative and thoughtful book, *Head to Head: The Coming Economic Battle Among Japan, Europe, and America,* cited the following questions as central to the global economic competition:

Who can make the best products? Who expands their standard of living most rapidly? Who has the best-educated and best-skilled work force in the world? Who is the world's leader in investment—plant and equipment, research and development (R&D), infrastructure? Who organizes best? Whose institutions—government, education, business—are world leaders in efficiency? (p. 23)

In his new book, *Building Wealth: New Rules for Individuals, Companies and Countries in a Knowledge-Based Economy,* Thurow (1999) acknowledges that as we enter the 21st century, the United States is economically out in front in the global competition. But there are anxieties. The middle class in the United States is shrinking. Although some people are making economic gains, many more are falling lower. For two thirds of the workforce, real wages are below where they were in 1973.

Thurow (1999) states that the developing industries at the heart of this global competition are all "brainpower industries":

Microelectronics, computers, telecommunications, new man-made materials, robotics, and biotechnology are spawning new industries and re-inventing old industries. . . . The science behind these new industries is revolutionizing our lives. Internet retailing supplants conventional retailing. Cellular telephones are everywhere. Genetically engineered plants and animals appear. . . . It is an era of man-made brain-power industries. For all of human history, the source of wealth has been the control of natural resources—land, gold, oil. Suddenly the answer is "knowledge." The world's wealthiest man, Bill Gates, owns nothing tangible—no land, no gold or oil, no factories, no industrial processes, no armies. . . . The world's wealthiest man owns only knowledge. (pp. xiv-xv)

Will the traditional U.S. curriculum provide the kind of knowledge and skills that our workforce needs to secure a strong future for all? Regular education is aligning *curriculum* and instruction to national and state standards to raise academic levels. Tests, rewards, and sanctions are supposed to motivate excellence. But states vary greatly in the degree to which their standards require conceptual understanding of content knowledge. Some standards are so factually oriented that thinking won't get off the basement floor—"Identify the first governor of _____." Some are so broad and conceptual that it is anyone's guess as to the essential, transferable understandings—"Examine systems." And some are just right—clear and powerful conceptual understandings with enough specificity to bring relevance to the district-defined curricula—"Understand that energy is a property of substances and systems and comes in many forms." Standards need to keep moving toward "just right" in the coming refinements if we are going to develop the kinds of thinking abilities and depth of content knowledge that are required for citizenship as well as work roles.

The rapid changes occurring in the workplace are also affecting the curriculum of school vocational programs by emphasizing problem solving, teamwork, and the use of technology in conjunction with "real-world" simulations and experiences. Robotics, bridge building, laser applications, and CO_2 cars have replaced birdhouses and boxes in the vocational classroom. The critical need for a quality workforce has been a major impetus for the development of high-level skills and student standards in the traditionally differentiated, academic, and vocational classrooms. Model programs blending vocational and academic programming

FIGURE 1.1. SCANS Competencies

Resources: Identifies, organizes, and allocates resources
  A. Time—selects goal-relevant activities, ranks them, allocates time, and prepares and follows schedules
  B. Money—uses or prepares budgets, makes forecasts, keeps records, and makes adjustments to meet objectives
  C. Material and facilities—acquires, stores, allocates, and uses materials or space efficiently
  D. Human resources—assesses skills and distributes work accordingly, evaluates performance, and provides feedback

Information: Acquires and uses information
  A. Acquires and evaluates information
  B. Organizes and maintains information
  C. Interprets and communicates information
  D. Uses computers to process information

Interpersonal: Works with others
  A. Participates as member of a team—contributes to group effort
  B. Teaches others new skills
  C. Serves clients and customers—works to satisfy customers' expectations
  D. Exercises leadership—communicates ideas to justify position, persuades and convinces others, and responsibly challenges existing procedures and policies

exist around the country, through *career paths,* applied academics programs, and tech prep programs. These trends to reinforce school-to-work transitions need to be supported.

The Global Labor Market

The U.S. Secretary of Labor formed a commission called SCANS, the Secretary's Commission on Achieving Necessary Skills (1991), to investigate what is required in today's and tomorrow's workplace and to determine the readiness of our high school students to meet those requirements. In June 1991, the commission issued a report that identified five competencies for workplace success. Figure 1.1 outlines the SCANS competencies.

The SCANS competencies have little to do with the traditional content of schooling. They are high-level personal competencies, and it is apparent they are

---

FIGURE 1.1. Continued

    E. Negotiates—works toward agreements involving exchange of resources and resolves divergent interests

    F. Works with diversity—works well with men and women from diverse backgrounds

Systems: Understands complex interrelationships

    A. Understands systems—knows how social, organizational, and technological systems work and operates effectively in them

    B. Monitors and corrects performance—distinguishes trends, predicts impacts on system operations, diagnoses deviations in systems' performance, and corrects malfunctions

    C. Improves or designs systems—suggests modifications to existing systems and develops new or alternative systems to improve performance

Technology: Works with a variety of technologies

    A. Selects technology—chooses procedures and tools or equipment, including computers and related technologies

    B. Applies technology to task—understands overall intent and proper procedures for setup and operation of equipment

    C. Maintains and troubleshoots equipment—prevents, identifies, or solves problems with equipment, including computers and other technologies

---

SOURCE: *What Work Requires of Schools: A SCANS Report for America 2000.* Washington, DC: U.S. Department of Labor.

---

the kinds of skills and aptitudes that make or break a worker. More people lose jobs because of poorly developed competence in these areas than because of a lack of content knowledge. It is also evident that these are leadership competencies. This means that workers of the future must be independent thinkers, as well as team problem solvers, and should not expect to wait for the answers from a superior.

Salable Skills in the Global Market

In *The Work of Nations*, U.S. Secretary of Labor Robert Reich (1992) reminds us that schools in the 1950s reflected the national economy, with "a standard assembly-line curriculum divided neatly into subjects, taught in predictable units of time, arranged sequentially by grade, and controlled by standardized tests intended to weed out defective units and return them for reworking" (p. 226).

Reich's (1992) book outlines the transformation from a national to a global economy. Reich groups the majority of American jobs into three broad categories of contribution to the global economy. The first two categories are "routine production services" and "in-person services" (pp. 174-176). Routine production services encompass jobs that require repetitive routine, from assembly-line workers to low- and middle-level supervisors who routinely check work and procedures of subordinates. Routine production services do not require high levels of education.

In-person services also encompass simple and repetitive tasks. They do not require education beyond high school, except perhaps some vocational training. In-person service workers, such as waiters, janitors, secretaries, or security guards, interact directly with their customers (Reich, 1992).

Neither category will earn as high a wage as the third category—that of the "symbolic analysts." Symbolic analysts exhibit and refine four basic skills:

- ◆ *Abstraction*—discovering patterns and meanings; using models; constructing analogies, equations, and metaphors to make sense; and rearranging and creating new possibilities from the mass of information available

- ◆ *System thinking*—seeing reality as a system of interacting causes, consequences, and relationships

- ◆ *Experimentation*—applying thought and reason while systematically exploring different options in testing ideas and intuition against past results and assumptions

- ◆ *Collaboration*—working in groups to plan and solve problems and using the key skills of collaboration: communicating abstract ideas, using effective group process techniques, and achieving consensus on direction

Reich (1992) states that it is not necessarily the job title that determines whether a person will have saleable skills in the global marketplace. It is the degree to which a worker exhibits the skills of abstraction, *systems thinking,* experimentation, and collaboration. Secretaries can be symbolic analysts if they perform with the high-level skills, and lawyers can be routine production workers if they churn out standard forms with little thought (Reich, 1992).

Why are these skills so important for high-level success in the 21st century? Because they allow a person to use and manipulate information to invent, reinvent, and create. As Thurow (1999) states,

> Knowledge is the new basis for wealth. . . . [But] how do societies have to be re-organized to generate a wealth enhancing knowledge environment? What causes the entrepreneurs necessary to effect changes and create wealth to sprout? . . . What skills are needed? Where do natural and environmental resources fit into the new knowledge economy? How does one use "knowledge" to build a new wealth pyramid for the individual, for the company, and for society? (pp. xv, xvi)

Advances in technology have created a time warp, in which old methods and ways of thinking leave industries in the dust and in which expanded communication and interdependence demand big-picture thinking. In business and in our communities, we must now deal with the issues and complexities of global systems— economic, social, and political.

William Greider (1997), in *One World, Ready or Not: The Manic Logic of Global Capitalism,* states, "The national interest must now find expression in the far more complex context of the collective global interest." For example,

> The history of nation-states . . . has been a series of armed contests for territory and domination, but the traditional geopolitical assumptions are now quite confused as global commerce dilutes the meaning of national borders and constructs complex webs of interdependence. . . . It becomes increasingly difficult to select a proper enemy—someone who is not also a major customer or co-producer. (pp. 470-471)

State Governments

State governments are the second pressure group. They set up commissions and panels to evaluate and plan for a restructured system of education. Goals are defined and standards set. But have state governments required academic standards that would develop the conceptual and critical thinking abilities alluded to by Reich and Thurow? People who are ready to flexibly address the rapidly changing problems and issues of a complex, interdependent world? A review of state standards will show that some states realize that the job of state standards is to set a conceptual framework for nesting the specific content of the local districts. Other states have mandated standards that resemble the district curricular frameworks of old—right down to the last war, date, and general. If they only realized the impact in classrooms—as teachers race to cover more material, faster, the goal of intellectual pursuit is forced to compete with trivial pursuit.

Government in the United States has largely supported the idea of school competition—the panacea offered by business for the problems of education. So vouchers are offered to parents to "buy" the education of choice. A menu of schooling types spring up from religious private schools to business-run, for-profit schools to public schools.

The business-run schools have not yet convinced the nation that they know the way out of the forest. *Education Week* ("Report Card," 1999) states that in the extended evaluations of three private business enterprises to run schools, only the Edison Schools have shown truly positive academic gains so far. Edison Schools Corporation has been managing public schools for districts and charter groups for approximately 6 years. Based in New York City, Edison Schools now operates 79 schools around the country and serve approximately 38,000 students.

A review of the Edison School data by the American Federation of Teachers (AFT) concluded that the academic results appeared more mixed than suggested by the company, however. Nancy Van Meter, an associate director in the AFT's

Department of Organizations and Field Services, stated in *Education Week,* "We have looked at the track record of most of the for-profit education management organizations, and to date, we are fairly unimpressed with the educational programs they are offering" ("Report Card," 1999, p. 15). As we watch for-profits eagerly enter the field of education, we have to wonder the following:

◆ Where are they finding their teachers? Have they been trained at different preservice institutions than our regular public school teachers?

◆ Who is designing their curricula? How are they different from the curricula that are currently being taught in public schools? Is it just "more technology" and perhaps "foreign language earlier"? Or is it truly an insightfully designed masterpiece that meets the needs of developing learners of varying abilities?

◆ Do the for-profits accept all students—or do they find ways to be selective? There have been accusations of selectivity among private schools for many years.

◆ Who trains the teachers in for-profit schools, and what is the content of their inservice training? Are they getting the same training that public school teachers receive?

◆ Just what are the magic bullets that purport to make for-profit schools succeed over public schools?

As a result of the charter school movement, many public school districts such as Boston, Massachusetts, and Toledo, Ohio, have started their own innovative charter schools rather than pay money and lose students to the for-profits. It will be interesting to watch the results of these public charter schools.

One thing is certain—to prepare students for the new millennium curriculum, instruction must change from traditional models based on coverage and rote memorization. They must change because these old models do not develop the conceptual and critical thinking abilities that are now essential for complex problem solving.

So whether schools are public, private, or for-profit, they need a deeper understanding of how to redesign curriculum and instruction. Otherwise, the national frustration over schooling will continue.

Social Forces

Besides the pressure from business and government, schools are being affected by social forces: increasing immigration that brings many cultures and languages into the classroom, environmental pressures, drugs and alcohol, ongoing poverty, and increasing violence among children. In recent years, the United

States has experienced alarming gun violence in schools from Denver, Colorado to Paducah, Kentucky.

The United Nations International Children's Emergency Fund (UNICEF) issued a report in the fall of 1993 stating that the U.S. homicide rate for young people ages 15 to 24 is five times that of its nearest competitor, Canada. Nine out of 10 young people murdered in industrialized countries are killed in the United States. For young men of color, the homicide rate is particularly alarming. For all of our talk of equal opportunity and the American Dream, we are failing a large segment of our young people, and the consequences sting the conscience. The UNICEF (1999) report goes on to say that child poverty in the United States has increased from 15% in 1970 to 20% in 1992. The poverty rate for children in the United States is more than double that of any other major industrialized nation. Among the 10 wealthiest nations, only the United States and the United Kingdom have experienced declines in the social health indicators of children. Out of 27 industrialized nations, the United States ranks 19th in infant survival rates. The mortality rates among African American infants run high at 18 per 1,000 births. And although we are making progress for children in many areas, the overall statistics are still grim. According to the UNICEF report for 1999 supporting the Convention on the Rights of the Child, the United States still has one of the highest rates of hunger among children and suffers one of the highest infant mortality rates among industrialized countries. Nearly three quarters of all child murders in the industrialized world occur in the United States (UNICEF, 1999). At a time when schools are being called on to educate all children to high standards, the inequality at the starting gate is glaring.

Another factor in the growing poverty rate is the large increase in U.S. immigration. With 1.2 million legal and illegal immigrants coming across our borders each year, we are feeling the effects on schools and social systems. The seeds for conflict are present. But increasing migration of peoples worldwide is a reality.

Schools have been thrust to center stage as they wrap their arms around the children of the world. At times, a teacher may have six or more languages and cultures in the classroom. Yet our teachers have had very little training on how to effectively instruct such cultural diversity. Clearly, the schools need to have a focused agenda for meeting the needs of a growing multicultural population. The diversity of the United States is its greatness. No other country in the world has as rich a diversity in customs, perspectives, values, and beliefs. We can value the diversity and see it as a great opportunity, or we can resist.

International education is a critical element in a future-oriented curriculum. The single Eurocentric viewpoint is no longer conscionable as the only perspective to be presented on world issues. As students learn about other cultures, they grow to value diversity as an opportunity for expanded perspective and knowledge. At the same time, schools must teach the values and principles of democracy and a free society. Separating into ethnic enclaves, without the common bond of shared beliefs outlined in the U.S. Constitution and the Federalist Papers, puts us at risk for the internal ethnic and religious conflict so common in other parts of the world.

Media

Media are the fourth pressure group. They highlight the negative, whether crime, violence, corruption, or falling standardized test scores. It is interesting that in repeated national surveys, parents grade their own child's school as doing an A or B job, but the nation's schools in general are perceived as failing (Coles, 1999). How great a role does the media play in the national view? Research psychologist and educational writer, Gerald Bracey, in a report for the *Phi Delta Kappan* (1998, p. 113), discusses the negative reporting on education in the United States. He points out that writers who try to provide a positive or even balanced view of education are paid little attention in the press. He cites examples such as the book, *The Manufactured Crisis* by David Berliner and Bruce Biddle (1997), and articles by Princeton economist Alan Krueger (1998) and Peter Schrag (1997), retired editor of the *Sacramento Bee*. Both examined and presented data contrary to the notion that our public schools had failed. What if publishers insisted that a positive story in education had to be written for every negative story? The same should occur for our other institutions such as law enforcement and government. I fear that the ongoing negative diatribe is beginning to engender a breakdown of support for and potential collapse of our institutional social structure.

The truth is that education does need improvement but not because of teacher or administrator failures. The problem is based in rapidly changing societal needs that are centered on economics, demographics, and the rapid growth of information. We have a systems problem. The old system of education is not functional for delivering the highly cognitive, conceptual, and technical skills that are needed for the 21st century. And the old system cannot be changed without massive retraining of teachers and administrators and more effective curricular and instructional models. This retraining needs to include the teacher training institutions that are too often churning out the same old, same old. . . .

Parents

The final pressure group—the one that I feel the most concern for—is the parents. What a confusing time for them! Between the mixed messages coming from the media, business, the government, and the schools, parents often don't know what to think. No wonder so many parents are opting for private or home schooling. Never before has the need to include parents in the educational setting been more urgent.

Educational change will only occur in a cooperative, problem-solving partnership with business, the community, and parents. The current aura of blaming impedes progress by generating feelings of hopelessness. By addressing the needs at the building level, supporting teachers and administrators, dialoging as a community, and addressing the desired student outcomes with an analytical systems roach, we can align public schooling with societal and individual needs.

SHARING THE JOB OF QUALITY EDUCATION

Parents as Partners

Parents need to understand the changing world and how education is working to provide students with the skills for success in the 21st century. Progressive schools cooperatively plan the educational program with parents and see that they are involved in the educational process whether that be at the school site or as support to their children at home.

Traditionally in education, we have opened our doors only slightly to parents. We have engaged them as volunteers for various activities but have had difficulty communicating our plan for learning. Today, educators must find ways to include parents in defining the aims of education and show how the school learning plan is focused toward achieving those aims. Parents want and deserve to be active partners in their children's educational experience.

Parents are feeling heightened anxiety for the safety as well as the education of their children. In a society that is increasingly violent and threatening and in which guns appear to be as plentiful as bubble gum, parents naturally hold their children close. They want to see plans to ensure the safety and well-being of children in school. This must be an issue for the community as well as the school.

Community and Business as Partners

Education is a community venture with schools, churches, health, welfare, and law enforcement agencies working together to provide for the needs of children. In some communities, there are excellent communication networks between the public agencies. Help to families is focused and timely. In other communities, there is a breakdown in relationships. Families wait months for assistance from overburdened case workers or suffer from duplication of effort between agencies.

One particularly effective model in a small community in Montana calls together an interagency task force that includes representatives from the schools, health and human service agencies, law enforcement, and the clergy. This task force meets on a monthly basis to dialogue and develop ways to serve the many families they share more effectively and efficiently. Task force members become acquainted as professionals and open lines of communication to serve individual families efficiently.

Business, as another important segment of the community, also has an important role in education. Certainly, many of the requested changes in schooling are emanating from the needs of business. Businesses have changed their requirements for education. Now they need workers who can process and use knowledge in solving complex problems while working as members of a team.

Many businesses around the country today provide positive support to schools through business partnerships. These businesses aid schools through activities, such as allowing employees to speak to classes during the workday or providing funding to support the development of curriculum and technology in schools. The business world wants technologically literate workers, but computers and more advanced technologies are still in scarce supply in too many schools. Helping schools solve the problem of an inadequate supply of technology would be one of the best ways for businesses to help boost school change into the 21st century.

THE GOVERNMENT AS A PARTNER

The Dilemma of Time and Funding . . . in a Minute . . . With a Nickel

There are policymakers who have difficulty understanding why education is so slow to change. They believe that if educational standards and tests are developed for students and high stakes are set for both students and schools, the change process will occur naturally. But educators know that these changes are a major transformation in outcomes, teaching paradigms, techniques, and materials. They require long-term cooperation and commitment for training and funding.

Two examples come to mind to demonstrate the complexity of curricular and instructional change. The first one deals with the process of curriculum development related to state standards and subsequent classroom implementation.

Educators feel the pressure to meet state and local standards. The stakes are high. Some states, such as Florida, are giving letter grades to individual public schools based on their standardized test scores and factored criteria. Grades are published in the newspaper, and teachers' salaries are soon to be tied to student performance. Merit pay is on the horizon. With stakes this high, teachers deserve quality curricular documents. But the reality in many states is that the state standards to which local documents are "aligned" are very poor. In some states, the standards are so detailed and comprehensive that teachers could never even "cover" the information demanded, let alone help students intellectually process the information. Standards between disciplines also vary in the way they are written and in their expectations.

Because the national science standards are so well conceived and written, the state and local standards documents usually follow suit. They are concise and clear and can lead to deeper, conceptual understanding. The history standards in too many states, on the other hand, have fallen into the trap of trying to write specific curricula, usually as a set of traditional objectives: list, identify, and explain (causes and effects).

Teachers need explanations as to how standards are written, the expectations, and what the standards imply for instruction. We cannot assume that by handing these curricular documents to teachers, they will be understood and used effectively. The formats and expectations vary too much from discipline to discipline.

When state frameworks are poorly done, local curriculum committees need to know how to make adaptations to address the deficiencies. This is not easy work. After quality curricular and assessment programs have been developed, teachers need intensive in-service and time to develop new instructional pedagogy and skills for the classroom. It is imperative that school districts have quality leadership in curriculum and instruction at both the central and site levels. Principals cannot afford to be managers only. The heartbeat of schools is the curricular and instructional program for students.

The second example revolves around the definition of *depth of instruction.* Under the traditional fact-based paradigm, depth of instruction is too often thought of as "teaching more facts about a topic." In a concept-based paradigm, depth of instruction means using the fact base as a tool to teach for a deeper understanding of the key concepts and principles of a discipline. This shift in definition highlights the need for change in instruction as teachers challenge their own thinking to facilitate student thinking. Content serves not as an end product but as a tool for deeper thought.

The increasing emphasis on critical and conceptual thinking in schooling requires a level of staff development that goes far beyond "make it and take it" workshops or five early-release-day presentations by experts. The level of staff development that is necessary to effect the needed changes in curriculum, instruction, and systems planning is ongoing and weekly. If legislators are serious about wanting an improved educational system, they will concede the time needed for teachers and administrators to interact as professionals in learning new skills.

I have seen the greatest school improvements when teachers and administrators are given time to deal intellectually and in depth with the essential questions related to their profession in a changing world. The school year should be extended so teachers have one morning per week for professional dialogue, curriculum writing, and staff development. It is critical that educators be accountable for this time, however, by showing results to their community.

It is important to hold the staff and curriculum development time in the morning. The high level of staff development and curriculum work to be undertaken requires alert minds. The higher the quality of thinking that is brought to planning, the better the program for students. Results should show for students by the second year if the time is well used.

Some schools are following a model of early release days, but I have found this model to be insufficient. It is often only an hour or an hour and a half long. This is too short a time to complete any meaningful dialogue or work. Some teachers also feel compelled to attend to other business during that time, which erodes the school-based, professional focus.

Numerous schools in states such as Washington, Oregon, Florida, and Alaska are now banking time by extending the school day for a few minutes and shortening the passing time between classes. Banked time is turned into a 3-hour late arrival day for students on alternating weeks. We will not see the kind of school transformation we are seeking without this time. Teachers in Germany and Japan have longer school years but have much less contact time with students during the day. They have the time to dialogue, plan, and learn together.

Big business recognizes the need for quality training of its employees. Education is one of the largest businesses, and the job is human development. This job is far more complex than following a standard blueprint to build a standard product. The job of human development takes the individual child in whatever form and guides and nurtures the mind, body, and self-concept. If we raise the expectations for teachers and administrators, then we owe them the training they need to meet the changing requirements. We get what we pay for. If we expect major change, in a minute, with a nickel, we will get what we paid for—minute change.

MAKING CHANGE THE SYSTEMS WAY

Senge and Systems Thinking

Two recommended books for all policymakers, leaders, and organizations involved in change are *The Fifth Discipline* by Peter Senge (1990) and his follow-up book, *Dance of Change: The Challenge of Sustaining Momentum in Learning Organizations* (1999). Central to Senge's thesis in the first book is the view that

> learning organizations . . . where people continually expand their capacity to create the results they truly desire, where new and expansive patterns of thinking are nurtured, where collective aspiration is set free, and where people are continually learning how to learn together . . . develop in a culture which embraces systems thinking. (Senge, 1990, p. 2)

Systems thinking, states Senge, is a framework for looking at the interrelationships and patterns of change over time. Too often, events are perceived in isolation, and quick fixes for symptoms are applied. Systems thinking is the "integrating discipline" for seeing the underlying structures that need to be considered in making change (Senge, 1990, p. 69).

Senge (1990) calls the critical components for a learning organization "disciplines." The first four disciplines—personal mastery, mental models, building shared vision, and team learning—are integrated through the fifth discipline, systems thinking. Senge (1990, pp. 7-10) gives the following definitions:

- ♦ *Personal Mastery*—the discipline of continually clarifying and deepening our personal vision, focusing our energies, developing patience, and seeing reality objectively.

- ♦ *Mental Models*—deeply ingrained assumptions, *generalizations,* or even pictures or images that influence how we understand the world and how we take action.

♦ *Building Shared Vision*—the capacity to build and hold a shared picture of the future we seek to create. People with shared vision have . . . genuine commitment and enrollment rather than compliance.

♦ *Team Learning*—the ability to dialogue and suspend assumptions while entering into a genuine "thinking together." Team learning also involves learning how to recognize the patterns of interaction in teams that undermine learning.

A major difficulty in the restructuring of schools is a lack of the five disciplines in action. People work in their comfort zones, each tinkering with a piece of the whole. But a coordinated, systemic plan for change is too often absent. Policymakers insist on tests; assessment people comply. Principals encourage teachers to risk and try new ideas; teachers comply. A plethora of new buzzword innovations sweep into classrooms but are seldom evaluated for their contributions to increased student success. Teachers and principals request time to dialogue, plan, and design effective programs, but there is a breakdown in the system because this essential need remains but a whisper at the budget and policy tables. It is feared that parents would never support the scheduling change. Parents need to be informed as to the complexity of the changes being asked of us. We must gain their support for these reasonable requests for time.

The five disciplines as defined by Senge are about professional communication, interaction, and development. Learning organizations will be as effective as their wise and focused use of precious time in cultivating these five disciplines.

OVERCOMING OBSTACLES: OVER, UNDER, THROUGH, AND AROUND

Educators have an indomitable spirit. Despite a lack of coordinated problem solving and systems thinking in school districts, teachers and administrators strive to improve education for the students in their schools. A powerful point made by Senge (1990) is that learning organizations move forward on the collective vision and actions of people. They overcome obstacles and achieve their goals because they are all headed in the same direction, toward a shared vision.

Systems design considers all players when building a shared vision. When business works with government to require certain standards from schools, then business becomes part of the system. Parents, too, are part of the system. So are the community agencies that support children and families. It is admittedly difficult to effect a coordinated and coherent vision because of diverse perspectives and a natural resistance to change.

In *Dance of Change,* Senge (1999) reminds us of the scientific principle that nature presents inhibitors to change. That same principle applies to human change, says Senge. When learning organizations and leaders seek to create change, they need to remember that there will be inhibiting factors. It is not enough to implore people in the organization to "change, grow, try harder." Leaders must anticipate the inhibiting factors and address them preemptively. These inhibiting factors can be the naysayers: "We've done this before. It will never work. We don't have time or materials to do this." Or they may be systems issues—"How can we get everyone in different departments and institutions to work together on this?" Senge presents many suggestions and strategies for helping learning organizations with the change process in his most recent book.

The next chapter presents an introduction to the idea of concept-based curriculum design. Concept-based curriculum provides a more efficient model for handling the massive amounts of information available today, focuses teaching and learning to more sophisticated levels, and provides hope for truly raising standards in education. Without addressing the inherent problems in the basic structure of traditional curriculum designs, educational change will fall short of the goal of raising standards.

SUMMARY

Teachers and administrators are caught in the crosshairs of conflicting messages and actions from pressure groups. Everyone wants higher academic standards for schools, but legislators create cattle-prod policies of punishment and reward, vouchers, choice, and competition. They want educational excellence but encourage state standards that at times are antithetical to excellence because they promote low-level coverage over intellectual engagement. The focus is on assessment before teachers have been trained to teach to higher standards. Media have a field day reporting test scores and school letter grades, and parents question, worry, and shuffle their children around, shopping for the best deal.

A committed partnership between schools, parents, business, and the community is essential to a quality plan for education. A systems approach to the education of each child brings the parts into a coherent whole—and the children are the winners.

Curriculum and instruction are critical focal points for educational change. This job cannot be done effectively without providing quality time each week for professional dialogue, training of staff, and curriculum development. Teachers deserve quality *curriculum frameworks* that will allow them to raise intellectual and academic standards.

The purpose of educational change is to better meet the needs of our students today and to prepare them for the future. Change just for the sake of change is wheel spinning. Change for the sake of children is our job, and we are ready and willing.

EXTENDING THOUGHT

1. Why must education become a community partnership in the systems view?

2. What questions should parents ask of educators today?

3. How would you respond to those questions as an educator?

4. Describe your vision of an insightful and appropriate curricular and instructional program for students in the new millennium.

5. The dilemmas of little time and short funding are school realities. How can you creatively and practically "make time" and "find funding"?

6. What kind of training do teachers need to raise standards for all students?

7. What should be included in a "well-rounded" education for students today?

8. What are the main impediments to change in your school or district? How would you address those impediments as a leader?

9. How would *you* characterize leadership?

2 Concept-Based Curriculum

We are caught in a curious blend of old content and new. Societal trends have foisted a pot of mulligan stew at the schoolhouse door. Curricula for AIDS, personal safety, and drugs and alcohol, developed with the best of intentions, threaten to drive teachers to the brink. Add to these ingredients the breadth of content and skills delineated in national and state standards and district curricular frameworks. Principals cringe to hear that they must ask teachers to toss in just "one more thing." This continual addition of ingredients into the simmering curriculum stew has created a crisis. We are losing sight of the significant knowledge and ideas. They are drowning in the mix.

Process outcomes address the personal abilities that students will need for responding to the trends, but they do nothing to address the problems of subject area content. How do we make decisions on what content is most valuable to include in our limited school hours? And how do we ensure that meaningless content will be replaced?

♦ Community organizations develop full curricula on specific topics to help educate future citizens to their cause. Fire, water, energy, teeth, heart, fitness, smoking, personal development, safety, and recycling—all are socially valuable. But are we tossing together a curriculum of fragmented topics, rather than a reasoned, coordinated, and articulated plan for learning?

♦ Elementary teachers collect a myriad of instructional material through the years. But how can we use all that "stuff"? The current wisdom is "less is more."

♦ American history classes live in the past and race toward the future but often crash at the end of World War II. (Some determinedly speed through to Vietnam.) The dogged pursuit of a chronological compendium of events contributes to the loss of the significant understandings—the lasting lessons of history.

Figure 2.1. Traditional-Model Fact-Based Curricula

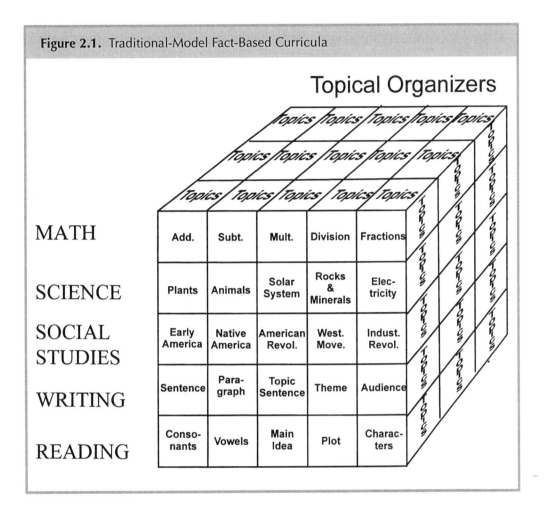

TRADITIONAL CURRICULUM

Many teachers still rely heavily on textbooks to tell them what to teach. Yet textbooks, because of their topic focus, usually cover too much content and fail to address the higher-level, lasting ideas that can be applied to current and future trends.

For the past 100 years, our curriculum has been governed by discrete subject areas and topical organizers for content. Figure 2.1 shows the traditional model of discrete subjects, topics, and content. The unwavering focus in schooling has been on memorization of an increasing body of facts and the practice of skills.

The problem with this model is that the information base in our world is challenging the best of microchips. School districts try to keep up with this information explosion by looking to state standards as the parameters for what to teach. But the design of local curriculum frameworks usually resembles the traditional booklets and lists of isolated student learning *objectives* that were prevalent in the early 1980s because that is what we know. Although we do need skill-based objectives, the format for writing content objectives usually tickles only the lowest cognitive levels and serves as fodder for a trivia pursuit intellect.

There are several effects of this lower-level love affair with trivia. Perhaps most significantly, studying topics and facts as information to be memorized fails to engage the deeper intellect of students. When students are encouraged to think beyond the facts and connect factual knowledge to ideas of conceptual significance, they find relevance and personal meaning. When students become personally and intellectually engaged, they are more motivated to learn because their emotions are involved. They are mind-active rather than mind-passive. Could the lack of personal, intellectual engagement be a major reason that so many students exhibit apathy toward their studies?

A second effect of "coverage" of content is that we miss the deeper, transferable understandings. Kings, queens, dates, and the presidents and all their men: What significance do they hold for understanding our world and the human condition? Certainly, they hold little significance as isolated bits of stored memory. But as key historical players in life's drama, their social situations, actions, and reactions hold lasting lessons for understanding the human condition today and for predicting the world of tomorrow.

There is ongoing debate between historians and social studies educators as to the best approach for teaching content. Both groups have developed a set of national standards for their discipline, and both integrate economics, politics, sociology, anthropology, and geography. The primary differences appear to be in pedagogy and approaches to content:

♦ Historians use specific events and people to teach historical thinking and avoid conceptual generalizations.

♦ Social studies educators use specific events and people to teach historical thinking but encourage students to identify the lessons of history and the human experience by relating specific content to conceptual generalizations.

Sam Wineburg (1999), professor of educational psychology and history at the University of Washington, wrote an article for the *Phi Delta Kappan* called "Historical Thinking and Other Unnatural Acts." Wineburg includes in the article a cogent explanation as to why historians basically eschew the practice of generalizing in history and balances this view with the realization that one cannot understand the past without relating to the thread of human experience.

The study of history pivots on a tension between the familiar and the strange, between feelings of proximity to and feelings of distance from the people we seek to understand. . . . [But] we discard or just ignore vast regions of the past that either contradict our current needs or fail to align easily with them . . . we contort the past to fit the predetermined meaning we have already assigned to it. . . . Yet, taken to extremes, regarding the past "on its own terms"—detached from the circumstances, concerns, and needs of the present—too often results in esoteric exoticism . . . which fails to engage the interest of anyone except a small coterie of professionals. (p. 490)

Wineburg (1999) goes on to quote the philosopher Hans-Georg Gadamer:

How can we overcome established modes of thought when it is these modes that permit understanding in the first place? . . . Trying to shed what we know to glimpse the "real" past is like trying to examine microbes with the naked eye: the very instruments we abandon are the ones that enable us to see. (p. 492)

Historians have a valid concern in one respect—generalizations may make it too easy for students of history to wrap the complexities of events, issues, and people from different times and places into neat little summary statements. I have seriously considered this argument. But then I look at the current history standards and am struck with the realization that historians want it both ways. They want students to develop historical thinking (a laudable aim), and they want students to know every war, date, and general (figuratively speaking). We can't have it both ways because each goal takes a great deal of time. If the breadth of content forces teachers to choose, they are going to emphasize the fact study because they perceive that is what will be tested. And in most cases, they are correct. It is harder to assess historical thinking because it includes factual knowledge, conceptual understanding, and reasoning ability. Yet it is historical thinking that will develop depth of understanding and the ability to critically reason.

As I have watched and worked with history teachers, I have seen the generalizations and guiding questions actually stimulate historical thinking abilities. When students (and teachers) consider specific events, issues, and historical figures through a conceptual lens, they are forced to analyze, evaluate, and investigate at deeper levels as they consider the transferable legitimacy of an idea.

Wineburg (1999) concludes in his article that our best chance at having students "understand" the past is to develop their "sensibility" to the time, culture, perspectives, and people. They must engage with primary source documents and literature that convey the emotions and perspectives of the time. They will naturally want to use their experience as a frame of reference, but we can broaden that frame by heightening their sensibilities. Wineburg points out that most history textbooks are written in a dispassionate, dry discourse and do little to develop historical sensibility. (And we wonder why history is one of the least favored subjects among students.)

The model presented in this book will show how the events of history can become lessons of history with the focused exploration of concepts and representative examples viewed through time. Culture, change and continuity, trade, justice, law and order, and diversity and commonality can serve as conceptual lenses. A

FIGURE 2.2. This Is Critical Content

SOURCE: Cartoon by David Ford. *david@twocrowcartoons.com*

conceptual lens forces students to think through and beyond the facts to consider the transferable lessons of history—the generalizations that highlight patterns and connections of human experience.

In *The Disciplined Mind,* Howard Gardner (1999) states,

> It should be clear by now why a "fact-based" approach will make even less sense in the future. One can never attain a disciplined mind simply by mastering facts—one must immerse oneself deeply in the specifics of cases and develop one's disciplinary muscles from such immersion. (p. 126)

Gardner is a leader in the popular view that understanding is a performance—a "public exhibition" of what one knows and is able to do.

Gardner (1999) provides many examples of quality performances in his book—performances that reflect conceptual or disciplinary depth and breadth. But the reality in many classrooms is that the rich "performances" Gardner advocates materialize as shallower "activities" that fall short of a demonstration of understanding. I believe this happens because our curriculum designs do not explicitly state the deeper ideas, and, consequently, classroom performances demonstrate a skill tied to a topic rather than to an understanding.

Some state standards unknowingly reinforce this confusion of activity for performance. For example, the following performance indicator might be suggested for teachers as evidence that a student understands that "governments influence the lives of citizens":

Performance indicator: Identify the rules that people are asked to follow.

This performance indicator shows us that students can identify rules but stops short of understanding governmental influence.

Concept-based curriculum raises the bar for curriculum design, instruction, and assessment in history because it forces students to use meta-analysis to evaluate historical issues. The big ideas, guiding questions, and related performances cause students to examine and understand the particular perspectives, emotions, causes, and effects of events and issues in different times and places.

CONCEPT-BASED CURRICULUM

Concepts are the foundational organizers for both *integrated curriculum* and for single-subject curriculum design. They serve as a bridge between topics and generalizations.

Hilda Taba, a visionary educator of the 1950s and 1960s, saw the value of conceptual organizers for content. Her research on developing higher levels of thinking was funded through a Federal Department of Education Research Project, which she completed in February 1966 at San Francisco State College. Today, more than ever before, we need to reexamine Taba's views and extend her work— because she provides positive direction for increasing the intellectual functioning of students. Development of critical and creative thinking is essential for the 21st-century challenge.

HISTORICAL PERSPECTIVE: HILDA TABA

Taba (1966) refers to concepts as "high level abstractions expressed in verbal cues and labels, e.g., interdependence, cultural change and causality" (p. 48). She knew that a person's understanding of a concept grows as he or she experiences increasingly complex, conceptual examples. In science, for example, a student might learn about the concept of force at Grades 4, 8, and 12, but the specific examples would represent increasingly complex principles as the child progressed (see Table 2.1).

Taba (1966) referred to "generalizations and principles" as the main ideas of the content under study. She differentiated generalizations from principles by stat-

TABLE 2.1 Gradated Examples of Force

Grade 4: General Science	Grade 8: Physical Science	Grade 12: Physics
Force as action/reaction	Newton's second law of momentum	Friction
		Hydraulics
Pulleys and force	Machines and gravity	Pneumatics
Gravity as a force	Pressure	Torque
Reduction of force	Energy transfer	Inclined plane
		Trajectory
		Force and planets

ing that generalizations usually include qualifiers in their statements, such as, "Conflict is often caused by differences in values and beliefs." Taba proposed that content coverage could be focused and delimited by letting the main ideas—the generalizations—determine the direction and depth for instruction. She held that specific content should be sampled rather than covered (Taba, 1966, p. 49).

Another insightful Taba truism was the observation that learning has multiple objectives—the learning of content and the learning of increasingly sophisticated behaviors in thinking, attitudes, and skills—and these objectives call for different forms of instruction at different levels of complexity.

Taba's (1966) study consisted of an experimental research design using a trained group of 12 teachers and a control group of 12 untrained teachers. All of the elementary grade teachers instructed students with a social studies curriculum that used topics and facts as a vehicle for teaching to major concepts and main ideas.

The trained teachers received 10 days of intensive instruction on using the social studies curriculum to develop students' cognitive processing abilities. Trained teachers learned to sequence and pace instruction to allow for maximum student response. The concept formation strategy required students to identify what they were seeing, formulate groupings of items by common characteristics, and label and subsume like items under organizing concepts.

Taba (1966) found that the cognitive maps of the teacher were critical to facilitating the cognitive development of the child. By *cognitive map*, Taba was referring to the levels of understanding related to the content under study, as well as the nature of the thinking processes. The teacher's task of "protecting the student's creative and autonomous thinking" while reinforcing the logic of content called for high sensitivity in the instructional setting (p. 60).

Taba's (1966) research found that students in the trained groups showed a greater number of thought units, which were also longer and more complex than the control groups. The trained students exhibited the convergence of low- and high-level thought units into logical generalizations (the main ideas) related to the content.

Although the greatest problem for the teachers was a feeling of pressure to cover the curriculum, test results demonstrated that the time spent on process teaching and learning did not impede strong achievement in learning the fact-based information (Taba, 1966).

CONCEPTUAL ORGANIZERS

A conceptually organized curriculum helps solve the problem of the overloaded curriculum. Concepts bring focus and depth to study and lead students to the enduring understandings. It is important to clarify the issue of concepts in general before we return to their value in curriculum organization.

What Is a Concept?

A universal concept is a mental construct that is timeless, universal, and abstract. Although the specific examples of a concept may vary, the general descriptors of the concept will be the same. "Symmetry," as a concept, has many different examples, but the descriptors of symmetry in all of the examples are the same. Examples of symmetry can be found across disciplines, as in art, life science, or music. The descriptors or characteristics include "balance" and "equivalence."

Concepts are a higher level of abstraction than facts in the structure of knowledge. They serve as cells for categorizing the factual examples. Conceptual understanding continues to grow more sophisticated as new examples fill each concept cell. Because higher-level concepts are timeless, they may be studied through the ages. Because they are universal, their examples may be derived from cultures around the world.

It is common in educational circles today to hear the word *theme* being used for the ideas I am defining as concepts. The problem I have found with this practice is that the definition of *theme* is so loose that topics sometimes become confused with concepts. This is a significant problem in integrated curriculum if the goal is higher-level, integrated-unit design. Units centered on a topic alone will only result in coordinated, multidisciplinary curriculum. This means that two or more subjects, or disciplines, are coordinated in instructional time and content to focus on a single topic. Integrated curriculum, described in detail in Chapter 4, requires a conceptual as well as a topical focus if thinking is to be integrated.

Where Do Concepts Fall in the Structure of Knowledge?

Figure 2.3 illustrates the relationship of concepts to topics and facts, generalizations, principles, and theories in the structure of knowledge. Traditionally in

FIGURE 2.3. The Structure of Knowledge

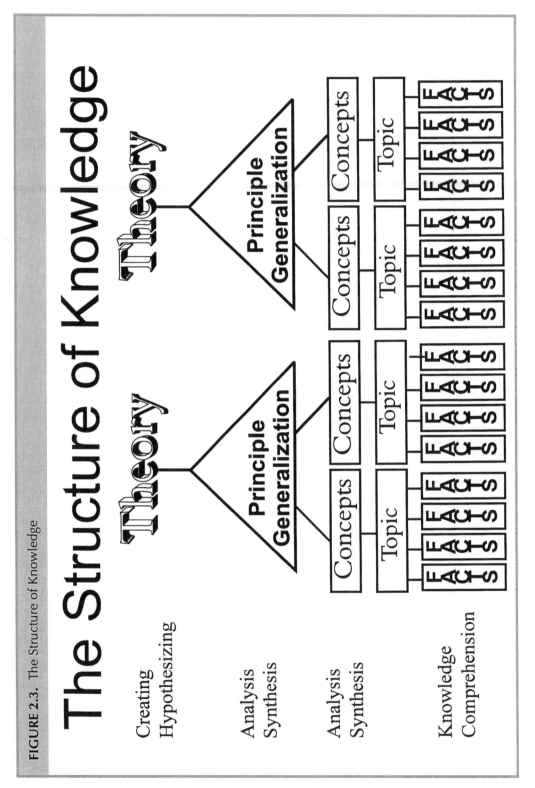

education, we have spent the majority of our content study on the lowest cognitive level, the memorization of isolated facts.

The often-quoted Third International Mathematics and Science Study (TIMMS) study that compared U.S. curriculum to higher achieving industrialized countries really characterizes the problem best: "American curriculum is an inch deep and a mile wide" (TIMMS, 1996). Although there is controversy over whether the TIMMS research is an unbiased and accurate international comparison, no one can argue that the United States covers far more content than other industrial nations. Common sense tells us that massive content coverage will be intellectually shallow when time is limited.

I was surprised to realize, through my work in curriculum, the generally shallow cognitive level most of us have experienced as students in our educational paths. I now think this is largely the result of fact-based rather than idea-based emphases in textbook and curriculum design. And we often teach as we were taught. Educators today, however, know that students must be actively and mentally engaged in their learning. As a result, they are adjusting the learning experience. Unfortunately, many textbook materials and some standards continue to be structured with low cognitive expectations and a continued emphasis on coverage over intellectual engagement.

Some people would argue that students cannot apply higher-level thinking processes until they have a wealth of foundational knowledge. But that is not so. As a first-grade teacher, I enlisted creative and critical thinking from my students in the solution of problems. For example, using the concept of *want* versus *need,* my students built new homes for our two imaginary pets, Chalk Mouse and Pencil Mouse. Chalk Mouse kept eating the teacher's chalk, and Pencil Mouse chewed on the pencils. They lost their homes in a natural disaster (the custodian accidentally disposed of them). The charge for students was to decide what Chalk Mouse and Pencil Mouse would "need" and "want" in a home.

All students gathered their own materials for the project and went to work. They had chalk and pencils for them to eat, water to drink, ladders for their use in climbing up and down from desks, and soft straw to lie on. Needless to say, this was the expression of critical and creative thinking at its finest. The room was buzzing with discussion of need versus want. The critical point is that the students were responsible for solving the problem. I'm sorry to say that Chalk Mouse turned to dust with the invention of the white board in classrooms.

Perhaps in the days of relatively unsophisticated technology and global isolationism, it was not as critical to think at high levels. But the game has changed. Global interdependence and sophisticated technologies require that we raise the intellectual as well as the academic standards in classrooms.

What Are Some Examples of the Subject Area Organizing Concepts?

Teachers frequently want to know if there is a "master list of concepts in the sky" for each subject area. Except for the field of science, there are no formal lists

FIGURE 2.4. Top Level of Knowledge

SOURCE: Cartoon by David Ford. *david@twocrowcartoons.com*

at this time, but it would be helpful to have national subject area organizations develop their lists of the most significant organizing concepts as frames for the critical content. Certainly, the dialogue among the professionals has started, but the task is not yet complete.

We need not wait, however. I have seen some of the most intense professional dialogue occur among subject area staff as they relate the content they teach to the organizing concepts. This process forces teachers to consider the most important ideas for instruction. Figure 2.5, as well as Resource A, shows some of the organizing concepts for different subject areas. I have included additional examples of subject area concepts in this edition to help further the work of curriculum committees and teachers.

Please note in Figure 2.5 that literature has two types of concepts. One type arises out of the literature itself—out of the "themes" of literature. Family, love, conflict, and so on are examples of the first type of concepts. The other type is drawn from the writer's craft. How does the author use concepts such character, symbolism, allegory, foreshadowing, and so on to convey meaning or create effects?

In Figure 2.5, note the "macroconcepts" that cut across disciplines. Because these concepts rise above the fact base and can be exemplified through multiple disciplines, they are often used as organizers for interdisciplinary, integrated curriculum, the focus of Chapter 4.

FIGURE 2.5. Examples of Subject-Specific Concepts

Science	Social Studies	Literature
Cause/effect	Cause/effect	Cause/effect
Order	Order	Order
Organism	Patterns	Patterns
Population	Population	Character
System	System	Interconnections
Change	Change/culture	Change
Evolution	Evolution	Evolution
Cycle	Cycle	Cycle
Interaction	Interaction	Interaction
Energy matter	Perception	Perception
Equilibrium	Civilization	Intrigue
Field	Migration/immigration	Passion
Force	Interdependence	Hate
Model	Diversity	Love
Time/space	Conflict/cooperation	Family
Theory	Innovation	Conflict/cooperation
Fundamental entities	Beliefs/values	
Replication		

Mathematics	Visual Art	Music
Ratio	Rhythm	Rhythm
Proportion	Line	Melody
Scale	Color	Harmony
Symmetry	Value	Tone
Probability	Shape	Pitch
Pattern	Texture	Texture
Interaction	Form	Form
Cause/effect	Space	Tempo
Order	Repetition	Dynamics
Quantification	Balance	Timbre
System	Angle	Pattern
Theory	Perception	Perception
Field	Position	
Gradient	Motion	
Invariance	Light	
Model		

The science concepts are taken from the national science standards (National Research Council, 1996). The macroconcepts are referred to as *integrating concepts* in the national science standards because they can be applied across all of the science disciplines—earth, life, and physical. They lead to the encompassing, enduring ideas that explain our world and universe. The microconcepts are the more discipline-specific concepts, although some of them also transfer across disciplines.

An excellent source for identifying discipline-based concepts is in the national standards for each discipline. In some standards, such as the national science standards, the concepts are easily identified and labeled. In other subjects, such as history, one must know the difference between a topic and a concept and draw them out. In Resources A and B, there are additional lists of concepts for different disciplines.

Identifying the major concepts for a topic of study is not as difficult as it seems. If you were asked to name the major concepts for a unit on U.S. trade, the economics concepts of *scarcity, supply and demand,* and, of course, *trade* would spring to mind. Once you have a list of terms related to the unit theme, you can run them through the "Concept Definition Test."

Concept Definition Test

Does the term you are considering as a higher-level concept serve as a mental frame or construct for a class of examples? Does it meet the following criteria?

♦ Broad and abstract

♦ Represented by one or two words

♦ Universal in application

♦ Timeless—carries through the ages

♦ Represented by different examples that share common attributes

  Example: Conflict, as a concept, has many different examples, but the examples share the characteristics of "opposing forces" and "friction."

Let's try it. Which of the following are concepts? Apply each of the following terms to the test:

– Conflict	– Persuasion
– Family	– Power
– Culture	– Revolution
– Change	– Model
– Fitness	– Dinosaurs
– Human rights	– Bears
– China	– Cooperation

FIGURE 2.6. Superman/Concepts

SOURCE: Cartoon by David Ford. *david@twocrowcartoons.com*

How did you do? If you recognized that China, dinosaurs, and bears are *topics* that hold learning to the fact and activity base, then you are correct. But remember that you can apply a concept to the study of a topic, and you will shift learning to a higher cognitive plane. In the following examples, consider the effects on instruction and learning when the conceptual lens is focused on the topics under study:

Topic Example	Possible Conceptual Lens
Dinosaurs	Extinction
Presidential elections	Communication/influence

Why Should Curriculum Documents Provide a Conceptual Structure for the Content of Different Subject Areas?

♦ A conceptual structure for curriculum is important because conceptual understanding requires content knowledge, but the reverse is not true. National and state standards include the statement, "Students will understand the concepts and principles of mathematics, science, social studies,

TABLE 2.2 Topics Versus Concepts

Topical Organizers	Conceptual Organizers
Frame a set of isolated facts	Provide a mental schema for categorizing common examples
Maintain lower level of thinking	Lead to a higher level of thinking
Hold learning to the fact or activity level	Aid in the development of higher-order generalizations
Have short-term use—to cover an event, issue, or set of facts	Serve as a tool for processing life events
Increase the overload curriculum	Reduce the overload curriculum by framing the most salient or critical examples of the concepts

etc." It is recognized that concepts and principles signify deeper under-standing.

♦ A conceptual structure is efficient for handling the growing body of infor-mation. Concepts focus and streamline the breadth of content.

♦ A conceptual structure forces students to think about topics and facts in terms of their transferable significance.

♦ A conceptual structure allows kindergarten through postsecondary teachers to become a team as they systematically build conceptual understanding and develop student intellect.

♦ A conceptual structure provides an instructional model that is "idea cen-tered," rigorous, and engaging for both students and teachers.

♦ A conceptual structure ensures that teachers are clear on the concepts and "big ideas" that students must understand at each level of schooling. It is not "assumed" that students and teachers will reach deeper understanding of ideas by covering the course objectives.

Why Are Concepts Better Than Topics Alone as Curricular Organizers?

Curriculum design in the United States today is flawed in most subject areas because it relies on topics alone to organize content. If we are to truly raise stan-dards, then a conceptual overlay for the topics and facts is critical.

Table 2.2 compares the value of concepts and topics as curricular organizers.

GENERALIZATIONS

What Are Generalizations? Why Are They So Important for 21st-Century Education?

Generalizations are the enduring understandings, the "big ideas," the answer to the "so what?" of study. They synthesize the factual examples and summarize learning.

An excellent discussion of generalizations can be found in *Teaching Strategies for Ethnic Studies* by James Banks (1991). Banks differentiates between lower-level, intermediate-level, and universal-level generalizations that are related to a factual example.

> Fact: The Chinese immigrants who came to San Francisco in the 1800s established the *hui kuan.*
>
> *Lower-level generalization:* Chinese immigrants in the United States established various forms of social organizations.
>
> *Intermediate-level generalization:* All groups that have immigrated or migrated to the Unites States have established social organizations.
>
> *Universal-level generalization:* In all human societies, forms of social organizations emerge to satisfy the needs of individuals and groups. (pp. 43-45)

It is interesting to note that Banks (1991) differentiates the levels by the statement's degree of generalizability. I would consider Banks's lower and intermediate levels facts rather than generalizations, however, because these two levels give specific noun subjects. The parts of the sentences that generalize are the conceptual phrases, but when these phrases are linked to specific nouns, I think they fall into the category of facts.

In this book, the focus is on universal generalizations—the enduring understandings that have wide applicability through time and across cultures. These are the lessons of history that can be used as *benchmarks* in considering and comparing new situational examples. Some possible generalizations for a unit on Native American culture and change might include the following:

♦ Cultures change over time.

♦ Cross-cultural interaction fosters the exchange of ideas, goods, and services.

♦ Social, political, or economic change can cause conflict within a society.

♦ Dominant cultures can disrupt minority cultures.

♦ Merging cultures create social, political, and economic change.

Teachers do not usually tell students the generalizations. They teach inductively to develop students' abstract thinking abilities as they relate specific facts to transferable understandings. Students will develop their own insights and as they learn to synthesize facts to the level of abstract relevance. It is important to ensure that student generalizations are supported with facts. At times, students may make inaccurate generalizations, leaps of abstraction in their zeal to "know the answer." Teachers must think on their feet as they foster the development of higher-level abstraction through reasoning and critical thinking. They teach students to use primary and secondary sources to support their generalizations. They question students to help them clarify their thinking. Chapter 7 discusses additional strategies and provides examples for teaching concept-based curriculum.

Because the path from specific topics to the concepts and generalizations is a new and somewhat difficult skill, teachers' first attempts may be very broad surface learnings, such as "Governments influence culture." But as they question the broad ideas with "how?" or "why?" and delineate the ideas more specifically, the statements become powerfully stated and clear. An example of a more specific idea might be, "Governments structure a society to maintain order." The learning curve for thinking from facts to big ideas is very sharp. Teachers around the country are becoming very skilled at writing clear and powerful generalizations for their instruction.

Some educators feel that young children are not capable of abstracting to the level of generalizations. But children are capable of abstract thought and generalization when they are called for in the context of *developmentally appropriate* content.

As one example, a group of kindergarten and first-grade teachers in Richmond, Indiana, developed a unit around the concept of "color" for their young students. The theme they chose was "The Value of Color in Our Rainbow World." They engaged students in many activities that demonstrated the theme such as the following:

- ◆ Scarf drapings to decide as a group whether each child looked best in winter, spring, summer, or fall colors

- ◆ Environmental walks to note and appreciate how the different colors create interest for the viewer

- ◆ Identifying how color is used to keep people safe

When asked how color helps us in our world, the children were able to generalize (with a little help on the lead-in): Color "can make us pretty," "makes our environment more interesting," and "keeps us safe."

Generalizations are summaries of thought and answer the relevancy question, "What do I understand as a result of my study?" Generalizations are deeper understandings that transfer through time and across cultures. They hold truth as long as they are supported by the situational examples. Banks (1991) explains that even though a generalization is capable of being tested or verified, it can never be proven absolutely to be correct. Because of the complexity of human behavior, generalizations in the social and behavioral sciences are necessarily tentative and often contain qualifiers such as *sometimes* or *usually*. They are important, however, as conceptual summaries of thought.

A Universal Generalization Defined

A generalization is defined formally as two or more concepts stated in a relationship. Universal generalizations have the same characteristics as a concept:

- Broad and abstract

- Universal in application

- Generally timeless—carry through the ages

- Represented by different examples, but the examples support the generalization

Apply the characteristics to the following idea: "Cultures regulate social behavior to maintain order." Does this idea meet the criteria to qualify as a generalization?

Universal generalizations, as they are written, use no past, past-perfect, or present-perfect tenses. To do so would set them in time as a fact. For example, "Poverty was a catalyst for migration" is past tense and may be a factual generalization related to a particular group or groups of people, but it is not a timeless, universal generalization as stated. How could we change this fact into a timeless generalization?

Although generalizations are usually timeless, they are more susceptible to demise than concepts. Concepts remain timeless, but because generalizations are interdependent variables in a relationship, they may change over time with the alteration of either variable's circumstances. For example, a current generalization could be, "A balanced diet supports a healthy lifestyle." But if our diet becomes affected too heavily by pollutants, the generalization will not hold.

Generalizations are helpful constructs for summarizing conceptual relationships, but their timeless validity must be tested continually through analysis of contemporary, factual examples.

Universal generalizations avoid proper and personal nouns. "Japanese trade affects the American economy" is a fact because it states the specific examples, Japanese and American. The universal generalization is written, "Trade affects an economy." This statement can be supported through time, by numerous examples. As students progress through the grades, the generalizations should become more sophisticated by drawing on more complex concepts. Concepts and generalizations provide a framework for the articulation and coordination of curriculum in both single-grade and multiage schooling structures.

Chapter 3 looks at state standards and considers their impact on local curriculum design. Do standards support or impede concept-based curriculum and instruction at the local level? Chapter 3 shares examples of district curricula that adhere to a concept-based design as they align to state standards.

SUMMARY

The use of universal and lasting concepts to structure the massive amount of content as we work with students provides a rational plan for teaching for the transfer of knowledge. Concept-based curriculum and instruction solve the problems of

- ♦ How to reduce an overloaded curriculum

- ♦ How to systematically articulate K-12 curriculum to engage higher-level, complex thinking and develop deeper understanding

- ♦ How to raise academic standards by bringing relevance and rigor to learning through idea-centered curricula

Concept-based curriculum design allows the teacher to control rather than be controlled by the subject matter and provides the flexibility to allow students to search for and construct knowledge.

EXTENDING THOUGHT

1. How does concept-based curriculum design reach beyond the memorization of isolated facts?

2. When students dialogue about issues at a conceptual level, they may be debating a variety of perspectives. What are the ramifications for instruction? Teachers' responsibilities?

3. What role do topics and facts play in a concept-based curriculum design?

4. Why is a conceptual schema important as a framework for learning in today's world?

5. What is the value of a "generalization" to the learning process?

6. What are the dangers of generalizing related to

- ♦ Shallow thinking and low-level generalizations?
- ♦ Leaps of abstraction without supporting data?
- ♦ Bias in generalizing?

State Academic Standards and Local Curriculum Frameworks

STATE STANDARDS

State *standards* are driving curriculum and instruction in the United States today. On the positive side, standards have dramatically increased the attention and time spent on curriculum development and assessment in schools and school districts. On the negative side, standards vary greatly in the quality of their design. And the design of curriculum does affect classroom instruction. In my previous book, *Concept-Based Curriculum and Instruction: Teaching Beyond the Facts* (Erickson, 1998), I address these issues related to national standards design in depth, so I will only reference that discussion here. But it is helpful to look at a few examples from state standards and consider how they will affect local curricular documents.

Although the implied or implicit content of state standards is virtually identical from state to state, the language of standards varies greatly. Some content standards are specific and factual; others are broad and abstract. It is important to understand how these standards are written because the impact on classroom instruction is significant. State curriculum committees and legislative oversight committees made a conscious decision to write the content standards either in the form of a "conceptual framework" or as a "delineated curriculum" of specific topics and skills. Some states emphasized the conceptual approach with science and the topic approach with history, following the lead of the national science and history standards. (Note: Skill-based standards, such as the language arts area, have not changed much over the years except in degree of emphasis for various skills. Skill-based standards are driven by verbs by necessity. This discussion of concept based versus topic based does not relate to these skill-based areas.)

Can you determine from the following examples of state standards whether the emphasis and expectations are for conceptual understanding or factual knowledge?

37

Social Studies: Virginia State Standards—Grade 5

The student will describe life in America before the 17th century by

- Identifying and describing the first Americans, their arrival from Asia, where they settled, and how they lived, including Inuits (Eskimos), Anasazi (cliff dwellers), Northwest Indians (Kwakiutl), Plains Indians, Mound Builders, Indians of the Eastern forest (Iroquois, etc.), Incas, and Mayans

- Explaining how geography and climate influenced the way various Indian tribes lived

- Evaluating the impact of native economies on their religions, arts, shelters, and cultures

Factual or conceptual? How will teachers address these standards in their instruction?

Science: Illinois State Learning Standards—1997

Early elementary
    12.B.1b Describe how living things depend on one another for survival.

Middle/junior high school
    12.B.3a Identify and classify biotic and abiotic factors in an environment that affect population density, habitat, and placement of organisms in an energy pyramid.

High school
    12.B.4b Simulate and analyze factors that influence the size and stability of populations within ecosystems (e.g., birth rate, death rate, predation, migration patterns).

Factual or conceptual? How will teachers address these standards in their instruction?

How will local committees design their curriculum when aligning these two approaches to standards? Will both use specific topics to ground the standard? Certainly! You cannot teach conceptual understanding without specific content topics. But should we write traditional content objectives at the state level, complete with the verbs from Bloom's taxonomy (Bloom, Engelhart, Furst, Hill, & Krathwohl, 1956)? Or should we write conceptual understandings at the state level and list critical content topics (without verbs) that must be included in the local curriculum documents? Which format, conceptual or topic driven, will facilitate deeper levels of thinking, transfer of knowledge, and active student engagement when translated into curriculum at the local level?

Objectives—Outcomes—Standards

Educational terms shift in the wind with each wave of reform. In the 1970s and early 1980s, the essential component for quality education was a set of "clear, specific, and measurable objectives" for each subject. Educators practiced writing objectives with just the right verb. Then the outcomes movement came roaring along in the mid-1980s. Objectives were out—outcomes were in. Outcomes were to show through performance what students could do with what they know. The philosophy held on, but the term *outcome* became a political harpoon, and we moved on to *standards*. This term is still surviving, and the intent is to have students demonstrate what they know, but when we get right down to it, we are back to the old "objectives" in most states. Add to this "goes around, comes around" phenomenon the high-stakes testing, and we find predicted results in classrooms: "Cover more faster" and "more discrete skill drill, less talk."

The trouble with traditional objectives is that they choose a verb, link it to a topic, and assume that teaching and learning will move beyond memorization. For example, consider the following typical objective (often called a *benchmark* in today's jargon): "Describe life in early America before and after European contact." Now consider the question, "Why?" We should ask this question every time we align to a content standard.

It is easy to "do the verb" with the topic—but is that really the point? Or do we want students to understand that "merging cultures create social, political, and economic change"? Too many standards "assume" that teaching and learning will go beyond the objective to arrive at a significant understanding. But I can assure you, based on 6 years of intensive work with teachers around the country, that thinking beyond the facts to the level of conceptual relevance is a difficult and new skill for most teachers. Our traditional curriculum design and lower-level assessments have not required going beyond the facts. And the structure of content objectives is a large part of the problem.

THE TRIPARTITE MODEL FOR CURRICULUM

To truly raise standards, we must move from a solely fact-based model to a *tripartite model of curriculum design*. Figure 3.1 shows the usefulness of the tripartite model for single-subject area curriculum design as well as for the integrated curriculum model, which will be described in Chapter 4.

In the traditional model of curriculum, the focus for teaching and learning is on the fact base. The facts are organized by topics, and as the world information base expands, more topics are added to the bulging curriculum. We lack a rational plan for reducing content, and teaching becomes a skim of surface information.

FIGURE 3.1. The Tripartite Model

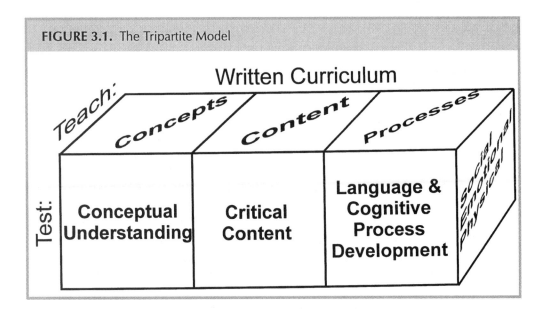

In the tripartite model, content topics are set within a conceptual framework. When you teach conceptually, the focus shifts from memorizing isolated facts as the end game to using facts as a tool for understanding the deeper, transferable concepts and principles. The aim is to develop conceptual understanding and build brain schema to intellectually manage the expanding information base.

Figure 3.1 shows the balance between conceptual understanding, critical content knowledge, and process development. If we are to increase the development of conceptual understanding, critical content knowledge, and process and skill abilities, then we must make more instructional time in the school day. This can only be accomplished by systematically reducing and focusing the content load. The standards movement can conceivably make this task more difficult. If teachers view standards as a set of objectives that they have to "check off" and race through, then learning will be shallow.

The move toward a more balanced curriculum of concept, content, and process development is really a move toward greater depth in teaching and learning as well as a focus on higher-level thinking. If we want all children to be successful in developing the conceptual understanding implied in many standards documents across the country, then we will design curriculum that moves from topic-based to concept-based curricula, from lower-order to higher-order *process skills,* and from meaningless to meaningful activities in learning experiences.

How Can Curriculum Developers and Committees Organize Content Related to the Major Concepts?

Before a district, school, or classroom can design a concept-based curriculum, it must identify the critical content topics that it is required to teach. These topics, along with processes and skills and assessments, are delineated through the pro-

TABLE 3.1 Curriculum-Mapping Format

Grade Level 4	September	October	November	December	January
Science topics					
Science skills					
Social studies topics					
Social studies skills					

cess of "curriculum mapping," so aptly described by Heidi Hayes-Jacobs (1997) in *Mapping the Big Picture.*

Curriculum mapping is a procedure for collecting data about the actual curriculum in a school district, using the school calendar as an organizer. Data need to be collected on the content being taught at each grade level, the processes and skills being emphasized, and the nature of assessments students are producing to show growth.

Curriculum maps help teachers to see what is actually going on in curriculum through the grades; adjust for gaps, overlaps, and redundancies in content topics and skills; and see where connected topics can work together in an integrated, interdisciplinary unit.

CURRICULUM MAPPING

Table 3.1 shows a typical curriculum-mapping format.

Once the critical content has been identified by topics on curriculum maps, it is helpful to identify related concepts. A simple format is the matrix. Figures 3.2 and Tables 3.2 and 3.3 show examples from K-6 science curriculum, as well as high school chemistry and economics. These examples were developed by teachers in the Federal Way, Washington School District. Although these matrices have been replaced over the years with other curriculum documents, they do illustrate an effective method for relating critical content topics to key concepts in different disciplines.

(text continues on page

FIGURE 3.2. Elementary Science Kits Excerpt

	Second Grade	
	Second Grade	

CONCEPT UNITS	CYCLES	SYSTEM
	Butterfly cycle	Open and closed systems
	Mealworm cycle	Aquariums as a system
	Calendar cycles	Circulatory system
	Water cycles	Subsystems
	Plant life cycles	Ecosystems
	Population cycles	Fitness systems
	Seasonal cycles	School systems
	Recycle	Transportation systems
	Human impact on cycles	Solar system

Fourth Grade

CONCEPT UNITS	SYMMETRY	FORCE
	Symmetry in crystals	Force as action/reaction
	Importance of symmetry in flight	Force and distance
	Symmetry in the plant world	Pulleys and force
	Symmetry in the animal world	Inclined planes
	Symmetry in magnetism	Force and resistance
	Mirror images and symmetry	Gravity as a force
	Creating symmetry	Reduction of force
	Lines of symmetry	Force and pressure
		Forces in our environment

Sixth Grade

CONCEPT UNITS	ORGANISM	POPULATION
	Attributes of an organism	Identifying populations
	Fungi as organisms	Classifying populations
	Growing organisms	Limiting factors of populations
	Distinguishing between living and nonliving	Ecosystems
	Classifying organisms	Competition for resources
	Recording organisms	Sampling populations
	Microscopic organisms	Predator/prey
	Environmental factors that affect organisms	Graphing populations
		Environmental effects on populations

SOURCE: Federal Way Public Schools, Federal Way, Washington.

TABLE 3.2 Chemistry: Concepts and Critical Content

Content Strands

Concept	Processes and Methods	Energy/ Thermodynamics	Atomic Theory	Bonding	Matter	Kinetic Theory	Reactions
Cause and effect	Controlled experimentation Safety	Entropy activation and potential energy	Significance of electron configuration Periodicity	Attachment between atoms		Heat and temperature Factors affecting reaction rate	Ionic reactions Molecular reactions
Change	Dimensional analysis	Conversion of energy Phase changes Entropy			Physical change Chemical change	Phase changes	Stoichiometry oxidation reduction reactions
Energy matter	Naming compounds	Forms of energy	Light emission Absorption Ionization	Bond energy	Varieties of matter Physical or chemical properties	Heat and temperature Phase changes Enthalpy Entropy	Energy and chemical reactions
Equilibrium	Chemical formulas Solutions	Phase changes			Conservation of matter Conservation of atoms	Phase changes	Le Chatelier principle
Fundamental entities	Mole		Atoms Molecules Electron Proton Neutron	Electrical interaction	Mole		Balancing equations Mole, pH scale

(continued)

TABLE 3.2 Continued

			Content Strands				
Concept	Processes and Methods	Energy/Thermodynamics	Atomic Theory	Bonding	Matter	Kinetic Theory	Reactions
Interaction		Ionization		Ionic bonds Covalent bonds Hydrogen bonds Polar bonds	Solubility Colligative properties	Factors affecting reaction rate	Limiting reaction Acid/base reaction
Model	Problem solving		Dalton model Thomson model Bohr model Quantum model Charge cloud Electron configuration	VSEPR model Lewis structure	Conservation of mass	Gas laws Collision theory Hess's law	Collision theory Acid/base reaction
Probability	Percentage error		Electron distribution Energy levels				
Quantification	Percentage composition Graphing SI units Significant figure precision Concentrations of solutions	Scientific notation Measurement heat	Atomic weight Mass		Mole Percentage composition		Stoichiometry

SOURCE: Federal Way Public Schools, Federal Way, Washington.

TABLE 3.3 Economics: Concepts and Critical Content

Concept	Content	Generalizations and Principles
Scarcity	Opportunity costs Choices Personal Country	The basic economic problem is scarcity. At any given time, each society has a given amount of labor, capital, and natural resources. People's wants for goods and services are greater than what can be produced. Because we cannot do or have everything all at once, we must make choices. Much of economics deals with analyzing how and why individuals, institutions, and societies make the choices they do.
Comparative systems	Command economy Communism Socialism Market economy Business cycles Capitalism	Every economic system institutionalizes the manner in which people decide what to produce, how to produce, and for whom to produce. Each economic system uses different means to answer these questions, based on its prevailing philosophic assumptions. Several economies rely more heavily on government and less on markets. The major ideas developed in this course will be to develop the concepts of the market economy as they are used in the United States.
Investments	Stocks Bonds Mutual funds Others	Investment capital comes from the people buying stocks and bonds from companies who use the needed capital to expand their production capacities and increase their productivity.

(continued)

TABLE 3.3 Continued

Concept	Content	Generalizations and Principles
Supply and demand	Competition Utility Equilibrium	Markets are institutional arrangements that enable buyers and sellers to exchange goods and services. Changes in supply, demand, or both will cause changes in prices in and in the amounts of goods or services produced and demanded. Competition thus forces the use of resources in an efficient manner.
Government regulation	Budget, debt Taxation Controls	Government guides the market in decision making by forcing it to respond to rules and regulations that are designed to achieve the objectives society has set and to answer its basic economic questions of what to produce, how to produce, and for whom to produce.
Monetary/fiscal	Federal Reserve Government	Monetary policy attempts to regulate the general level of economic activity through the Federal Reserve system. It regulates the money supply by its activities. Congress and the president decide fiscal policy through taxing and spending policies.
Labor	History Unions Bargaining	The American labor movement exemplifies the working supply and demand in the job market. Unions are formed to maintain some control over jobs and lives and keep fairness in the workplace through collective bargaining.
International trade	Comparative advantage Balance of trade Restrictions versus free trade	The concept of comparative advantage explains why nations benefit from specialization and trade with each other. Comparative advantage can allow goods and services for the least cost to be exchanged. However, this specialization might force a nation to become dependent on others for basic needs. As a consequence, government often steps in with regulations designed to balance the flow of trade to ensure jobs and resources for itself.

SOURCE: Federal Way Public Schools, Federal Way, Washington.

In the examples for K-6 science and chemistry, note that the concepts are repeated, but the related topics become more specialized and sophisticated as students progress through the grades. This format for organizing content allows for meaningful K-12 content articulation and provides a framework that supports concept-based curriculum. A concept-content matrix also allows the teacher to visually assess the "content load" of the course. If there are too many topics to "cover," there will be less time for the student to develop the essential processes and skills for accessing, interpreting, and displaying knowledge.

Three criteria are especially helpful in deciding which topics qualify as critical content (topics/facts) to be included on the matrix:

♦ What do students need to know to be successful at the next level of learning? Multiplication, for example, is necessary prior knowledge for success with division.

♦ What do you, as a professional, feel that students need to know to understand the discipline? For example, in U.S. history, the American Revolution and the Civil War are two topics critical to an understanding of the subject.

♦ What critical content topics are reasonably expected and identified in state and national standards?

SCOPE AND SEQUENCE CHARTS FOR PROCESSES AND SKILLS

Processes and skills noted on the curriculum maps need to be articulated in a scope and sequence format. Processes and skills also need to be aligned to state (and national) standards to prevent gaps. Some disciplines such as mathematics and art are both skill based and concept based. Yet, too often, the curriculum documents address directly only the skill component and make an assumption that students will infer the key concepts and principles of the discipline. But this is fallacy. Why is it that so many people feel that they are weak in mathematics or art knowledge? Is it because they never really developed understanding of the deeper knowledge base—the key concepts and principles? Could they "do" mathematics but never really understood "why" the mathematics worked? And how could they really show sophisticated performance in art without being able to use the "language of art" to articulate their understandings?

Meridian School District in Meridian, Idaho, is developing concept/process curricula for all subject areas K-12. Figure 3.3 and Table 3.4 share excerpts from the curricular frameworks of two subject areas that traditionally tend to focus more on the skills and activities in curriculum documents. Key concepts are italicized in the generalizations.

Districts such as Meridian, which are taking on the intellectual challenge of identifying the deeper, conceptual understandings, are to be commended. It is hard

FIGURE 3.3. Math—Elementary

Generalizations (enduring understandings)

▶ *Numbers* are *quantities.*

▶ *Numerals* represent *quantities.*

▶ *Numbers* name *things* and place things in *order.*

▶ *Mathematical operations* (+ – ×) help solve *problems.*

▶ *Quantities* can be *added together* or *taken apart.*

Introduce	Develop	Master
Numeral recognition to 200	Numeral recognition to 200	Numeral recognition to 100
	Counting 0-100+	Counting 0 -100+
	Counting backward from 10	Counting backward from 10
	Matching numeral to number 5 ◯◯ 2 ◯◯◯◯	Matching numeral to number 5 ◯◯◯◯◯ 2 ◯◯
Place value to 100—counting days in school, grouping 1s to 10s and 10s to 100	Place value to 100—counting days in school, grouping 1s to 10s and 10s to 100	
		Numeral writing 1-100
Ordinal numbers 6th to 10th and vocabulary	Ordinal numbers 1st to 10th and vocabulary	
	Count by 2, 5, 10, to 100	Count by 5 and 10 to 100
Addition—connecting concrete form to symbolic form (5 + 2 = 7)	Addition—connecting concrete form to symbolic form (5 + 2 = 7)	Addition—connecting concrete form to symbolic form (5 + 2 = 7)
Addition—2 digit without carrying	Addition—2 digit without carrying	
Addition—single-digit sums to 18	Addition—single-digit sums to 18	Addition—single-digit sums to 10
Subtraction—symbolic form (5 – 2 = 3)	Subtraction—symbolic form 5 – 2 = 3	Subtraction—symbolic form 5 – 2 = 3

FIGURE 3.3. Continued

Introduce	Develop	Master
Subtraction—2 digit without regrouping	Subtraction—2 digit without regrouping	
Subtraction—single-digit differences from 18	Subtraction—single-digit differences from 18	Subtraction—single-digit differences from 10
Concept of zero in addition and subtraction facts as a quantity	Concept of zero in addition and subtraction facts as a quantity	Concept of zero in addition and subtraction facts as a quantity
Doubles (2 + 2 to 9 + 9)	Doubles to 9 + 9	Doubles to 5 + 5
Doubles +1 (2 + 2 = 4, so 2 + 3 = 5)	Doubles +1 (2 + 2 = 4, so 2 + 3 = 5)	
Greater than, less than, equal to—terms, not symbols	Greater than, less than, equal to—terms, not symbols	

Sample Generalizations

Fourth Grade	Fifth Grade	Sixth Grade	Seventh Grade
The placement of a *number* determines its *value.*	*Long division* is a *repeated-step* *process*	Estimation approximates exact values	*Rational numbers* can be written as *fractions* or *decimals.*
The *decimal placement* determines *place value* in *addition* and *subtraction.*	The placement of the *decimal* in a *product* is determined by the *parts of the whole* that are multiplied.	*Division* splits a *whole* into *equal parts.*	*Relationships* exist between *factors, multiples,* and *rules of divisibility.*
The *borrowing process* depends on a *comparative value* of the *numbers.*		*Divisibility rules* control *factoring* and *dividing.*	*Fraction* and *decimal numbers* can be *expressions* of the same *quantity.*

SOURCE: Meridian Mathematics Committee, Meridian Joint School District No. 2, Meridian, Idaho. Used with permission.

TABLE 3.4 Secondary Mathematics

Prealgebra	Algebra 1/2	Precalculus
Proportion expresses an equivalent relationship between two parts.	The distributive property allows options in problem solving.	Logarithms represent exponents and follow exponential rules of operation.
Scientific notation is an efficient way to represent extended numbers.	Absolute value measures the distance from zero. Variables represent unknown quantities.	All real and imaginary numbers can be written as complex numbers.
The properties of numbers and the order of operations establish a universal language.	Rational numbers are a subset of the real number system.	Conjugates are used to simplify complex rational expressions.

SOURCE: Meridian Mathematics Committee, Meridian Joint School District No. 2, Meridian, Idaho. Used with permission.

work to think beyond the facts and activities to answer the relevancy questions: "Why?" "How?" and "So what?" These excerpts are drawn from draft documents in Meridian and will continue to be refined by their curriculum committees in the coming months.

The mathematics curriculum in Meridian provides the necessary scope and sequence based on skills to be "introduced, developed, and mastered." But the mathematics committee also looked for the key concepts implied in the skills to be mastered and asked themselves, "What are the key, conceptual ideas (generalizations) that students need to internalize?" The scope and sequence charts and the generalizations were written for the following mathematics strands:

Number

Patterns, functions, algebra

Measurement, geometry, spatial sense

Data analysis, statistics, and probability

Figure 3.3 shows an excerpt from the Meridian first-grade scope and sequence for the number strand only. The generalizations at the top of the page are the *enduring understandings*—the key conceptual ideas framing the skills to be mastered. Meridian chose to make the generalizations for Grades K-3 the same, but the skills become more sophisticated to bring depth to the understandings. At Grade 4 and

FIGURE 3.4. Meridian Music Generalizations

Grade	Melody	Rhythm	Harmony	Form
K-2	Melody has direction.	Rhythmic patterns exist in the natural and constructed worlds.	Combining two or more pitches creates harmony.	Music has structure.
3-6	Melodies are organized into tonalities.	Manipulation of rhythm creates musical patterns.	Combining two or more sounds in different ways creates variety in harmony.	Musical structure is caused by repetition and contrast of same and different parts.
6-12	Distinct melodic patterns indicate culture and style.	Distinct rhythmic patterns differentiate musical styles.	Harmonic movement through chord construction and progression follows a deliberate order.	Structure creates order and clarity in music.

Grade	Timbre	Texture	Expressive Elements
K-2	Sounds have recognizable/distinguishing characteristics.	Music has layers of sound.	Music has a variety of expressive elements.
3-6	Timbre conveys mood and culture.	Layers of sound (texture) are associated with historical musical periods.	Dynamics, tempo, articulation, and text express and enhance the message of music.
6-12	Timbre can be modified to reflect style, mood, and culture. The authentic recreation of style requires appropriate timbre.	Manipulation of textures creates complexity and interest—aural, visual and kinesthetic.	The message of music elicits an emotional response. Expressive elements drive the artistry in music.

SOURCE: Meridian Joint School District No. 2, Meridian, Idaho. Used with permission.

each grade thereafter, the generalizations become more sophisticated as additional concepts enter the curriculum.

Table 3.4 excerpts the increasingly sophisticated generalizations from Grades 4 through precalculus as students work with the concept of number.

Figure 3.4 on the previous page, also from Meridian, Idaho, shows an excerpt of the generalizations for music. The basic elements of music are the organizing concepts that structure the knowledge and provide the language to discuss music. When students can perform the skills and deepen their conceptual understanding of the content and language of music, they move toward artistry. Notice how this curriculum benchmarks the enduring understandings by grade bands for each organizing concept. The music committee is also developing a scope and sequence of the music skills to be taught in the different grade bands.

Visual art is another discipline that traditionally has been reflected in curriculum documents as skills to be learned and applied. Yet the content of art is structured with a language that students need to understand at a conceptual and skill level.

Tacoma public schools in Tacoma, Washington, are designing a K-12 visual arts curriculum that addresses conceptual understanding as well as skills. Figures 3.5 through 3.7 share excerpts from classroom lessons related to the concept of "line" at different grade levels. The generalization and essential question set the focus for the lesson. As students learn and practice the skills, they build conceptual understanding. The art generalizations become more sophisticated as students progress through the grades. Teachers need to have the generalizations clearly stated in the grade-level curricula. We cannot assume that doing the skills will produce the conceptual understanding. Instruction needs to follow through to the conceptual level. Susy Watt, art instructor for elementary and secondary education at Pacific Lutheran University in Washington state, and consultant for the Tacoma visual art curriculum, shares her thoughts on concept-based art: "Whether looking at, talking about, or making visual art, a concept-based approach to teaching gives teachers a clear, intentional focus and students the resulting opportunity to apply new knowledge and skils in their everyday living. Generalizations and essential questions advance art in the classroom from a singular activity to vital study for school, work, and home. Long after the excitement of art making, students recognize the practice of art in their lives. Students learn a concept, practice the concept again in a new context, change the subject of their art, change the art materials, and are still left with enduring understandings" (personal communication, February 2000).

Figure 3.7 shows an excerpt from the Tacoma high school course, "Drawing 2." Notice that the students are still working with the concept of line, but their prior knowledge of the concept and related skills allows them to perform with greater sophistication and deeper understanding. The generalizations that describe conceptual relationships are more complex. This curriculum design is strong because it brings relevance to skills by highlighting the related concepts and transferable understandings.

There are many different formats for designing district-level curricula to meet state and national standards. This chapter shares examples of district frameworks

(text continues on page 61)

FIGURE 3.5. Tacoma Kindergarten Art Lesson

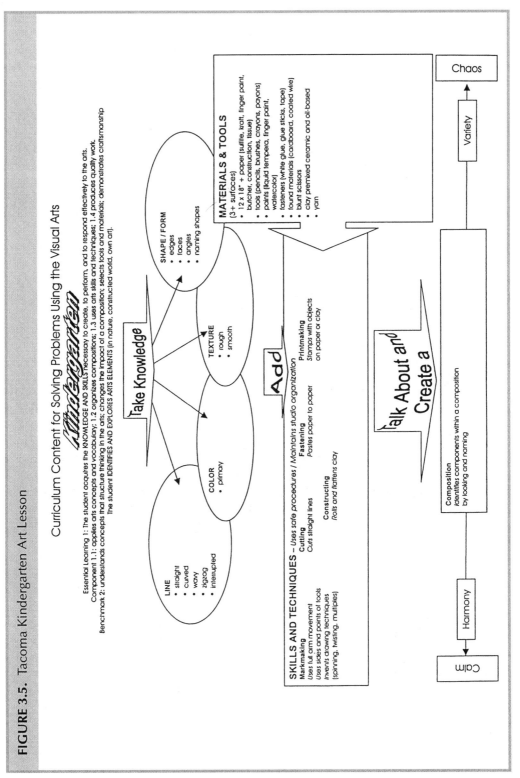

Curriculum Content for Solving Problems Using the Visual Arts

Kindergarten

Essential Learning 1: The student acquires the KNOWLEDGE AND SKILLS necessary to create, to perform, and to respond effectively to the arts.
Component 1.1: applies arts concepts and vocabulary; 1.2 organizes compositions; 1.3 uses arts skills and techniques; 1.4 produces quality work.
Benchmark 2: understands concepts that structure thinking in the arts; changes the impact of a composition; selects tools and materials; demonstrates craftsmanship.
The student IDENTIFIES AND EXPLORES ARTS ELEMENTS (in nature, constructed world, own art).

Take Knowledge

LINE
• straight
• curved
• wavy
• zigzag
• interrupted

COLOR
• primary

TEXTURE
• rough
• smooth

SHAPE / FORM
• edges
• faces
• angles
• naming shapes

MATERIALS & TOOLS
(3+ surfaces)
• 12 x 18" + paper (sulfite, kraft, finger paint, butcher, construction, tissue)
• tools (pencils, brushes, crayons, paints)
• paints (liquid tempera, finger paint, watercolor)
• fasteners (white glue, glue sticks, tape)
• found materials (cardboard, coated wire)
• blunt scissors
• clay premixed ceramic and oil-based
• yarn

Add

Printmaking
Stamps with objects on paper or clay

SKILLS AND TECHNIQUES – *Uses safe procedures / Maintains studio organization*

Markmaking
Uses full arm movement
Uses sides and points of tools
Invents drawing techniques (spinning, twisting, multiples)

Cutting
Cuts straight lines

Constructing
Rolls and flattens clay

Fastening
Pastes paper to paper

Talk About and Create a

Composition
Identifies components within a composition by looking and naming

Calm — Harmony — Variety — Chaos

(continued)

FIGURE 3.5. Continued

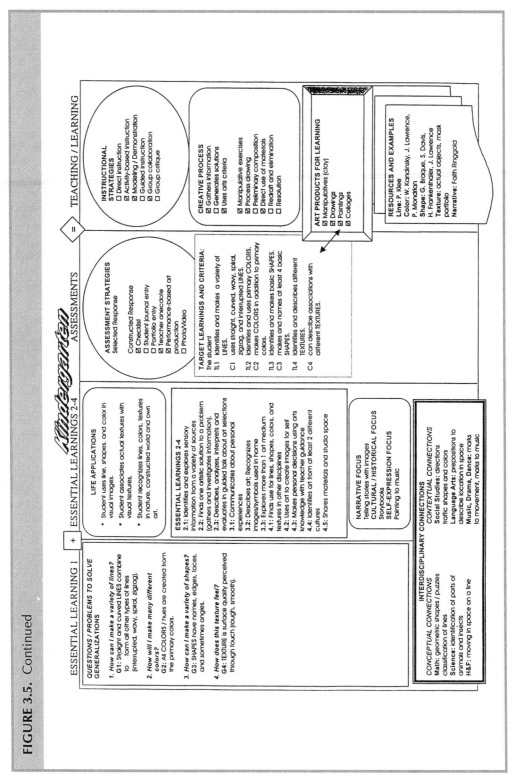

Kindergarten

ESSENTIAL LEARNING 1 + ESSENTIAL LEARNINGS 2-4 = TEACHING / LEARNING

ASSESSMENTS

ESSENTIAL LEARNING 1

QUESTIONS / PROBLEMS TO SOLVE GENERALIZATIONS

1. *How can I make a variety of lines?*
G1: Straight and curved LINES combine to form all other types of lines (interrupted, wavy, spiral, zigzag).

2. *How will I make many different colors?*
G2: All COLORS / hues are created from the primary colors.

3. *How can I make a variety of shapes?*
G3: SHAPES have names, edges, faces, and sometimes angles.

4. *How does this texture feel?*
G4: TEXTURE is surface quality perceived through touch (rough, smooth).

ESSENTIAL LEARNINGS 2-4

LIFE APPLICATIONS
• Student uses line, shapes, and color in visual images.
• Student associates actual textures with visual textures.
• Student recognizes lines, colors, textures in nature, constructed world and own art.

ESSENTIAL LEARNINGS 2-4
2.1: Identifies and explores sensory information from a variety of sources
2.2: Finds one artistic solution to a problem (gathers and investigates information).
2.3: Describes, analyzes, interprets and evaluates in guided talk about art selections
3.1: Communicates about personal experiences
3.2: Describes art; Recognizes images/symbols used in home
3.3: Explores more than 1 art medium
4.1: Finds use for lines, shapes, colors, and textures in other disciplines
4.2: Uses art to create images for self
4.3: Makes personal decisions using arts knowledge with teacher guidance
4.4: Identifies art from at least 2 different cultures
4.5: Shares materials and studio space

NARRATIVE FOCUS
Telling stories with images
CULTURAL / HISTORICAL FOCUS
Storybooks
SELF-EXPRESSION FOCUS
Pointing to music

INTERDISCIPLINARY CONNECTIONS

CONCEPTUAL CONNECTIONS
Math: geometric shapes / puzzles classification of lines
Science: identification of parts of animals and insects
H&F: moving in space on a line

CONTEXTUAL CONNECTIONS
Social Studies: directions traffic shapes and colors
Language Arts: prepositions to describe location in space
Music, Drama, Dance: marks to movement, marks to music

ASSESSMENTS

ASSESSMENT STRATEGIES
Selected Response

Constructed Response
☐ Checklist
☐ Student journal entry
☐ Portfolio entry
☑ Teacher anecdote
☑ Performance-based art production
☐ Photo/Video

TARGET LEARNINGS AND CRITERIA:
The student
TL1 Identifies and makes a variety of LINES.
C1 uses straight, curved, wavy, spiral, zigzag, and interrupted LINES.
TL2 Identifies and uses primary COLORs.
C2 makes COLORS in addition to primary colors.
TL3 Identifies and makes basic SHAPES.
C3 makes and names at least 4 basic SHAPES.
TL4 Identifies and describes different TEXTURES.
C4 can describe associations with different TEXTURES.

TEACHING / LEARNING

INSTRUCTIONAL STRATEGIES
☐ Direct instruction
☑ Activity-based instruction
☑ Modeling / Demonstration
☐ Guided instruction
☐ Group collaboration
☐ Group critique

CREATIVE PROCESS
☑ Gathers information
☑ Generates solutions
☑ Uses arts criteria
☑ Manipulative exercises
☐ Process drawing
☐ Preliminary composition
☐ Direct use of materials
☐ Recraft and elimination
☐ Resolution

ART PRODUCTS FOR LEARNING
☑ Manipulatives (clay)
☑ Drawings
☑ Paintings
☐ Collages

RESOURCES AND EXAMPLES
Line: P. Klee
Color: W. Kandinsky, J. Lawrence, P. Mondrian
Shape: G. Braque, S. Davis, H. Frankenthaler, J. Lawrence
Texture: actual objects, mask portfolio
Narrative: Faith Ringgold

FIGURE 3.5. Continued

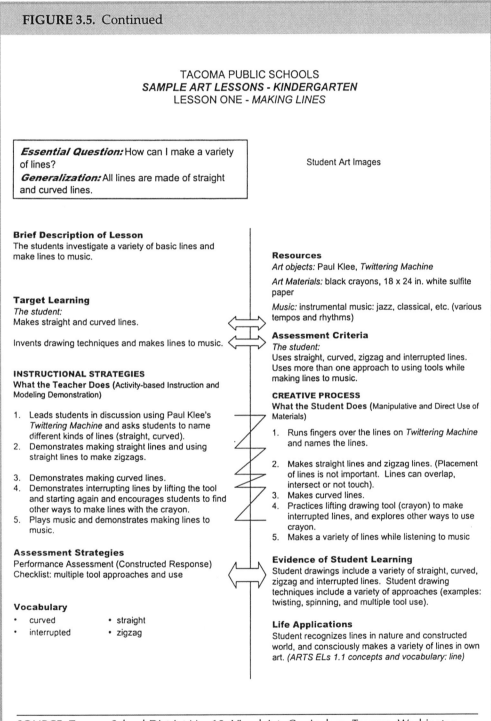

TACOMA PUBLIC SCHOOLS
SAMPLE ART LESSONS - KINDERGARTEN
LESSON ONE - *MAKING LINES*

Essential Question: How can I make a variety of lines?
Generalization: All lines are made of straight and curved lines.

Student Art Images

Brief Description of Lesson
The students investigate a variety of basic lines and make lines to music.

Resources
Art objects: Paul Klee, *Twittering Machine*

Art Materials: black crayons, 18 x 24 in. white sulfite paper

Music: instrumental music: jazz, classical, etc. (various tempos and rhythms)

Target Learning
The student:
Makes straight and curved lines.

Invents drawing techniques and makes lines to music.

Assessment Criteria
The student:
Uses straight, curved, zigzag and interrupted lines.
Uses more than one approach to using tools while making lines to music.

INSTRUCTIONAL STRATEGIES
What the Teacher Does (Activity-based Instruction and Modeling Demonstration)

1. Leads students in discussion using Paul Klee's *Twittering Machine* and asks students to name different kinds of lines (straight, curved).
2. Demonstrates making straight lines and using straight lines to make zigzags.
3. Demonstrates making curved lines.
4. Demonstrates interrupting lines by lifting the tool and starting again and encourages students to find other ways to make lines with the crayon.
5. Plays music and demonstrates making lines to music.

CREATIVE PROCESS
What the Student Does (Manipulative and Direct Use of Materials)

1. Runs fingers over the lines on *Twittering Machine* and names the lines.

2. Makes straight lines and zigzag lines. (Placement of lines is not important. Lines can overlap, intersect or not touch).
3. Makes curved lines.
4. Practices lifting drawing tool (crayon) to make interrupted lines, and explores other ways to use crayon.
5. Makes a variety of lines while listening to music

Assessment Strategies
Performance Assessment (Constructed Response)
Checklist: multiple tool approaches and use

Evidence of Student Learning
Student drawings include a variety of straight, curved, zigzag and interrupted lines. Student drawing techniques include a variety of approaches (examples: twisting, spinning, and multiple tool use).

Vocabulary
* curved
* interrupted
* straight
* zigzag

Life Applications
Student recognizes lines in nature and constructed world, and consciously makes a variety of lines in own art. *(ARTS ELs 1.1 concepts and vocabulary: line)*

SOURCE: Tacoma School District No. 10, Visual Arts Curriculum, Tacoma, Washington. Used with permission.

FIGURE 3.6. Tacoma Third-Grade Art Lesson

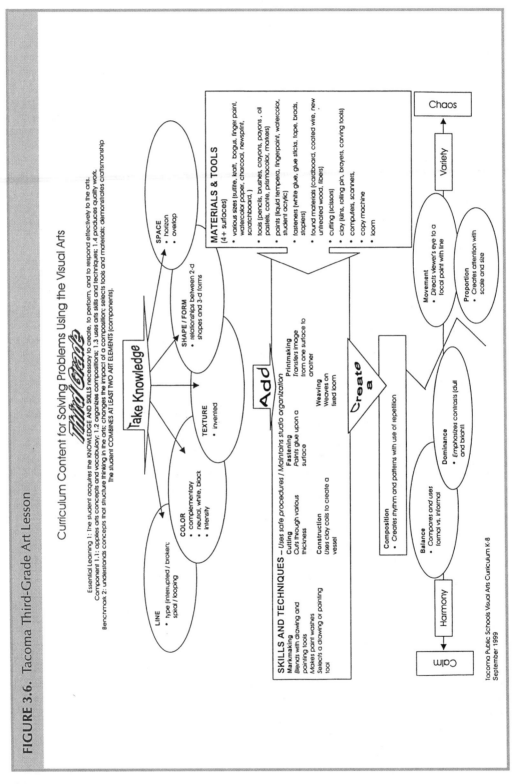

Curriculum Content for Solving Problems Using the Visual Arts

Third Grade

Essential Learning 1: The student *acquires* the KNOWLEDGE AND SKILLS necessary to create, to perform, and to respond effectively to the arts.
Component 1.1: applies arts concepts and vocabulary; 1.2 organizes compositions; 1.3 uses arts skills and techniques; 1.4 produces quality work.
Benchmark 2: understands concepts that structure thinking in the arts; changes the impact of a composition; selects tools and materials; demonstrates craftsmanship
The student COMBINES AT LEAST TWO ART ELEMENTS (components).

Take Knowledge

LINE
• type (interrupted / broken; spiral / looping

COLOR
• complementary
• neutral, white, black
• intensity

TEXTURE
• invented

SHAPE / FORM
• relationships between 2-d shapes and 3-d forms

SPACE
• horizon
• overlap

MATERIALS & TOOLS
(4+ surfaces)
• various sizes (sulfite, kraft, bogus, finger paint, watercolor paper, charcoal, newsprint, scratchboard,)
• tools (pencils, brushes, crayons, crayons, oil pastels, conte, prismacolor, markers)
• paints (liquid tempera, fingerpaint, watercolor, student acrylic)
• fasteners (white glue, glue sticks, tape, brads, staplers)
• found materials (cardboard, coated wire, new untreated wood, fibers)
• cutting (scissors)
• clay (kilns, rolling pin, brayers, carving tools)
• computers, scanners,
• copy machine
• loom

Add

Cutting
Cuts through various thickness

Fastening
Paints glue upon a surface

Printmaking
Transfers image from one surface to another

Construction
Uses clay coils to create a vessel

Weaving
Weaves on fixed loom

SKILLS AND TECHNIQUES – *Uses safe procedures / Maintains studio organization*

Markmaking
Blends with drawing and painting tools
Makes paint washes
Selects a drawing or painting tool

Create a

Composition
• *Creates* rhythm and patterns with use of repetition

Balance
• *Compares and uses* formal vs. informal

Dominance
• *Emphasizes* contrasts (dull and bright)

Movement
• *Directs* viewer's eye to a focal point with line

Proportion
• *Creates* attention with scale and size

Harmony

Calm

Variety

Chaos

Tacoma Public Schools Visual Arts Curriculum K-8
September 1999

FIGURE 3.6. Continued

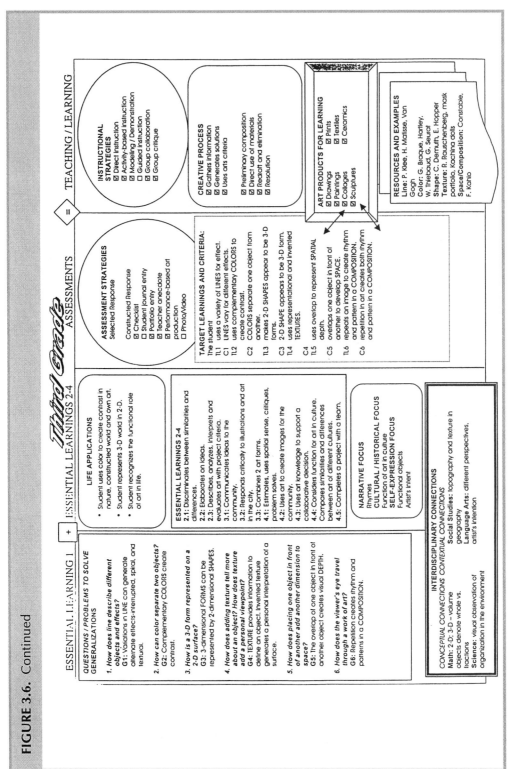

ESSENTIAL LEARNING 1   +   ESSENTIAL LEARNINGS 2-4   =   TEACHING / LEARNING

Third Grade

ASSESSMENTS

QUESTIONS / PROBLEMS TO SOLVE GENERALIZATIONS

1. *How does line describe different objects and effects?*
   G1: Variations in LINE can generate alternate effects-interrupted, spiral, and texture.

2. *How can color separate two objects?*
   G2: Complementary COLORS create contrast.

3. *How is a 3-D form represented on a 2-D surface?*
   G3: 3-dimensional FORMS can be represented by 2-dimensional SHAPES.

4. *How does adding texture tell more about an object? How does texture add a personal viewpoint?*
   G4: TEXTURE provides information to define an object. Invented texture generates a personal interpretation of a surface.

5. *How does placing one object in front of another add another dimension to space?*
   G5: The overlap of one object in front of another object creates visual DEPTH.

6. *How does the viewer's eye travel through a work of art?*
   G6: Repetition creates rhythm and patterns in a COMPOSITION.

LIFE APPLICATIONS
- Student uses color to create contrast in nature, constructed world and own art.
- Student represents 3-D world in 2-D.
- Student recognizes the functional role of art in life.

ESSENTIAL LEARNINGS 2-4
2.1: Discriminates between similarities and differences.
2.2: Elaborates on ideas.
2.3: Describes, analyzes, interprets and evaluates art with project criteria.
3.1: Communicates ideas to the community.
3.2: Responds critically to illustrations and art in the city.
3.3: Combines 2 art forms.
4.1: Estimates, uses spatial sense, critiques, problem solves.
4.2: Uses art to create images for the community.
4.3: Uses art knowledge to support a collaborative decision.
4.4: Considers function for art in culture. Compares similarities and differences between cultures of different cultures.
4.5: Completes a project with a team.

NARRATIVE FOCUS
Rhymes
CULTURAL / HISTORICAL FOCUS
Function of art in culture
SELF-EXPRESSION FOCUS
Functional objects
Artist's intent

ASSESSMENT STRATEGIES
Selected Response

☐ Constructed Response
☐ Checklist
☐ Student journal entry
☐ Portfolio entry
☑ Teacher anecdote
☑ Performance-based art production
☑ Photo/Video

TARGET LEARNINGS AND CRITERIA:
The student
TL1   uses a variety of LINES for effect.
C1   LINES vary for different effects.
TL2   uses complementary COLORS to create contrast.
C2   COLORS separate one object from another.
TL3   makes 2-D SHAPES appear to be 3-D forms.
C3   2-D SHAPE appears to be 3-D form.
TL4   uses representational and invented TEXTURES.
C4   uses overlap to represent SPATIAL depth.
TL5   overlaps one object in front of another to develop SPACE.
C5   repeats an image to create rhythm and pattern in a COMPOSITION.
TL6   repetition in art creates both rhythm and pattern in a COMPOSITION.
C6

INSTRUCTIONAL STRATEGIES
☑ Direct Instruction
☑ Activity-based Instruction
☑ Modeling / Demonstration
☐ Guided Instruction
☑ Group collaboration
☑ Group critique

CREATIVE PROCESS
☑ Gathers Information
☑ Generates solutions
☑ Uses arts criteria

☑ Preliminary composition
☑ Direct use of materials
☑ Rework and elimination
☑ Resolution

ART PRODUCTS FOR LEARNING
☑ Drawings   ☑ Prints
☑ Paintings ☑ Textiles
☑ Collages   ☑ Ceramics
☑ Sculptures

RESOURCES AND EXAMPLES
Line: P. Klee, H. Matisse, Van Gogh
Color: G. Braque, Hartley, W. Thiebaud, G. Seurat
Shape: C. Demuth, E. Hopper
Texture: R. Rauschenberg, mask portfolio, Kachina dolls
Space/Composition: Constable, F. Kahlo

INTERDISCIPLINARY CONNECTIONS
CONCEPTUAL CONNECTIONS   CONTEXTUAL CONNECTIONS
Math: 2-D; 3-D – volume   Social Studies: topography and texture in objects denote whole vs.   geography
fractions   Language Arts: different perspectives,
Science: visual observation of   artist's intention
organization in the environment

(continued)

57

FIGURE 3.6. Continued

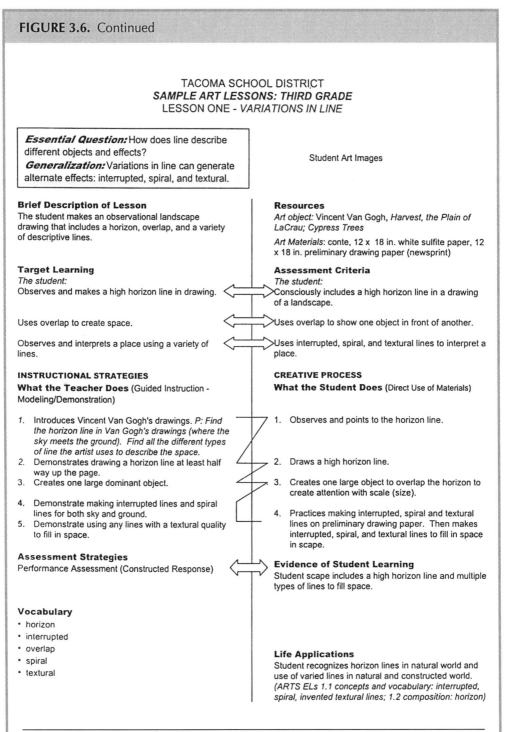

TACOMA SCHOOL DISTRICT
SAMPLE ART LESSONS: THIRD GRADE
LESSON ONE - *VARIATIONS IN LINE*

Essential Question: How does line describe different objects and effects?
Generalization: Variations in line can generate alternate effects: interrupted, spiral, and textural.

Student Art Images

Brief Description of Lesson
The student makes an observational landscape drawing that includes a horizon, overlap, and a variety of descriptive lines.

Resources
Art object: Vincent Van Gogh, *Harvest, the Plain of LaCrau; Cypress Trees*
Art Materials: conte, 12 x 18 in. white sulfite paper, 12 x 18 in. preliminary drawing paper (newsprint)

Target Learning
The student:
Observes and makes a high horizon line in drawing.

Uses overlap to create space.

Observes and interprets a place using a variety of lines.

Assessment Criteria
The student:
Consciously includes a high horizon line in a drawing of a landscape.

Uses overlap to show one object in front of another.

Uses interrupted, spiral, and textural lines to interpret a place.

INSTRUCTIONAL STRATEGIES
What the Teacher Does (Guided Instruction - Modeling/Demonstration)

1. Introduces Vincent Van Gogh's drawings. *P: Find the horizon line in Van Gogh's drawings (where the sky meets the ground). Find all the different types of line the artist uses to describe the space.*
2. Demonstrates drawing a horizon line at least half way up the page.
3. Creates one large dominant object.
4. Demonstrate making interrupted lines and spiral lines for both sky and ground.
5. Demonstrate using any lines with a textural quality to fill in space.

CREATIVE PROCESS
What the Student Does (Direct Use of Materials)

1. Observes and points to the horizon line.

2. Draws a high horizon line.

3. Creates one large object to overlap the horizon to create attention with scale (size).

4. Practices making interrupted, spiral and textural lines on preliminary drawing paper. Then makes interrupted, spiral, and textural lines to fill in space in scape.

Assessment Strategies
Performance Assessment (Constructed Response)

Evidence of Student Learning
Student scape includes a high horizon line and multiple types of lines to fill space.

Vocabulary
• horizon
• interrupted
• overlap
• spiral
• textural

Life Applications
Student recognizes horizon lines in natural world and use of varied lines in natural and constructed world. (*ARTS ELs 1.1 concepts and vocabulary: interrupted, spiral, invented textural lines; 1.2 composition: horizon*)

SOURCE: Tacoma School District No. 10, Visual Arts Curriculum, Tacoma, Washington. Used with permission.

FIGURE 3.7. Tacoma Drawing 2

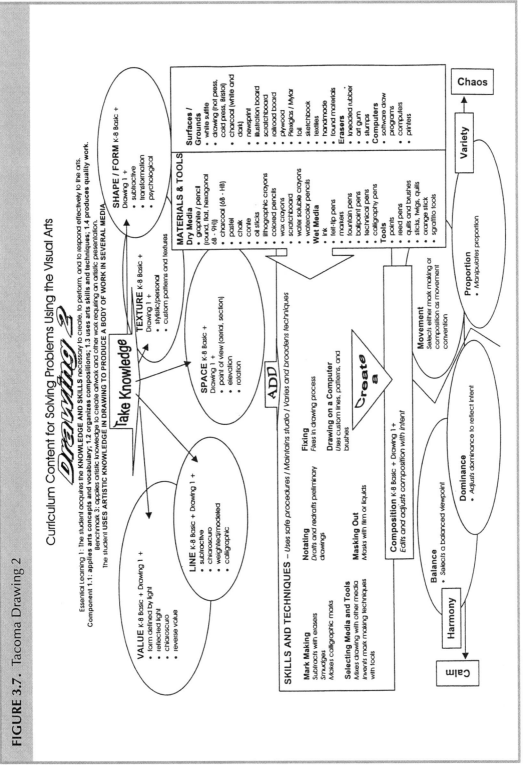

Curriculum Content for Solving Problems Using the Visual Arts

Drawing 2

Essential Learning 1: The student acquires the KNOWLEDGE AND SKILLS necessary to create, to perform, and to respond effectively to the arts.
Component 1.1: applies arts concepts and vocabulary; 1.2 organizes compositions; 1.3 uses arts skills and techniques; 1.4 produces quality work.
Benchmark 3: applies artistic knowledge to create artwork and other work requiring an artistic presentation.
The student USES ARTISTIC KNOWLEDGE IN DRAWING TO PRODUCE A BODY OF WORK IN SEVERAL MEDIA

Take Knowledge

SHAPE / FORM K-8 Basic +
Drawing 1 +
• subtractive
• transformation
• psychological

TEXTURE K-8 Basic +
Drawing 1 +
• stylistic/personal
• custom patterns and textures

SPACE K-8 Basic +
Drawing 1 +
• point of view (aerial, section)
• elevation
• rotation

VALUE K-8 Basic + Drawing 1 +
• form defined by light
• reflected light
• chiaroscuro
• reverse value

LINE K-8 Basic + Drawing 1 +
• subtractive
• chiaroscuro
• weighted/modeled
• calligraphic

MATERIALS & TOOLS
Dry Media
• graphite / pencil (round, flat, hexagonal 6B - 9H)
• charcoal (6B - HB)
• pastel
• chalk
• conte
• oil sticks
• lithographic crayons
• colored pencils
• wax crayons
• scratchboard
• water soluble crayons
• watercolor pencils

Wet Media
• ink
• felt-tip pens
• markers
• fountain pens
• ballpoint pens
• technical pens
• calligraphy pens

Tools
• points
• reed pens
• quills and brushes
• sticks, twigs, quills
• orange stick
• sgraffito tools

Surfaces / Grounds
• white sulfile
• drawing (hot press, cold press, Bristol)
• charcoal (white and dark)
• newsprint
• illustration board
• scratchboard
• railroad board
• plywood
• Plexiglas / Mylar
• foil
• sketchbook
• textiles
• handmade
• found materials

Erasers
• kneaded rubber
• art gum
• stumps

Computers
• software draw programs
• computers
• printers

ADD

Create a

Drawing on a Computer
Uses custom lines, patterns, and brushes

SKILLS AND TECHNIQUES – *Uses safe procedures / Maintains studio / Varies and broadens techniques*

Mark Making
*Subtracts with erasers
Smudges
Makes calligraphic marks*

Notating
Drafts and redrafts preliminary drawings

Fixing
Fixes in drawing process

Selecting Media and Tools
*Mixes drawing with other media
Inverts mark making techniques with tools*

Masking Out
Masks with film or liquids

Composition K-8 Basic + Drawing 1 +
Edits and adjusts composition with intent

Balance
• Selects a balanced viewpoint

Harmony

Calm

Dominance
• Adjusts dominance to reflect intent

Proportion
• Manipulates proportion

Movement
Selects either mark making or composition as movement convention

Variety

Chaos

(continued)

FIGURE 3.7. Continued

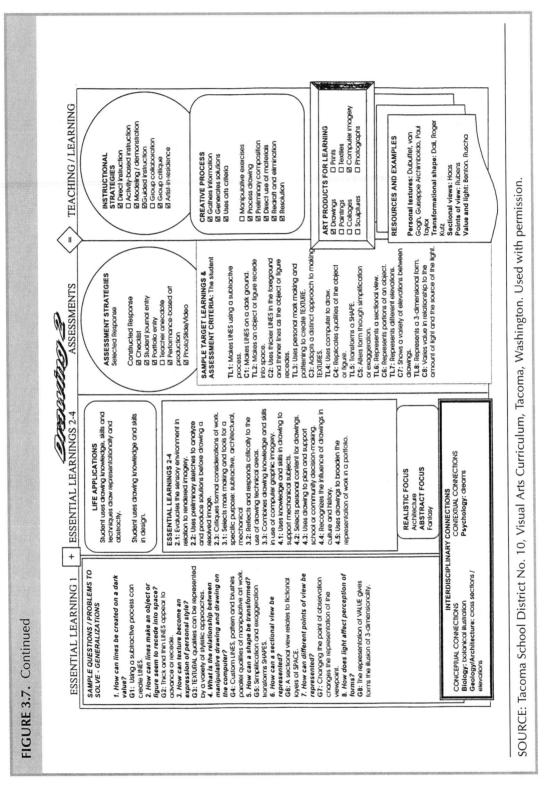

SOURCE: Tacoma School District No. 10, Visual Arts Curriculum, Tacoma, Washington. Used with permission.

that express all three components of the tripartite curriculum model: conceptual, factual, and processes/skills. It is important for subjects that have a heavy skill emphasis such as mathematics, language arts, fine arts, and vocational areas to delineate the curriculum for their own discipline before they integrate into social studies or science units.

Once a discipline has identified their subject area concepts, generalizations, critical content, and processes/skills, they can work with social studies or science teachers to create integrated units. Some local districts have chosen to develop curriculum frameworks for each subject area at the district level through teacher committees. They encourage teachers at the building to design integrated classroom units (interdisciplinary or intradisciplinary). It is expected that the classroom units will be aligned to the district curricular frameworks. Other school districts are using teacher committees to develop interdisciplinary units for the system in social studies and science. Mathematics, art, and the language arts committees articulate curriculum frameworks for their individual disciplines, but then they integrate their concepts and skills into the science and social studies units whenever possible. The next chapter deals with integration in greater detail.

SUMMARY

As school districts design local curricular frameworks, they rely on state or national standards to clarify what students must know and be able to do. But the standards vary in the way they are written—from broad, conceptual language to specific, topic-driven objectives. Teachers need to understand the language of standards because they drive different expectations and types of instruction in the classroom.

Some educators think that the more specific and factually oriented the standards, the better they are. But actually, well-written concept-based standards have a better chance of raising standards. Conceptually driven standards cause curriculum committees at the local level to determine how the grade-level content can be used to teach to the deeper understanding of the concepts and principles specified in the state standards. Conceptually framed state standards value the intellectual pursuit and deeper understanding of knowledge.

Curriculum mapping is a necessary strategy for determining what teachers are currently teaching. These maps will provide the information for looking at gaps and redundancies in content and skills when aligned to expectations from standards.

Curriculum maps also provide a base for identifying content that can be brought together for interdisciplinary units, for linking content to discipline-based concepts, and for assisting in the articulation of processes and skills for areas such as mathematics, art, or language arts.

EXTENDING THOUGHT

1. How can you identify whether a standard is factual, conceptual, or skill based?

2. How are the standards in your state written in the area of science? History? Are they more conceptually driven or factually driven?

3. How do local curriculum committees use their grade-level topics and content to align to conceptually driven standards? Relate a topic from your own curriculum to the following history standard: "Understand that as the economy of a nation expands, the demand for goods and services increases."

4. What value do curriculum maps have in the articulation of critical content and skills?

5. Why is it important to articulate discipline-based curriculums for subjects such as mathematics, art, physical education, and other skill-based subjects prior to interdisciplinary integration?

6. Why do skill-driven subjects such as mathematics and art also need to identify grade-level generalizations?

Designing Interdisciplinary, Integrated Curricula

Teachers in elementary schools jump in and tenaciously pursue integrated unit teaching. The thought of reducing the burden of content by integrating subject matter across disciplines is an appealing motivator. But the task has not been easy. A lack of well-articulated models has caused teachers to piece together integration techniques from trials and tidbits of training.

Heidi Hayes-Jacobs, a popular leader in the integrated curriculum movement, states that integrated curriculum is not new. It was prevalent in the early 1970s but was not successful because the structure of disciplines was lost, and the abundance of activities in the unit contributed to a "potpourri" problem (Hayes-Jacobs, 1989).

The disparate activities in these early forms of integration deflected learning from the deeper understanding of content, and process became the focus. And in those days, there was little assessment for the quality of process performance.

Student benefits from curriculum integration have become more apparent as teachers continue to explore the idea, and secondary teachers are now joining the quest. An **interdisciplinary,** integrated curriculum is a more difficult undertaking at the secondary level because of the traditional rigidity of subject area content expectations, some teacher attitudes toward change, class schedules, and issues related to collaboration and teaming.

This chapter will address the definition and value of integrated curriculum and present a step-by-step model for getting started. The chapter will end with answers to integration questions raised by elementary and secondary teachers.

DEFINING INTERDISCIPLINARY, INTEGRATED CURRICULA

A common precursor to content integration is coordinated, **multidisciplinary** curriculum. This model relates facts and activities across subject areas to a common topic, such as dinosaurs, bears, Africa, or the Revolutionary period in American history (see Figure 4.1). Students learn facts about the topic and develop their

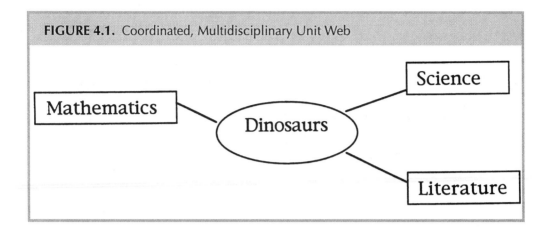

FIGURE 4.1. Coordinated, Multidisciplinary Unit Web

process skills through the varied activities, but a conceptual focus to force the integration of thinking is usually missing. Teachers often begin learning about curricular integration using the coordinated model and then progress to the higher form.

It is important for primary grade teachers to be assured that teaching units on bears or dinosaurs is fine as a supplementary unit, if they recognize that the major benefit will be the development of language skills around a motivational topic. And certainly, all students love bears and dinosaurs. But teachers will also want to provide units that challenge the higher-level thinking abilities of their students. They could achieve both language development and higher-level thinking in the same unit by linking a relevant concept to the topic study, such as hibernation, as a conceptual lens for the theme of bears in winter or extinction as a lens for the study of dinosaurs (see Figure 4.2).

The higher form of concept-based curriculum integration presented in this chapter rests on the following definition.

Concept-based integration examines a topic of study (theme) through a conceptual lens such as interdependence or conflict. The goal of concept-based, integrated curriculum is to cause students to integrate their thinking at a conceptual level. The key concepts and principles of each discipline develop brain schema as students meet new information. As students integrate new information, they deepen their factual and conceptual understanding. Students see patterns and connections between factual knowledge and transferable, conceptual ideas.

Interdisciplinary, as used in this chapter, refers to a variety of disciplines sharing a common, conceptual focus. The interdisciplinary focus on the conceptual lens—and theme, problem, or issue—contributes to deeper understanding and differentiates interdisciplinary from multidisciplinary.

Multidisciplinary refers to a variety of disciplines coordinating to a specific topic of study. A thematic unit on contemporary Russia is multidisciplinary unless a conceptual lens such as stability/instability is employed to force the disciplines to work together to develop a deeper, conceptual understanding.

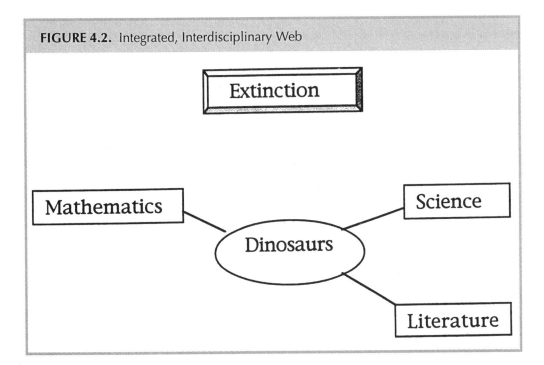

FIGURE 4.2. Integrated, Interdisciplinary Web

The common focus on the conceptual lens does not mean, however, that all disciplines only teach to the lens through the unit theme. Each discipline also teaches to its subject-specific concepts—but it develops these discipline-based concepts through the unit theme (directly or indirectly). It may or may not always relate directly to the lens. For example, if I am an art teacher participating in the unit on "Contemporary Russia: Stability/Instability," I might use artwork that illustrates social instability in some way, but I will have students explore how the artist used the conceptual elements of line, shadow, or form to express mood.

If I am a mathematics teacher, I may not be illustrating the lens of stability/instability directly, but I will choose an economics topic from social studies to illustrate a mathematics principle. I may have students do a mathematical projection of the economic trends based on applicable government statistics. I am teaching to mathematics concepts such as statistics, trends, and projections through the unit topics. I am indirectly supporting the lens.

Integration can also occur within a single discipline (**intradisciplinary**). Figure 4.3 illustrates a within-discipline history unit that uses a template to compare 20th-century conflicts illustrating the lens of freedom/independence. Chapter 5 provides another example of an intradisciplinary unit within the subject of biology.

Susan Drake, coordinator of the Integrated Studies Program for Brock University in Ontario, Canada, in *Creating Integrated Curriculum* (1998), presents a comprehensive review of different models and perspectives on the meaning of integrated curriculum. This book is quality reading for those people working to refine their own ideas and model for integration.

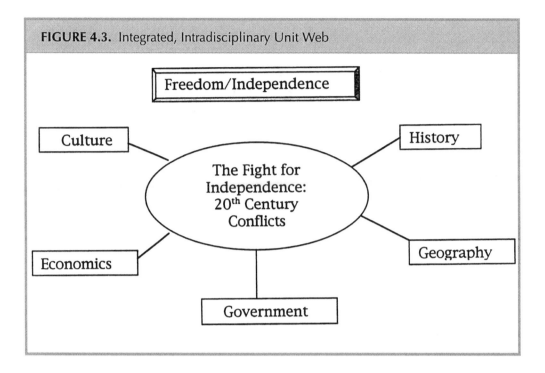

FIGURE 4.3. Integrated, Intradisciplinary Unit Web

In addition to the various levels of content integration, teachers make use of process integration that is referred to as integrated language arts. Integrated language arts is the coordinated application of the language skills of reading, writing, listening, speaking, and thinking to a particular area of study, whether a piece of literature, an interdisciplinary content unit, or a motivational single-topic unit focused on language development (see Figure 4.4). This chapter will deal with the design of the integrated, interdisciplinary content unit and discuss the application of language process skills.

THE INTEGRATED, INTERDISCIPLINARY CURRICULUM MODEL

The concept-based, integrated curriculum model presented in Figure 4.5 demonstrates that content from separate disciplines can be integrated when focused on a common problem, theme, or issue viewed through a conceptual lens. It is the lens that draws thinking to higher cognitive levels. This model also shows that process skills are addressed in planning as a component apart from the content because they are nurtured and assessed quite differently from content. The process skills interact with content in instructional activities and performances, however, to enhance conceptual and content understanding, as well as process and skill development. Integration using Gardner's (1993) multiple intelligences is another example of process integration enhancing know, understand, and do. These forms of process integration provide invaluable support for concept-based integration.

FIGURE 4.4. Process Integration and Content Integration

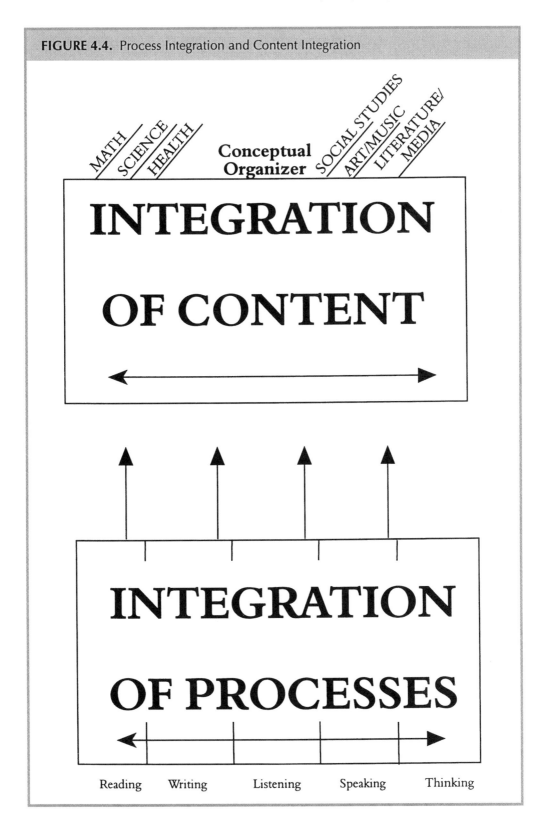

FIGURE 4.5. Integrated Concept/Process-Based Model

Conceptual Themes, Problems, Issues

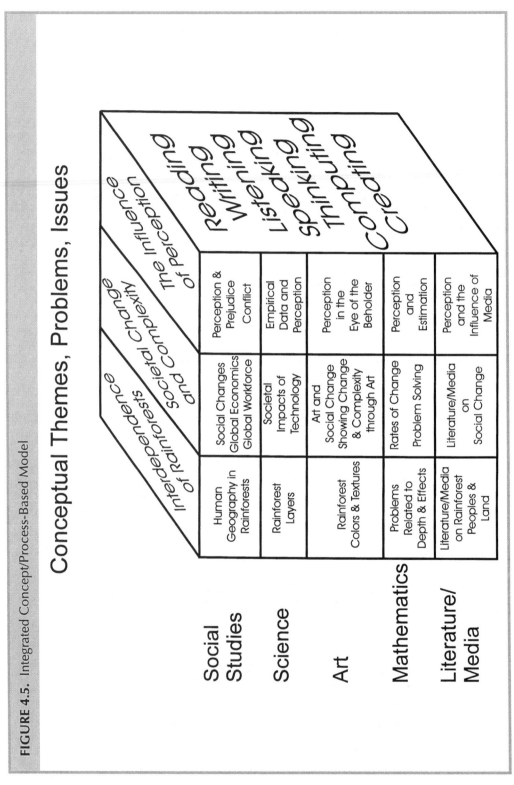

	Interdependence of Rainforests	Societal Change and Complexity	The Influence of Perception
Social Studies	Human Geography in Rainforests	Social Changes Global Economics Global Workforce	Perception & Prejudice Conflict
Science	Rainforest Layers	Societal Impacts of Technology	Empirical Data and Perception
Art	Rainforest Colors & Textures	Art and Social Change Showing Change & Complexity through Art	Perception in the Eye of the Beholder
Mathematics	Problems Related to Depth & Effects	Rates of Change Problem Solving	Perception and Estimation
Literature/ Media	Literature/Media on Rainforest Peoples & Land	Literature/Media on Social Change	Perception and the Influence of Media

Reading
Writing
Listening
Speaking
Thinking
Computing
Creating

Purpose and Value

Some educators feel that integrated curriculum should obliterate the separate disciplines to avoid fragmentation of knowledge. I agree with Gardner (1999), however, that the separate disciplines have value and should not be sacrificed in the name of integration.

One of the problems with a "seamless" curriculum is that even though disciplines have many foundational concepts in common, they also have discipline-specific concepts that would leave gaps in critical content knowledge if not addressed. Mathematics, for example, has the concepts of number, order, ratio, and proportion, which hold heavy content meaning. If subjects such as mathematics, literature, and art lose their unique conceptual structure, they will perform poorly whether within or outside of integrated units.

The purpose of integrated curriculum goes back to the definition stated previously—to cause students to integrate their thinking at a conceptual level by seeing the patterns and connections between transferable, conceptual ideas and the topic under study.

Integration of curriculum should proceed at a pace that allows for developing understanding and consideration of the following questions:

♦ Which concepts, critical content, and skills, by subject area, do national and state standards consider to be essential as we enter the 21st century?

♦ What framework or criteria will we use to decide on the significant themes, problems, or issues around which curriculum is integrated?

♦ How many interdisciplinary, integrated units should be taught in a year at the elementary and secondary levels? When should content and skills not be taught in the context of interdisciplinary units?

♦ How do we address discipline-based standards and benchmarks in integrated units?

♦ How will we ensure that we are maintaining the integrity of concepts, critical content, and skills from the separate disciplines as we integrate?

♦ If we move toward an issues orientation to the design of an integrated curriculum, what curriculum framework will ensure developing sophistication of conceptual understanding, critical content, and personal process skills?

As we continue to explore curriculum integration, the answers to the above issues become clearer. There is no question that integrated curriculum offers great value for teaching and learning. Table 4.1 lists often-cited benefits.

Because the integrated curriculum format draws from a wider information base than the single-subject area textbook, the teacher cannot hope to know all of the information prior to instruction. This provides an environment of greater freedom and flexibility to learn. It also ensures that students take responsibility for thinking and answering questions rather than depending on the teacher to dispense all knowledge.

TABLE 4.1 Benefits of Concept-Based Integrated Curriculum

Student Benefits	Rationale
Reduces curricular fragmentation	Facilitates curriculum connections
Provides depth to teaching and learning	Depth of thought and ideas, not depth of facts stacked higher
Provides teaching and learning focus	Teaching and learning are guided by the high-level generalizations arising from the concepts and critical content.
Engages students in active learning	Students search for and construct knowledge using a variety of learning styles and modalities.
Challenges higher levels of thinking	The conceptual lens and generalizations force thinking to the analysis and synthesis levels.
Help students connect knowledge	The best minds rise above the facts and see patterns and connections as they transfer knowledge.
Addresses significant problems, issues, concepts	Teacher-designed units typically address critical real-life issues.
Forces an answer to the relevancy question, "Why study these facts?"	Facts are not the end but means to deeper understandings.
Draws on multiple styles of learning	Auditory, visual, and kinesthetic activities are designed to engage many different modalities.

SOURCE: Arizona Department of Education.

In addition to the benefits for students, teachers find that the process of designing units facilitates their own development as learners. As they work collaboratively to plan units, teachers challenge their thinking in defining the critical outcomes for content and process development and in anticipating enduring content understandings—the key generalizations. Integrated units provide pathways for creating new knowledge for teachers as well as for students.

DESIGNING INTEGRATED TEACHING UNITS

Teachers who seek information on how to design integrated curricula ask for a step-by-step process that provides a model yet challenges their critical and creative thinking. Although I cringe to think that the model presented in this section

FIGURE 4.6. Steps for Designing an Integrated Teaching Unit

1. Decide on a **unit theme,** which will allow all team members to enter the integration process. The theme is the centering topic for study.

2. Identify a major **concept** to serve as a suitable **integrating or conceptual lens** for the study. The conceptual lens draws thinking above the disciplines to the integration level. Integrated thinking sees the conceptual and transferable patterns and connections of knowledge. Changing the conceptual lens changes the unit focus (e.g., "Systems" of the human body to "Structure and Function" of the human body).

3. Web the **topics** for study, by subject or area, around the concept and theme. Topics listed around the content/concept web will sometimes be specific (heart rate, diabetes, etc.), or they may be subconcepts (substance abuse, disease, etc.). After brainstorming specific topics and concepts for the web, underline all of the concepts. These become the fuel for writing developmentally appropriate and powerful enduring understandings.

4. Write a **unit overview** to engage student interest and introduce the unit.

5. Brainstorm some of the **enduring understandings** (generalizations/essential understandings) that you would expect students to derive from the study. Enduring understandings answer the question, "So what? Why should I learn these facts?" Enduring understandings go beyond the facts to the conceptual and transferable level of understanding. (This facilitates conceptual thinking and deep understanding.)

6. Brainstorm **guiding questions** to facilitate the student's thinking toward the enduring understandings. Guiding questions combine specific "what, why, or how" questions related to specific topics within the unit, with open-ended "why" and "how" questions to develop conceptual thinking and deep under-

(continued)

will be looked on as another Hunter-like set of steps, I also trust that teachers will see its value as a flexible springboard for engaging students in the design of integrated units as well as engaging them in relevant unit activities.

Figure 4.6 lists 12 steps for designing integrated teaching units. I have worked with elementary and secondary grade teachers around the country for the past 6 years to develop and refine these steps. Clarifying notes follow the steps.

Figure 4.7 provides a set of unit planning pages to use with the steps for designing a concept-based unit as one model. It is not necessary to use this model for laying out a unit, however. The various unit components can be arranged in a variety of formats. Teachers want a unit format that is coherent and usable for them.

To move from the overall unit plan to classroom lessons, the teacher may want to use the lesson planning pages similar to the example in Figure 4.8. I would suggest using these planning pages for a week's view rather than a daily plan.

FIGURE 4.6. Continued

standing. A unit may have one or two philosophical debate questions, which have no right or wrong answer but develop interest and defense of a position.

7. Identify the **specific knowledge (key facts) and skills** that a student must internalize. Students will "know" and exhibit "critical skills." The specific knowledge is drawn from the topics being studied; the skills are drawn from standards and curricular frameworks.

8. Code the knowledge and skills with **assessment codes (AC)** to show the other evidence that is planned beyond the culminating performance task. Include these other assessments in your unit packet.

9. For each week in the unit, **write an instructional plan or instructional activities** to address critical knowledge, understandings, and skills. Note: Engagement with the questions and activities should develop the enduring understandings. Incorporate the knowledge and skills from Step 7 into the plan or activities.

10. Write the **culminating performance task** to show the depth of learning. The performance task answers the question, "What do I want students to know, understand, and be able to do as a result of this unit of study?" Use the formula "what, why, and how" in writing to ensure that the performance assesses to the level of deep understanding (the "why"). You may decide to use more than one performance task in the unit.

11. Design the **scoring guide** (criteria and standard) to assess the performance task. For each criterion assessed in a given mode, ask yourself, "What does it look like?" at each level of the performance.

12. Identify **unit resources** and include **teacher notes** to assist with instruction.

Resource A provides two alternative formats for unit plans. These alternative formats are often preferred by secondary teachers.

Unit Design Steps—Questions and Answers

Questions arise as teachers work together to design concept-based units. To answer some of these questions, let's take each of the unit design steps and discuss major issues. The following material from my previous book, *Concept-Based Curriculum and Instruction: Teaching Beyond the Facts* (Erickson, 1998), has been updated with new examples.

1. The Unit Theme

A. **What is the difference between a *theme* and a *concept*?**

A concept meets the following criteria: a one- or two-word mental construct that is broad and abstract, timeless, universal, and represents a variety of examples that all share the attributes of the concept.

(text continues on page 82)

FIGURE 4.7. Unit Planning Pages

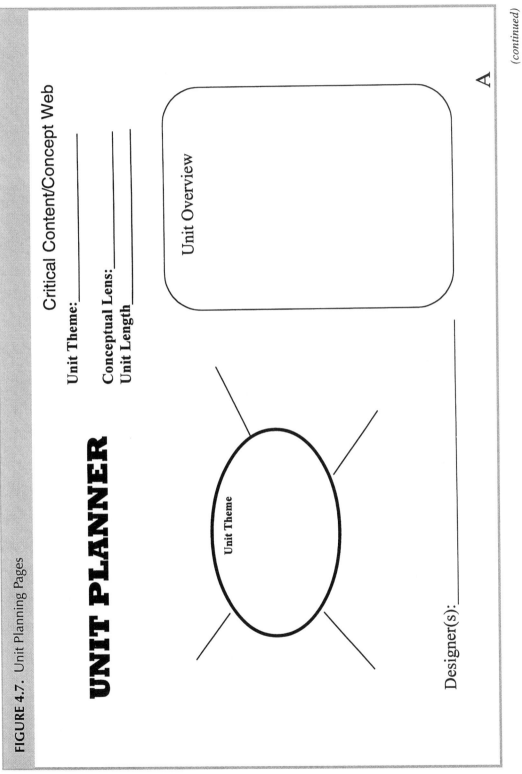

Critical Content/Concept Web

UNIT PLANNER

Unit Theme: _____

Conceptual Lens: _____
Unit Length _____

Unit Overview

Unit Theme

Designer(s): _____

A

(continued)

FIGURE 4.7. Continued

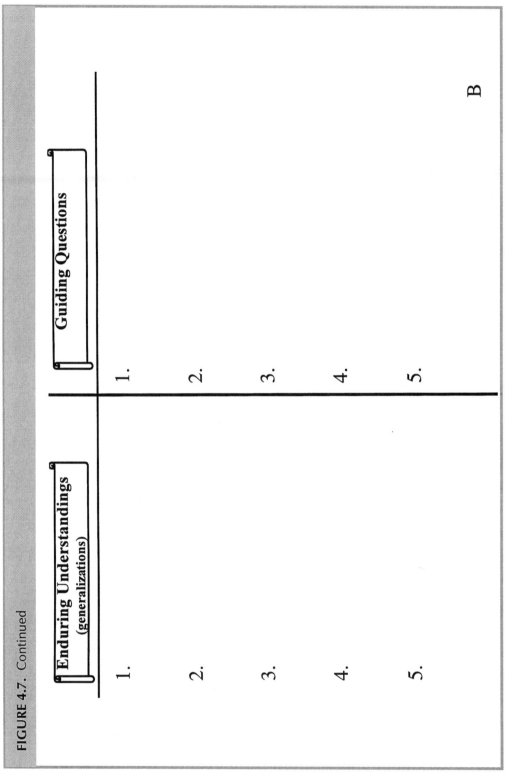

Guiding Questions

1.

2.

3.

4.

5.

Enduring Understandings
(generalizations)

1.

2.

3.

4.

5.

B

FIGURE 4.7. Continued

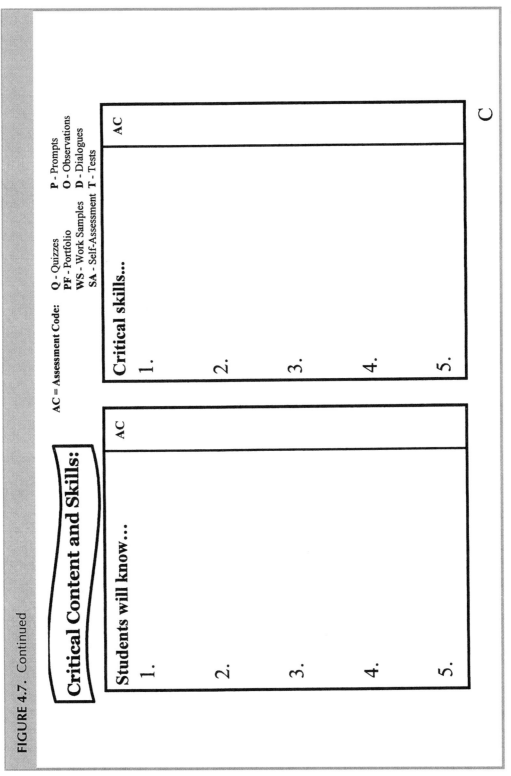

Critical Content and Skills:

AC = Assessment Code:
Q - Quizzes   **P** - Prompts
PF - Portfolio   **O** - Observations
WS - Work Samples   **D** - Dialogues
SA - Self-Assessment   **T** - Tests

Critical skills...

	AC
1.	
2.	
3.	
4.	
5.	

C

Students will know...

	AC
1.	
2.	
3.	
4.	
5.	

(continued)

75

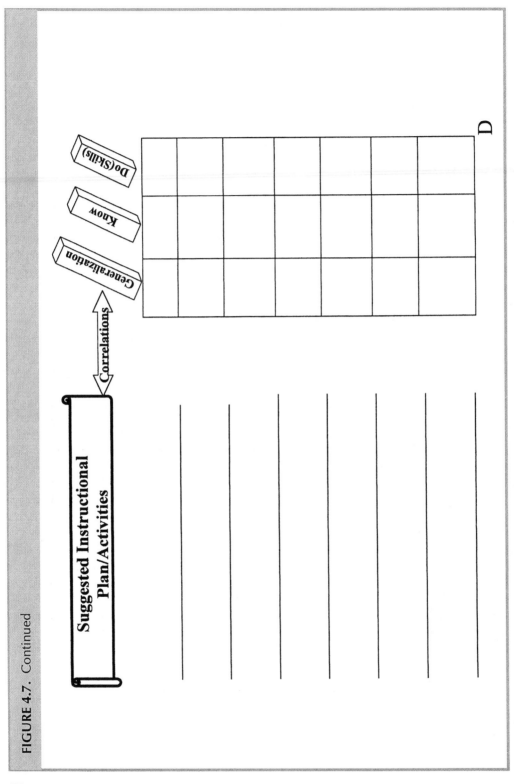

FIGURE 4.7. Continued

FIGURE 4.7. Continued

Culminating Performance Task Planner:

What: Investigate...

Why: in order to understand that...

How: (performance)

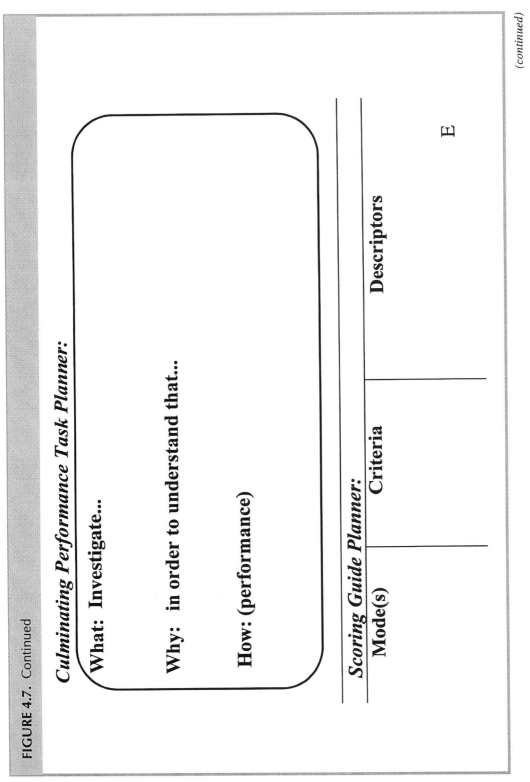

Scoring Guide Planner:

Mode(s)	Criteria	Descriptors
		E

(continued)

FIGURE 4.7. Continued

Scoring Guide

Performance:

Mode:

Criteria	Excellent	Highly Competent	Competent	Novice

F

FIGURE 4.7. Continued

Teacher Notes

Unit Resources

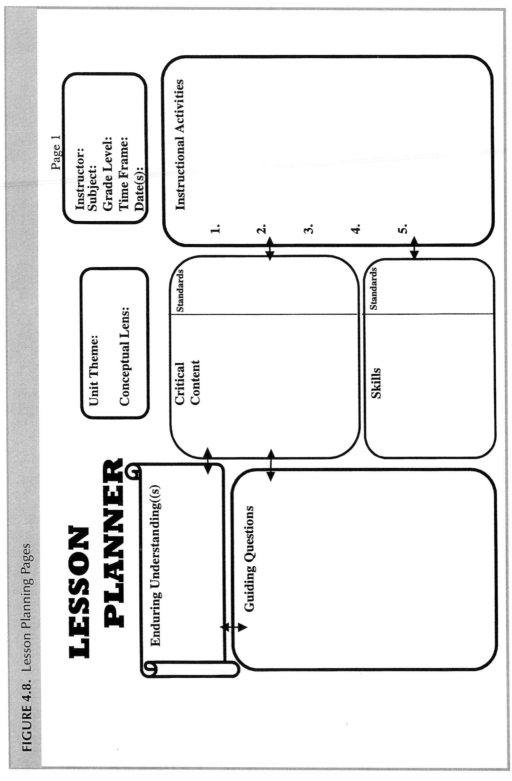

FIGURE 4.8. Lesson Planning Pages

LESSON PLANNER

Page 1

Instructor:
Subject:
Grade Level:
Time Frame:
Date(s):

Instructional Activities

1.

2.

3.

4.

5.

Unit Theme:

Conceptual Lens:

Standards

Critical Content

Standards

Skills

Enduring Understanding((s)

Guiding Questions

FIGURE 4.8. Continued

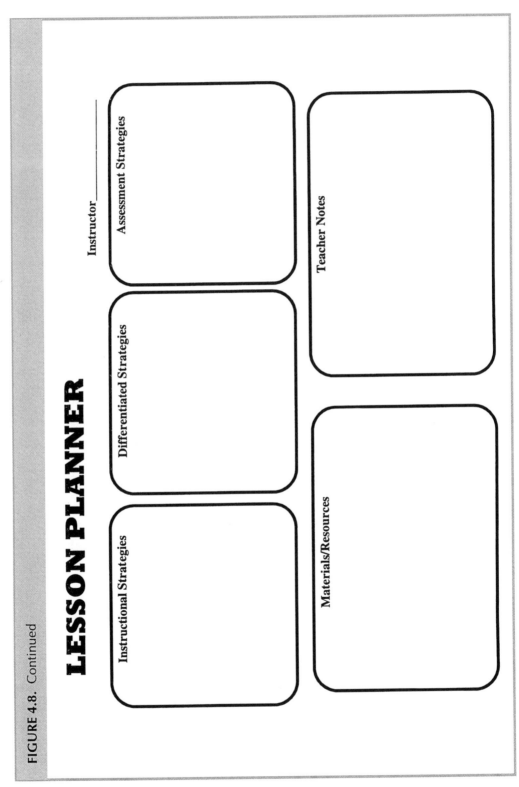

LESSON PLANNER

Instructor _____

Instructional Strategies

Differentiated Strategies

Assessment Strategies

Materials/Resources

Teacher Notes

A theme can be a **topical theme** such as "The U.S. Presidency" or a **conceptual theme** such as "The Changing Role of the U.S. Presidency." Including the conceptual lens of "change/role" as part of the unit title changes a topical theme into a conceptual theme. Which type of theme requires a greater degree of complex thinking? Why? Did you discover that conceptual themes take thinking to the transferable level, which requires a greater degree of complex thinking? Congratulations! You understand a basic premise of concept-based instruction.

You can state your unit focus as a topical theme, but for higher-level integrated thinking, you will also want to identify a conceptual lens for the unit.

B. How do the number of disciplines participating in a unit affect the unit theme?

Generally, the more subjects involved in the unit, the broader and more abstract the theme. To allow each discipline to enter the integration process, the theme has to be broad enough to encompass the different curricula. For example, I could do a unit titled "Wildlife Populations in the Northwestern United States" with a conceptual lens of habitat, but if I want to include social studies in the same unit, then I would have to make the theme more abstract and broad, such as "Populations in the Northwestern United States." As you can see, this makes the theme so obtuse that it provides little focus, and the unit will lack coherence. Beware the pit of "thematic obtusity" or you will end up with unfocused coverage over depth. There would also be the problem of the habitat lens. It would have to be broadened to something like "interdependence" to cross disciplines.

2. Concept (Conceptual Lens)

A. Why use a conceptual lens for my topic of study?

- A conceptual lens forces thinking to the integration level. Students see patterns and connections at a conceptual level as they relate the topic to the broader study framed by the lens.

- Without a conceptual lens, a topic of study remains at a lower cognitive level, and students seek to memorize the "facts" related to the topic.

- The focus concept facilitates and requires deep understanding and allows for the transfer of knowledge.

B. How do I select a suitable conceptual lens?

Examine the theme of your unit and select a conceptual lens that will provide a direction for the thinking process. For example, do you want thinking to center on "interdependence between nations" or "competition between nations"? For beginners in concept-based unit design, it sometimes helps to refer to the concepts suggested in Figure 2.5 (or Resource B), realizing that there are other choices available that are not shown on the sample lists. You may use either macro- or microconcepts for the lens, depending on the thematic focus. Sometimes, a microconcept, such as "Identity," produces deeper conceptual thinking.

C. Shouldn't I decide on my conceptual lens before I decide on the theme of my unit?

Not usually. How would you know which lens would provide the greatest thinking power unless you relate it to the specific theme you are studying? Occasionally, you can decide as a teaching team that a particular concept is so important that you want to focus the study on that concept and the lessons related to it. In these special cases, the theme might be selected after the lens is identified.

3. Webbing the Topics for Study

A. Should the categories around the web always be different subject areas?

No. There are two key considerations when deciding on categories to display the specific topics of study related to the theme:

— Is the unit interdisciplinary? If it is, then show the different subject areas that are participating in the unit as your categories.

— Is the unit intradisciplinary? If so, then show the different disciplines of study that appear within the subject area field as your categories. For example, if I am doing a unit within the field of social studies, my categories would be the disciplines of history, geography, economics, government, and culture. An intradisciplinary study of this type would benefit from the inclusion of literature/media and mathematics, however. To study any topic within the social studies or science fields without considering the related literature/media and applications of mathematics, greatly shortchanges the study for students.

Another intradisciplinary method for webbing is to determine the categories that best break down the theme into its significant components. For example, foreign language teachers may choose to do a unit related to the concept of culture (e.g., "Spanish Influence on American Culture") and would define the categories around the web by the elements of culture: language, customs, music and art, and so on.

4. The Unit Overview

A. Is there a specific pattern for writing the unit overview?

No. The key is to convey the thematic focus of the unit in an engaging way. The overview would include the unit theme and a description of the unit, but this can be done with a combination of narrative and engaging, provocative questions if you wish.

5. Generalizations (Enduring Understandings)

A. What are generalizations?

- Generalizations fall on the synthesis level of thinking in the structure of knowledge (see Figure 2.3). They may be referred to as *enduring understandings* because they are the deeper, transferable ideas that arise from fact-based studies.

- Generalizations are statements of conceptual relationship.

- Generalizations transfer through time and across cultures. They are exemplified through the fact base but transcend singular examples.

B. How do we identify generalizations for our topics of study?

In units of study, use the content web to look for concepts that can be paired to make statements of enduring understanding. Why are you studying this theme? What do you want students to understand at a conceptual, transferable level—beyond the specific topic?

C. How do we write generalizations?

- When first learning, it is helpful to use the sentence starter, "Students understand that. . . ." Complete the sentence by pairing two or more concepts from your unit of study into a sentence conveying an important idea that will transfer through time and across cultures.

- When writing generalizations, do not mention your topic of study. In other words, do not use proper or personal nouns. Move beyond the example provided by your topic and look for the transcendent ideas.

- When writing generalizations, use active, present-tense verbs to convey the timeless characteristic. Avoid passive voice and past-tense verbs. Try and avoid the use of *to be* verbs (*is, are, have*). A pitfall in writing generalizations, which are statements of conceptual relationship, is to write them as simple definitions of concepts. An example might be the statement, "A *ratio* is a *relation* in *degree* or *number* between two *things*." This statement has many concepts (italicized) but is mainly a definition of the concept of ratio. The use of a *to be* verb is often a clue that a definition has been offered. The danger would be in overusing definitions and missing the deeper conceptual ideas of the discipline. A few definitions are fine for baseline understanding but are better left for vocabulary study.

- Use qualifiers (*may, can, often*) if your generalization may not hold across all examples but is still significant as an understanding.

Let's put two or more of the following concepts together and state a generalization. (You can get at least five generalizations out of these concepts.) You may use other concepts if you need to add to the list for your idea.

Organisms
Migration
Survival
Resistance
Change
Disease
Environment
Populations
Adaptation

The student understands that

_____

_____

Is your idea important for students to understand in a broader context? Did you remember to use an active, present-tense verb? Do you have a full sentence? Did you avoid using proper and personal nouns? Did you use a qualifier (*often, may, can*) if the generalization is important but may not hold across all examples? ("Organisms often exhibit an evolutionary logic.")

D. What is the difference between a generalization and a principle?

Generalizations are statements of conceptual relationship that transfer across examples. They must be continually tested for truth because they may not hold over time. Some generalizations meet the test of timelessness, but they may not be ideas that hold as much significance as principles in the structure of a discipline. Principles are always true and have significant roles in a discipline. They are the cornerstones for understanding and applying the knowledge of a discipline. They carry the weight of universal and timeless truth, such as Newton's laws of gravity or the axioms of mathematics.

E. How do we tell the difference between less sophisticated and more sophisticated generalizations?

If we think of generalizations according to "levels" of sophistication, then we can look at what characteristics differentiate Level 1 (less sophisticated) to Level 3 (sophisticated) generalizations. The following generalizations, which might be appropriate for the elementary grades, show three different levels of sophistication.

Level 1: People use **machines** to do **work.**

Level 2: **Machines** supply **energy** and/or **special functions** to complete **tasks** efficiently.

Level 3: **Work efficiency** increases **productivity** and **revenues.**

As we move forward from Level 1, the generalizations become more specific, and the concept load becomes heavier. The concepts (in bold) require more background knowledge to understand as the levels increase. As the levels progress, we won't necessarily find more concepts in the sentence, but the idea presented will be more cognitively challenging.

Let's look at a set of generalizations that would be developmentally appropriate at the high school level:

Level 1: *Governments* regulate the exchange of *goods.*

Level 2: A national imbalance in the *supply* and *demand* of *goods* can lead to an *economic dependence* on *foreign products.*

Level 3: *Economic dependence* on foreign countries to meet *basic needs* can jeopardize the *political* and *economic stability* of a *nation.*

F. How do we "scaffold thinking" to write generalizations at more sophisticated levels?

To take thinking to more sophisticated levels in writing generalizations, one should use open-ended guiding questions, just as you would do in the teaching situation. Notice the guiding questions following each generalization in the examples below. The questions are formed by asking a "how" or "why" (not a "what") question related to the generalization. In the unit planning process, teachers discuss the possible answers to the essential question and listen for any concepts that could be used to form a more sophisticated essential understanding (generalization). Make certain that the generalizations answer the essential question and avoid the error of restating the previous generalization in different words.

Notice that the generalizations become more concept specific as the levels increase, but the concepts require greater background knowledge.

Elementary grades:

Level 1: *Organisms* survive in *changing environments.* (How do organisms survive in changing environments?)

Level 2: *Organisms* adapt (*adaptation*) to *changing environments.* (So what? Why must organisms adapt?)

Level 3: *Organisms* that do not adapt to *changing environments* will not survive (*survival*).

Secondary Schools—Art:

Level 1: *Texture* can be *real* or *implied.* (How do artists create implied texture?)

Level 2: Artists imply *texture* through *repeated patterns* of *lines, shapes,* and *spaces.* (So what? Why do artists create texture in visual art?)

Level 3: *Texture* adds *variety* and *balance* to *visual art forms* and can create *visual complexity* and *interest.*

Take the Level 1 generalization provided below and scaffold by asking a "how" or "why" question that will take the thinking to the next level. Notice that the Level 1 generalization in this and some of the previous examples use a *to be* verb. This often occurs at Level 1 because the idea is a broad and usually quite obvious conceptual idea. As the generalizations become more sophisticated, other verbs carry more power for the idea expressed. Using *is, are,* or *have* at Level 1 is acceptable but not preferred.

Level 1 Generalization: "Art is a method of communication."
Essential Question: "Why. . . . _____
_____?

Level 2 Generalization: _____
_____

Essential Question: _____

Level 3 Generalization: _____
_____

Did you experience difficulty moving from Level 2 to Level 3? This is often difficult at first. I think it is because our traditional curriculum design does not require much thinking beyond Level 1 or Level 2, and teachers feel so pressured to cover the content that there is little time in classrooms to probe students' thinking. So here is a tip to help you reach Level 3. After you have written the Level 2 generalization, ask the significance question, "So what? What importance or significance does this understanding (Level 2 generalization) have for society, the individual, and so on?" After thinking about and discussing the significance, write the importance in the form of a Level 3 generalization.

G. Aren't generalizations too abstract to mean very much? Isn't it more important to have clarity and topic specificity?

The most specific and clear piece of information is a fact (see following example), but is it the desired end for teaching and learning? What do

FIGURE 4.9. I Just Can't Stop Scaffolding

you think? Why? What role do facts play in concept/process curriculum and instruction?

■ Fact: According to census data, the United States population is growing.

■ Generalization: Increasing *populations* can lead to *environmental stress* and depletion of *natural resources.*

Do not underestimate the power of a seemingly bland generalization. The questions that are generated from the generalization challenge thinking and discussions to deeper levels. The generalizations are the summary of higher-level thought. They bring closure to previous learning and also invite further questions.

H. Why should we scaffold generalizations?

When teachers are asked why they are teaching a topic, the first answer is usually a summary of the facts they want students to know. After learning how to identify and write generalizations, teachers begin to state the important transferable "ideas" they want students to understand. But this new skill takes practice. The first generalizations are more often Level 1, no matter what the grade level. The learning curve is very steep, however, and after a few practice sessions, the generalizations become more sophisticated. Learning how to scaffold thinking also helps the thinking and writing processes. Learning to use language precisely to state generalizations (enduring understandings) brings focus to teaching and learning. The words *influence, affect, impact,* or *to be* verbs often indicate a Level 1 generalization because the statements tend to be so general that they say very little.

It is important to scaffold those generalizations that are so simplistic that they beg to be carried forward. You have students in your classrooms that fall at all levels of conceptual sophistication. If you identify and teach to all three levels of generalizations, you will be able to differentiate curriculum and instruction for the different ability levels while still centering on the same topics. This helps in this age of inclusionary programming. Scaffolding helps tap the depth and breadth of enduring understandings.

Wiggins and McTighe (ASCD, 1998) in *Understanding by Design* provide another technique for tapping the depth or "uncovering" the overarching generalizations (enduring understandings). They suggest six "facets" for ensuring deeper understanding[1]:

■ Facet 1: Explanation—students build, test, and verify theories or explanations.

■ Facet 2: Interpretation—students build their own interpretations, translations, and narratives from primary source texts, events, and experiences.

■ Facet 3: Application—students apply what they have learned to real or realistic situations.

■ Facet 4: Perspective—students take multiple points of view on the same issue. They must develop and use critical-thinking skills to determine, on their own, the strengths and weaknesses of the theories, explanations, proofs, and arguments they confront.

■ Facet 5: Empathy—students are confronted with types of direct experience designed to develop greater openness and empathy for experiences and worldviews other than their own.

■ Facet 6: Self-Knowledge—students engage in ongoing self-assessment about what they know and . . . make their thinking explicit as they examine the underlying assumptions for their ideas.

Wiggins and McTighe's intellectually provocative book is a must-read for educators interested in the connections between concept-based curriculum and the design for deep understanding.

I. **Why should I determine so many of the generalizations for a unit? Why not let the students come up with their own generalizations?**

If a student comes up with a generalization in the group discussion, then celebrate! You have a thinking student! But if you are just beginning to work with concept-based curriculum, the more likely scenario will be students who think to the level of facts (we have trained them well) and who resist thinking beyond the facts. (Do some of your brightest students come to mind?)

The reason teachers identify most of the unit generalizations is that we are learning how to think conceptually ourselves and need the practice, but, more important, we are "systematically" teaching students how to think. This is ultimately an inductive teaching model using guiding questions and activities to direct thinking toward enduring understandings. To teach students how to think conceptually, we have to know where the thinking is going (at least a direction), so that we can plan a questioning path. We do not want to be so rigid that we miss "teachable moments," when a student discovers a big idea that we can build on or when student questions take the discussion in a certain direction. But we cannot always wait and see where students want to go if we want to teach conceptual thinking and illuminate "enduring understandings" for a unit of study.

6. Guiding Questions

A. What are guiding questions?

Guiding questions are a critical driver for teaching and learning. They engage students in the study and create a bridge between performance-based activities and deeper, conceptual understandings.

B. Why are guiding questions important in the teaching/learning process?

There are a number of reasons why guiding questions are important:

■ They can help students discover patterns in knowledge and solve problems.

■ They support inductive teaching—guiding students to discover meaning, which increases motivation to learn.

■ They are one of the most powerful tools for helping students think at more complex levels.

■ They engage the personal intellect—something that traditional objectives usually fail to do.

Read the following objectives directing the learning of famous people. Do these objectives have a familiar ring?

Famous People in American History: Objectives

■ Identify famous historical figures in American history.

■ Identify significant events related to these historical figures.

■ Recall how the following historical figures shaped the course of American history: George Washington, John Adams, Adam Smith, Martin Luther King.

Now read the guiding questions related to the same topic.

Famous People in American History: Guiding Questions

■ What does it mean to be a leader?

■ Who were some of the famous leaders in American history?

■ Why are they considered famous?

■ How did John Adams shape the future of America?

■ How did Martin Luther King Jr. influence the views of a nation?

■ Why do we remember leaders long after their lives have ended?

■ Are all leaders good?

■ Can you think of a leader in the world today that America does not support? Why do we not support this leader?

■ What are the characteristics of a good leader?

■ Can ordinary citizens be leaders?

What did you notice as you read the questions that differed from reading the objectives? Did you find that your mind was on "autopilot" as you read the objectives but that you were "thinking" as you read the questions? Did the questions engage your interest because you wanted to know how you would answer the questions based on your own knowledge and perspectives? Looking at factual content through a conceptual lens, such as "leadership," engages the personal intellect. Why do so many curriculum documents attempt to drive content teaching through the use of objectives when they create so little passion for thinking and learning? Could it be that objectives are easier to test and score? We definitely need skill objectives, but do we really need content objectives if we have identified clearly the following?

(a) The critical content topics (without verbs) that students are to study

(b) The enduring conceptual understandings to be drawn from content

(c) The key processes (complex performances) and skills

C. Why are guiding questions so difficult to write?

We can only pull so many questions out of the air related to a topic. Consequently, most of the questions end up being "what" questions directly related to the topic of study. However, overemphasizing "what" questions won't guide thinking to deeper waters.

One reason that some teachers have trouble writing guiding questions is that they have not consciously identified the conceptual understandings that the questions should drive toward. Consequently, the questions keep flowing toward the specific topic. In a concept-based curriculum, it is not enough to teach only the facts related to a specific topic; we want to use questions to take thinking to the level of conceptual understanding and help students build a schema for knowledge transfer. We need "why" and "how" questions, as well as "what" questions to extend thinking.

Although fact-based questions are important to ensure the foundations of knowledge, the open-ended, conceptually based questions challenge the thinking of students beyond the facts. Open-ended questions that contain two or more concepts usually specify the essential understanding as an embedded statement. It is the use of these questions as a follow-up to specific, topic-related questions that will help students bridge to deeper understanding.

7. Specific Knowledge and Skills

A. How should we identify the specific knowledge for the unit?

The specific knowledge is a list of the critical content topics to be studied in the unit. These topics can be pulled off of the web and delineated further with bullets, or they can be listed as key facts that you feel students must know.

FIGURE 4.10. The Next Essential Question

SOURCE: Cartoon by David Ford. david@twocrowcartoons.com

B. Where do the skills come from?

The skills can be drawn from the curriculum documents for the different subject areas such as language arts, mathematics, or science. The skills listed need to have been taught directly either as a part of the unit or at another time during the day. Notice that we are not yet writing activities. We are just identifying the key skills that will be taught directly by the teacher. The activities, which link the skill with a topic, are developed in Step 9.

8. Assessment Codes

A. What are the assessment codes?

The assessment codes allow you to plan and identify the different ways you wish to assess knowledge, skills, and understandings within your unit. You will need to develop and include the different assessments in your unit packet. Different assessment types are suggested by the codes, but you may choose to add some other types. These assessments are in addition to the performance task, which is designed in Step 10.

9. Instructional Plan/Suggested Activities

A. What is the purpose of the instructional plan/activities?

Teachers have a choice in this step. They can either suggest activities to explore and develop the critical content and enduring understandings, or they can list the instructional steps for carrying out the unit plan. What would you do first in implementing this unit? Second? The instructional plan uses a teacher frame of reference; the activities are from the students' frame of reference.

There should be a coherent link between the understandings, the questions, and the activities. The purpose of the instructional plan and the guiding questions is to develop the enduring understandings based on the specific content examples. Students will learn specific content knowledge and also develop deeper, conceptual understanding when there is evident coherence. (If you include suggested activities, include the skills identified on the specific knowledge/skills page of the unit plan.)

B. How do the secondary school unit-planning pages differ from the elementary pages?

The secondary school remains quite departmentalized across the country, though many have moved to interdisciplinary teams and block schedules. With the reality of departmentalization, the unit-planning pages are used somewhat differently at the secondary level. Although the interdisciplinary team works together to develop the unit theme, conceptual lens, and web; the other unit components, up to the culminating performance, can be completed independently by teachers in each discipline. This is because secondary teachers in a departmentalized situation will be teaching their own subjects within their classrooms. They will still be providing "integrated instruction" with their team because they share a common theme and conceptual lens. There will be a few major generalizations that all disciplines support, but it is critical that each discipline maintain instructional integrity by also teaching to their own generalizations, reached through discipline-driven questions and activities. The activities will draw on the processes and skills important to each discipline. Once the unit planning pages have been completed by each discipline, it is important that the interdisciplinary team come back together once again to share their work and discuss what the overall student learning experience will be throughout the unit. Teachers will want to maintain a holistic sense of the integrated learning experience for students.

10. Culminating Performance Task

A. What is the culminating performance task?

The culminating performance allows you to make a final assessment on how well students relate content to transferable, conceptual ideas and on how well they are able to perform with their knowledge. It answers the question, "What do I want students to know, understand, and be able to do as a result of this unit of study?" We are assessing understanding of one or more major ideas (generalizations) for the unit, supported by critical content knowledge and demonstrated through a complex, authentic performance.

B. How do we evaluate the culminating performance?

A **scoring guide** is developed as part of the unit planning process to assess the level of performance. It is important to realize that students could easily get overloaded with major projects due in all classes at the same time in integrated units. This problem can be eased if teachers plan a common performance (e.g., a play) that would draw from the different disciplines or if they work together to stagger the due dates. Another option would be a unit **portfolio,** developed throughout the length of a unit, which would include the work of the different disciplines. The assessment criteria might differ by discipline.

C. Is the culminating performance the only assessment in the unit?

Definitely not. Throughout a unit, you will use an array of assessments that match the kinds of learning students are to demonstrate. Interviews, true/false assessments, multiple choice, writing tasks, oral presentations, and projects are just a few examples of assessments that provide information about different kinds of learning. These other assessments are noted in Step 8 with the assessment codes.

D. How do we write the culminating performance?

A major problem with many performance tasks is that there is too often little or no display of deep understanding. I think this is once again because our traditional curriculum design only takes us to the superficial level of

---

FIGURE 4.11. Culminating Performance Task

WHAT: investigate . . . (unit theme) _____

_____

WHY: to understand that . . . _____

_____

_____

HOW: _____

_____

_____

_____

---

topics and facts. How, then, can we write assessments for deep understanding? Figure 4.11 shows a simple model for writing a demonstration of culminating performance. This format ensures an assessment of deep understanding.

Complete the formula in Figure 4.11 as follows:

What do you want students to do?

WHAT: Begin this statement with a cognitive verb such as *investigate* and tie it directly to the theme of your unit. The theme of the unit in the example following is "The Holocaust: Man's Inhumanity to Man."

> **Example:**   Investigate the Holocaust.

WHY: to understand that. . . . Complete this statement by thinking beyond the topic to the importance or significance of the study. What is the transferable lesson to be taken from this particular study?

> **Example:**   To understand that leaders may abuse political or social power

HOW: Begin a new sentence that frames how you want students to demonstrate their understanding of the "why" statement. This is the critical step. If you want to measure deep understanding, then this "how" statement needs to demonstrate the "why"—not just knowledge of the facts learned in the "what" statement.

> **Example:** You are a prosecutor with the War Crimes Tribunal. Prepare a case trying Adolph Hitler for his alleged war crimes against the Jewish people in Germany during the Holocaust. Research primary and secondary documents and build your case around the themes of "crimes against humanity" and "abuse of power." Using multimedia and clear and specific arguments, present your case to the court.

Notice that the performance, the "how" statement, demonstrates understanding of the "why" statement. This takes the performance beyond a simple recitation of facts related to the Holocaust.

What are the complex performances required in this task? Can you underline them? What kinds of criteria will be used in the scoring guide related to the multimedia presentation? (Clarity of presentation, organization, depth and breadth of knowledge, etc.)

Write a culminating performance that links the "how" (presentation, project, etc.) directly to the deep understanding specified in the "why" statement.

Check back over the directions to make certain the performance demonstrated the "why" statement—the "deep understanding."

11. Scoring Guide for Culminating Performance

A. What is a scoring guide?

A scoring guide (**rubric**) assesses performance on a task according to defined criteria and a scaled set of performance **indicators.** A scoring guide assesses student progress toward the standard. The standard is the expected quality of performance.

Perhaps the most difficult part of writing scoring guides is finding effective and precise language to describe performance at the various levels. Too often, the defining language sounds "wishy-washy," such as *always, often, sometimes,* or *seldom.* We need to keep working on this language problem. We can find descriptive terms that are more precise and helpful to students, but it means that teachers will need to help students develop a mental construct for what these terms "look like" in the performance or product.

Students need to see specific exemplars, representative examples, of work. They need practice in applying the various descriptors that will be used in the assessment of their own work. This process of internalizing the "look" of various levels of performance through the descriptors must be engaged prior to the student's own work on a culminating performance. It is helpful if

- Teachers use the descriptors throughout the year on a variety of different **performance assessments**

- Teachers on a grade level agree to a common language of descriptors and applications to the various levels of performance

- Students can participate in choosing and defining the various descriptors of performance

Chapter 6 provides examples of scoring guides developed by teachers for classroom performances.

12. Unit Resources and Teacher Notes

A. Do I have to list all unit resources?

Unit planners need to think through the generalizations, questions, suggested activities, and skills and try and identify relevant and obtainable resources. Certainly, all teachers who implement the unit will add their own resources or continue to select the best resources over time. The Internet is a valuable tool for locating unit resources.

B. What is the purpose of the teacher notes?

These notes help the teacher implement and facilitate instruction. Again, these notes will be added to by any teacher who uses the unit.

Lesson-Planning Pages

The lesson planning pages can take the unit plan into classroom instruction. These pages are a tool for teachers: Which "big ideas," topics, questions, skills, and so on will be put together to form the actual lessons for a week? The second page allows teachers to differentiate instruction and assessment for special-needs students.

Chapter 5 shares some unit excerpts from the elementary and secondary grade levels.

SUMMARY

Perspectives on the design of integrated, interdisciplinary curricula continue to evolve. The views of this author have developed over the past 14 years in intensive work with teachers around the country. This chapter shares a concept-based model for content integration that values the support of process integration to develop deeper understanding and skills. Unit design formats can vary from district to district. The design steps and unit- and lesson-planning pages in this book are provided to show a set of critical components for a quality concept-based design.

EXTENDING THOUGHT

1. What is the value of integrated curriculum and instruction for students? Teachers?

2. What is the difference between *coordinated, multidisciplinary* and *integrated, interdisciplinary* curriculum?

3. What is the difference between content integration and process integration? Do units benefit from incorporating both types of integration?

4. Why is a conceptual lens essential for content integration?

5. What is the difference between *macroconcepts* and *microconcepts*? Why do instructional units need to identify enduring understandings at both the macro- and microlevels?

6. How does *intradisciplinary* differ from *interdisciplinary* in unit design? Can both be integrated? What is the key to integration?

7. Why is "scaffolding" a helpful skill in writing powerful, crisp, and clear generalizations?

8. How can you ensure that performance tasks go beyond simple activities to the level of deep, enduring understanding?

NOTE

1. From McTighe, J., & Wiggins, G. (1998). *Understanding by Design* (pp. 105-106). Alexandria, VA: Association for Supervision and Curriculum Development. Copyright © 1998 ASCD. Reprinted by permission. All rights reserved.

5 Concept-Based Units

Samples and Questions

FROM COORDINATED TO INTEGRATED UNITS

It is a simple matter to rework a topically based unit into a concept-based unit by deciding on a conceptual lens to draw thinking from the factual to the conceptual level. For example, an integrating conceptual lens for a supplementary unit on butterflies might be "Life Cycles." In a supplementary unit on African art, in the upper grades, the teacher might choose the lens of "Form and Function."

At this point, it might be helpful to review some definitions that are critical to understanding this section:

♦ Concept—A mental construct that is timeless and abstract. Specific examples of the concept may vary, but the descriptors are the same. For example: Cycle is a timeless concept. We can cite specific examples that differ—water cycle, rock cycle, historical cycle—but they all have the descriptor of a "repeating, circular pattern."

♦ Generalizations/enduring understandings—Two or more concepts stated in a relationship. Example: *Living organisms* adapt to *changing environments*.

♦ Conceptual lens—The integrating concept for a unit of study. The conceptual lens forces thinking to the conceptual, transferable level.

♦ Topical theme—The title of a unit of study. A topical theme does not include a concept in the title. Example: Cubist art.

♦ Conceptual theme—The title of a unit of study. A conceptual theme includes the conceptual lens in the title. Example: *perspective* in Cubist art.

♦ Subtopics—The content to be experienced through the unit activities. The
subtopics are brainstormed on the overview web under each subject or area
surrounding the theme.

Figure 5.1 shows a concept/content web for a concept-based, integrated unit.
This web-planning tool shows a theme, "Ancient Egypt," which is viewed through
the conceptual lens of "People, Places, and Environments." This design forces
thinking to the conceptual level as students are led through unit questions and
activities to enduring understandings of social change and cultural identity. A
major goal in concept-based instruction is to teach students how to think beyond
the facts—to conceptualize and understand the lasting significance of content
study.

The design in Figure 5.1 meets the criteria of a strong interdisciplinary, integrated unit using the definition of integrated curriculum presented in Chapter 4.
This unit also meets the additional criteria of a strong, integrated unit because each
of the subject areas has depth of study—it is not composed of a few activities. The
conceptual lens brings cohesion and focus to the unit study. The students know the
focus for learning, but the search for understanding is their responsibility.

Figures 5.2 through 5.13 are additional examples of the brainstormed concept/
content webs that elementary and secondary teachers have developed in planning
interdisciplinary, integrated units. Each figure has been chosen to illustrate one or
more of the steps for design. Accompanying each figure is a discussion of the
illustrative points.

The webs show the initial brainstorming efforts in planning the content focus
for the unit study. It is important to realize that these figures do not intend to convey the personal process skills that students will develop and apply to the content
study. Those will appear in the daily lessons through a variety of process activities
such as drama, debates, panel presentations, technology displays, plays, or musical, oral, or written presentations.

Figure 5.2 is a kindergarten unit on transportation. Although transportation is
actually a concept, the teacher has chosen to use the more sophisticated lens of
"motion" to begin developing student understanding of the concepts of energy
and force.

Figure 5.3 is a common unit at the fourth-grade level. This unit is commonly
webbed as a "template" that can be applied to each region of the United States
since the topics are basically the same. Each region would have some unique generalizations, however, addressing significant characteristics.

Figure 5.4 shows that teachers are drawn to issues of social significance when
asked to design units of study. These issues need to be addressed in classrooms.
Violence in America is certainly a theme of great concern to students, parents, and
teachers today. This is one of the best uses of integrated curriculum. Students view

(text continues on page 112)

FIGURE 5.1. Ancient Egypt, Grade 6 Social Studies Unit

People, Places, Environments
(Conceptual Lens)

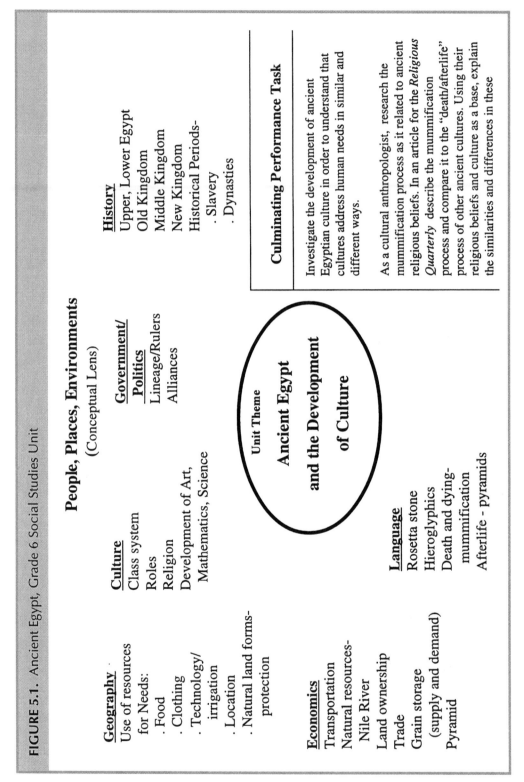

Unit Theme

Ancient Egypt
and the Development
of Culture

Geography
Use of resources
for Needs:
. Food
. Clothing
. Technology/
  irrigation
. Location
. Natural land forms-
  protection

Economics
Transportation
Natural resources-
Nile River
Land ownership
Trade
Grain storage
  (supply and demand)
Pyramid

Culture
Class system
Roles
Religion
Development of Art,
Mathematics, Science

Language
Rosetta stone
Hieroglyphics
Death and dying-
  mummification
Afterlife - pyramids

Government/
Politics
Lineage/Rulers
Alliances

History
Upper, Lower Egypt
Old Kingdom
Middle Kingdom
New Kingdom
Historical Periods-
  . Slavery
  . Dynasties

Culminating Performance Task

Investigate the development of ancient
Egyptian culture in order to understand that
cultures address human needs in similar and
different ways.

As a cultural anthropologist, research the
mummification process as it related to ancient
religious beliefs. In an article for the *Religious
Quarterly* describe the mummification
process and compare it to the "death/afterlife"
process of other ancient cultures. Using their
religious beliefs and culture as a base, explain
the similarities and differences in these

FIGURE 5.1. Continued

Enduring understandings and Guiding Questions

- 1. All cultures share basic elements such as food, shelter, clothing, and language.
  - – How did rivers play a vital role in the development of early civilizations?
  - – How did the Nile River affect the lives of the people of Egypt?
  - – How did alliances with other cultures enable the Egyptians to obtain resources?
  - – What impact did hieroglyphics have on the development of the Egyptian culture?
  - – In what ways did the geography of the region influence the development of Egyptian culture?

- 2. Cultures develop and progress through the exchange of ideas and products.
  - – What influence did Egyptian culture have on other civilizations?
  - – What limitations in Egyptian resources led to far-reaching trade?
  - – How did trade develop based on internal and external needs?
  - – How did Egyptian conquests improve the standard of living?
  - – How did the development of mathematics, science, and art change the standard of living in Egypt?
  - – How does the exchange of ideas and products across cultures stimulate progress?

- 3. Cultures address human needs in similar and different ways.
  - – How was land ownership a source of social, economic, and political power?
  - – In what way do societies assign power to individuals groups or institutions?
  - – What was the selection process for pharoahs?
  - – How did the structure of social classes in Egypt meet societal needs?
  - – What are the positive and negative effects of "social classes?"
  - – Should societies have social classes?

- 4. Geographical and political unification affect the development of civilizations and cultures.
  - – What is meant by "unification?"
  - – How did unification impact the growth of Egyptian civilizations?
  - – In what ways did geography play a role in unification?
  - – How did unification impact the development the class system in ancient Egypt?

SOURCE: Wayne Zalaski, Jody Muldoon, Phil Mannarino, Frank Bogdan. Plainville Community School District, Plainville, Connecticut. Used with permission.

FIGURE 5.2. Transportation Unit

Grade Level: Kindergarten

Motion
Conceptual Lens

Social Studies

Types of transportation-
- boats, bus
-land, water, air
-airplane, walking
-trucks, bikes,
- hot air balloons
- trains

Unit Theme

TRANSPORTATION

Literature
Sheep in a Jeep
(shared/guided)
On the Go
(shared/guided)
Wheels on the Bus
(read aloud)
Dan the Flying Man
(shared)
To Town
(shared)
Trucks
(read aloud)
What Makes Things Move
(shared)

Mathematics
Graphing   Speed
Estimation   Size
Sorting   Geometrical
Categorizing   Shapes
Measurements   Counting
Patterns   Lengths

Field Trips
Airport
Train Station

Culminating Performance Task

What: Investigate, observe, and
analyze three forms of
transportation: land, sea,
air and determine how
each mode of transportation
moves

Why: ...in order to prove that for
something to move there must
be a source of energy.

How: Create three moving vehicles:
land, sea, and air. Your vehicle
designs must move from one
place to another. Build and
decorate your vehicle with
materials found in the
classroom. Demonstrate and
explain how energy powers
your vehicle.

FIGURE 5.2. Continued

Enduring Understandings
(generalizations)

1. Energy causes objects to move.

2. Motion and power create energy.

3. Friction produces power which creates a push/pull movement.

4. Different types of transportation move at different speeds.

5. People depend on transportation.

Guiding Questions

1. What things in your house use energy? What is energy? Do you have a toy that can move because of energy? How does the energy cause it to move? What is power? Where does power come from?

2. When a car moves is it in motion? When a river runs is it in motion? What is motion? Can you think of other things that show motion? Will more power create more motion? Can you think of something that would show how more power and motion create more energy?

3. Why do many forms of transportation use wheels? What makes wheels work?

4. Why do airplanes move faster than cars? Which has greater energy? Which has the least energy: bicycles, trains, or cars?

5. Why is transportation important? Which form of transportation do you use most often?

B

SOURCE: Southwood Elementary School, Orange County School District, Orlando, Florida. Used with permission.

FIGURE 5.3. Critical Content/Concept Web

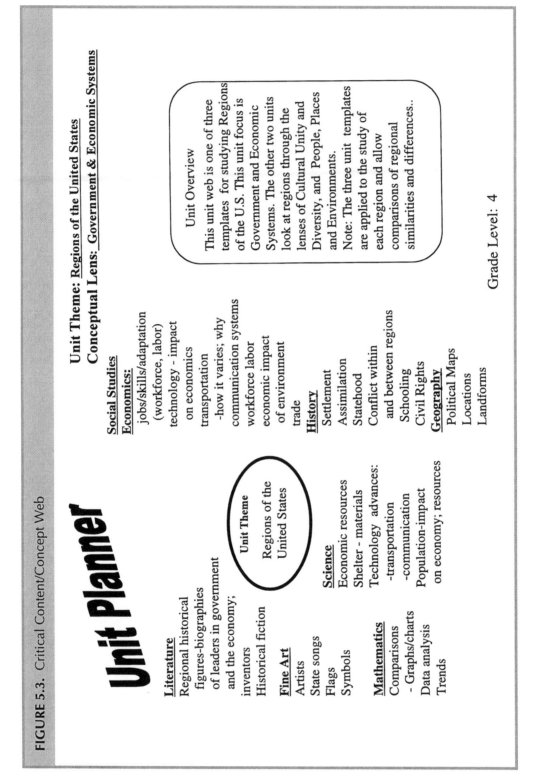

Unit Planner

Unit Theme: Regions of the United States

Conceptual Lens: Government & Economic Systems

Unit Theme
Regions of the United States

Social Studies
Economics:
jobs/skills/adaptation
(workforce, labor)
technology - impact
on economics
transportation
-how it varies; why
communication systems
workforce labor
economic impact
of environment
trade

History
Settlement
Assimilation
Statehood
Conflict within
and between regions
Schooling
Civil Rights

Geography
Political Maps
Locations
Landforms

Literature
Regional historical
figures-biographies
of leaders in government
and the economy;
inventors
Historical fiction

Fine Art
Artists
State songs
Flags
Symbols

Mathematics
Comparisons
- Graphs/charts
Data analysis
Trends

Science
Economic resources
Shelter - materials
Technology advances:
-transportation
-communication
Population-impact
on economy; resources

Unit Overview

This unit web is one of three
templates for studying Regions
of the U.S. This unit focus is
Government and Economic
Systems. The other two units
look at regions through the
lenses of Cultural Unity and
Diversity, and People, Places
and Environments.
Note: The three unit templates
are applied to the study of
each region and allow
comparisons of regional
similarities and differences..

Grade Level: 4

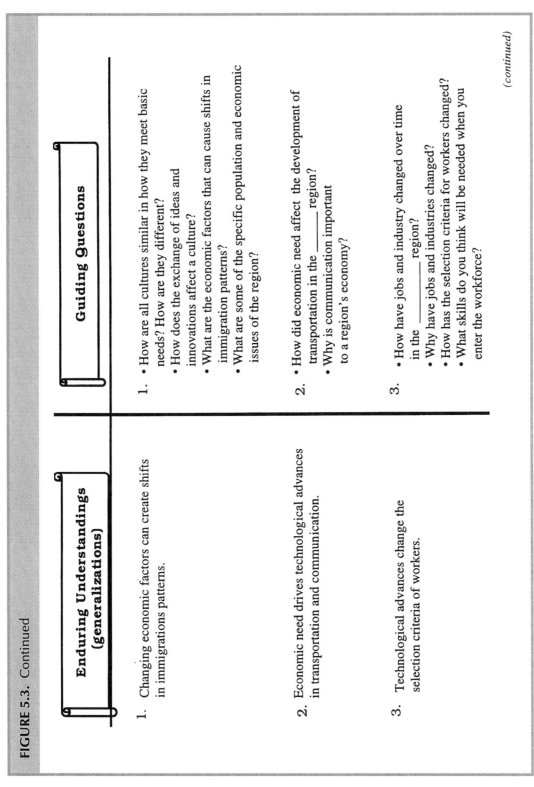

FIGURE 5.3. Continued

Enduring Understandings (generalizations)

1. Changing economic factors can create shifts in immigrations patterns.

2. Economic need drives technological advances in transportation and communication.

3. Technological advances change the selection criteria of workers.

Guiding Questions

1. • How are all cultures similar in how they meet basic needs? How are they different?
   • How does the exchange of ideas and innovations affect a culture?
   • What are the economic factors that can cause shifts in immigration patterns?
   • What are some of the specific population and economic issues of the region?

2. • How did economic need affect the development of transportation in the _____ region?
   • Why is communication important to a region's economy?

3. • How have jobs and industry changed over time in the _____ region?
   • Why have jobs and industries changed?
   • How has the selection criteria for workers changed?
   • What skills do you think will be needed when you enter the workforce?

(continued)

FIGURE 5.3. Continued

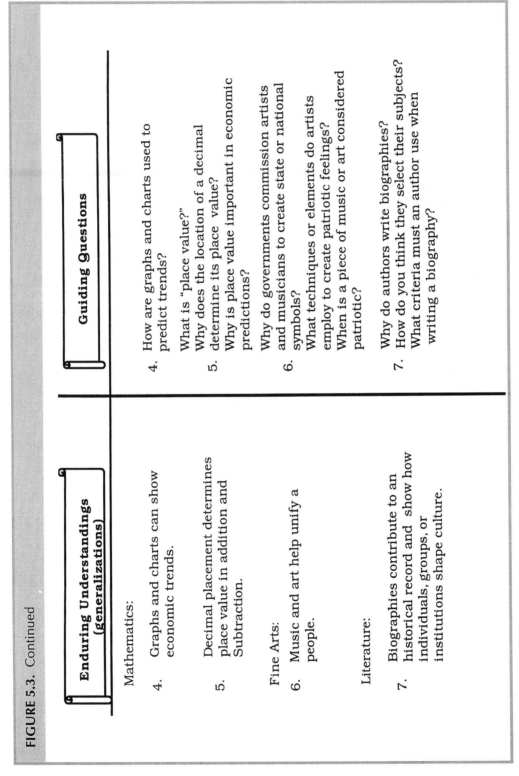

**Enduring Understandings
(generalizations)**

Mathematics:

4. Graphs and charts can show economic trends.

5. Decimal placement determines place value in addition and Subtraction.

Fine Arts:

6. Music and art help unify a people.

Literature:

7. Biographies contribute to an historical record and show how individuals, groups, or institutions shape culture.

Guiding Questions

4. How are graphs and charts used to predict trends?

What is "place value?"
Why does the location of a decimal determine its place value?
5. Why is place value important in economic predictions?

Why do governments commission artists and musicians to create state or national symbols?
What techniques or elements do artists employ to create patriotic feelings?
6. When is a piece of music or art considered patriotic?

Why do authors write biographies?
7. How do you think they select their subjects?
What criteria must an author use when writing a biography?

FIGURE 5.3. Continued

Critical Content and Skills:

AC = Assessment Code:

Q - Quizzes	P - Prompts
T - Tests	O - Observations
WS - Work Samples	D - Dialogues
SA - Student Self-Assessment	

Students will know...

	AC
1. Key facts related to the government and economics of the Northeast, Southeast, Midwest, Northwest, and Southwest regions of the United States	Q T D
2. Geographical locations for each region	
3. Major landforms and resources contributing to the economics of each region	

Students will be able to do...

Social Studies:

1. Identify and label
2. Use map key, compass rose, and distance scale
3. Use primary source documents to compare perspectives
4. Use the internet to locate information

Language Arts:

5. Read historical fiction and biographies to gain and compare information
6. Generate questions for study and interest
7. Organize and recall information
8. Use electronic sources and tools to research and communicate

Mathematics:
9. ----------

(continued)

FIGURE 5.3. Continued

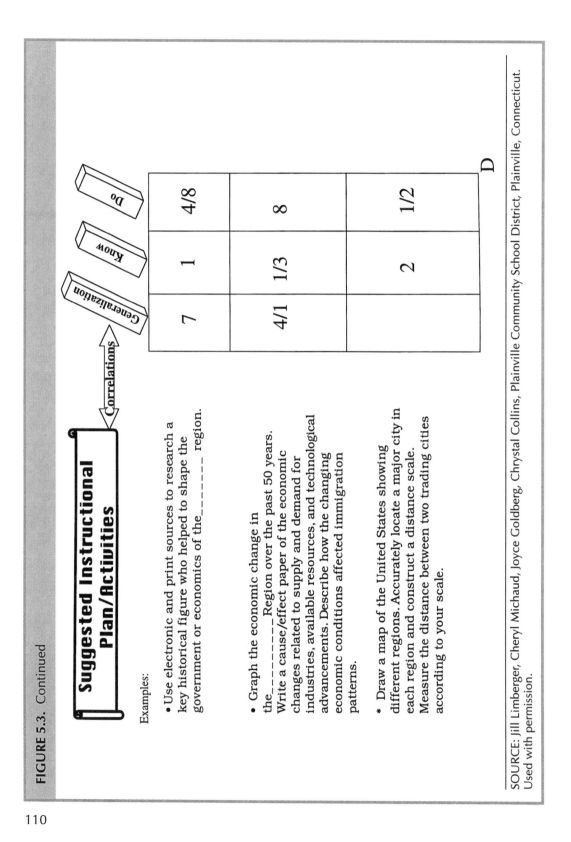

Suggested Instructional Plan/Activities

Correlations

Examples:

• Use electronic and print sources to research a key historical figure who helped to shape the government or economics of the _ _ _ _ _ _ region.

• Graph the economic change in the _ _ _ _ _ _ Region over the past 50 years. Write a cause/effect paper of the economic changes related to supply and demand for industries, available resources, and technological advancements. Describe how the changing economic conditions affected immigration patterns.

* Draw a map of the United States showing different regions. Accurately locate a major city in each region and construct a distance scale. Measure the distance between two trading cities according to your scale.

Generalization	Know	Do
7	1	4/8
4/1	1/3	8
	2	1/2

D

SOURCE: Jill Limberger, Cheryl Michaud, Joyce Goldberg, Chrystal Collins, Plainville Community School District, Plainville, Connecticut. Used with permission.

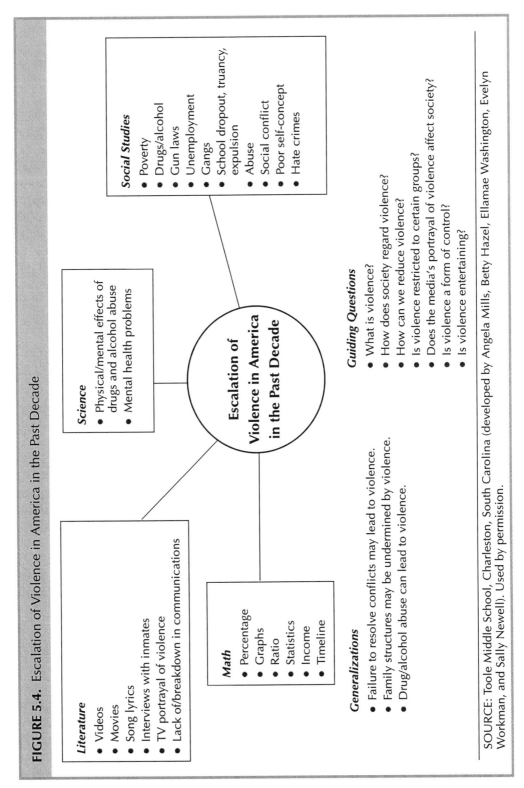

FIGURE 5.4. Escalation of Violence in America in the Past Decade

Literature
- Videos
- Movies
- Song lyrics
- Interviews with inmates
- TV portrayal of violence
- Lack of/breakdown in communications

Science
- Physical/mental effects of drugs and alcohol abuse
- Mental health problems

Social Studies
- Poverty
- Drugs/alcohol
- Gun laws
- Unemployment
- Gangs
- School dropout, truancy, expulsion
- Abuse
- Social conflict
- Poor self-concept
- Hate crimes

Escalation of Violence in America in the Past Decade

Math
- Percentage
- Graphs
- Ratio
- Statistics
- Income
- Timeline

Generalizations
- Failure to resolve conflicts may lead to violence.
- Family structures may be undermined by violence.
- Drug/alcohol abuse can lead to violence.

Guiding Questions
- What is violence?
- How does society regard violence?
- How can we reduce violence?
- Is violence restricted to certain groups?
- Does the media's portrayal of violence affect society?
- Is violence a form of control?
- Is violence entertaining?

SOURCE: Toole Middle School, Charleston, South Carolina (developed by Angela Mills, Betty Hazel, Ellamae Washington, Evelyn Workman, and Sally Newell). Used by permission.

complex social issues from multiple perspectives and develop problem-solving skills, which are essential to effective citizenship.

Cultural themes, such as the one shown in Figures 5.5 and 5.6, teach students how interacting cultures influence each other. Cultures are compared and studied through various cultural aspects, from language to trade to technology.

Primary grade units, such as Figure 5.7 on the family, are common. Notice how this teacher develops important enduring understandings with young students.

State standards require an in-depth knowledge of state history. Concept-based teachers teach important ideas in addition to teaching key facts about the state. Figure 5.8 is an example of a state unit.

Intradisciplinary, Integrated Unit Examples

The units shown in Figures 5.9 and 5.10 are intradisciplinary high school units. Notice how the generalizations guide the unit study. Students will discover other enduring understandings in their search for knowledge.

Figure 5.10 shows an intradisciplinary biology unit excerpt. This unit was created by Arnie Leslie, a teacher in the Lake Washington School District, in Redmond, Washington. Note the higher-level generalizations. Often, when teachers first begin writing generalizations, they are drawn from a surface level of thought. As they become more accustomed to synthesizing the learnings from content, the generalizations become more sophisticated. As students progress through the grades, the generalizations they derive should parallel the increasing depth of the content and concepts under study.

Figure 5.11 is a chemistry unit using the alternative format found in Resource A. This unit has clear generalizations and supportive questions.

Physics classes teach to enduring principles and concepts to facilitate the transfer of knowledge and a deeper understanding of the discipline. The unit excerpt in Figure 5.12 illustrates how the generalizations and questions work together.

MULTIAGE CLASSROOMS AND CONCEPT-BASED CURRICULUM

There is ongoing interest in multiage classrooms and nongraded education. Multiage classrooms combine two and occasionally three levels to provide a broader age span for the learning environment. There are benefits to these arrangements as long as the teacher has a solid understanding of how to approach curriculum and instruction with the increased span of abilities and maturity levels.

One of the questions that arises most frequently is, "How do we handle the multiple levels of curriculum within the multiage structure?" For multiage classes, the use of major concepts in social studies as K-6 organizers allows teachers to use

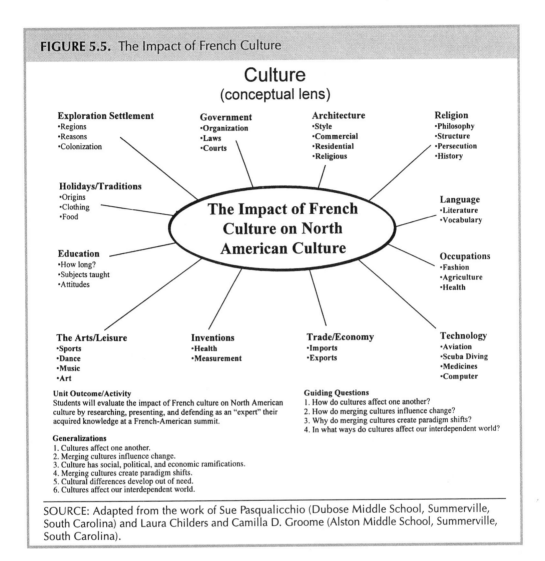

FIGURE 5.5. The Impact of French Culture

Culture
(conceptual lens)

Exploration Settlement
•Regions
•Reasons
•Colonization

Government
•Organization
•Laws
•Courts

Architecture
•Style
•Commercial
•Residential
•Religious

Religion
•Philosophy
•Structure
•Persecution
•History

Holidays/Traditions
•Origins
•Clothing
•Food

Language
•Literature
•Vocabulary

The Impact of French Culture on North American Culture

Education
•How long?
•Subjects taught
•Attitudes

Occupations
•Fashion
•Agriculture
•Health

The Arts/Leisure
•Sports
•Dance
•Music
•Art

Inventions
•Health
•Measurement

Trade/Economy
•Imports
•Exports

Technology
•Aviation
•Scuba Diving
•Medicines
•Computer

Unit Outcome/Activity
Students will evaluate the impact of French culture on North American culture by researching, presenting, and defending as an "expert" their acquired knowledge at a French-American summit.

Generalizations
1. Cultures affect one another.
2. Merging cultures influence change.
3. Culture has social, political, and economic ramifications.
4. Merging cultures create paradigm shifts.
5. Cultural differences develop out of need.
6. Cultures affect our interdependent world.

Guiding Questions
1. How do cultures affect one another?
2. How do merging cultures influence change?
3. Why do merging cultures create paradigm shifts?
4. In what ways do cultures affect our interdependent world?

SOURCE: Adapted from the work of Sue Pasqualicchio (Dubose Middle School, Summerville, South Carolina) and Laura Childers and Camilla D. Groome (Alston Middle School, Summerville, South Carolina).

related topical themes each year. As long as the concept stays the same, different themes can focus the content across age levels or grade spans. Teachers can have students working on different themes related to the concept in a classroom, or they can do a different theme each year for the same concept.

A Washington state example demonstrates the use of concepts, themes, and generalizations as an effective way to articulate the content curriculum in a multi-grade or multiage school setting.

This promising plan to write a global social studies curriculum was started in Washington state a number of years ago. Unfortunately, like many curricular projects, it was never completed because of district changes, but the design is worth sharing.

Realizing that students live in a globally interdependent world, the teachers developed a K-6 framework to address key concepts using examples from different

(text continues on page 133)

FIGURE 5.6. Ancient Mayan Culture Unit

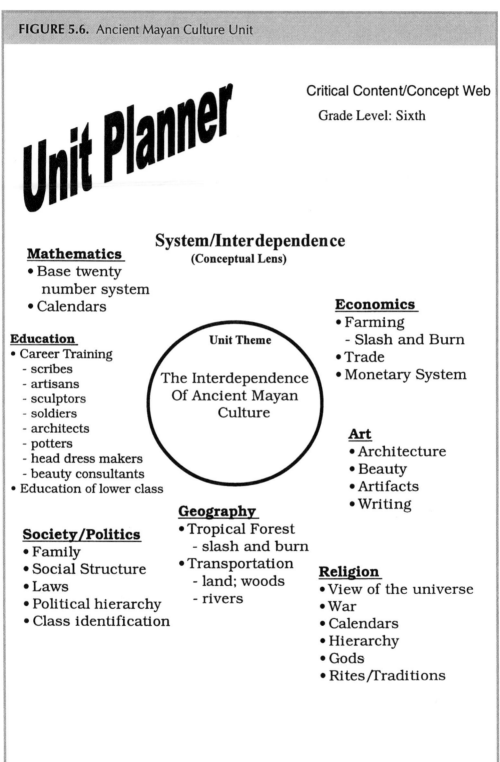

Critical Content/Concept Web

Grade Level: Sixth

Unit Planner

System/Interdependence
(Conceptual Lens)

Mathematics
- Base twenty number system
- Calendars

Education
- Career Training
  - scribes
  - artisans
  - sculptors
  - soldiers
  - architects
  - potters
  - head dress makers
  - beauty consultants
- Education of lower class

Society/Politics
- Family
- Social Structure
- Laws
- Political hierarchy
- Class identification

Unit Theme

The Interdependence Of Ancient Mayan Culture

Geography
- Tropical Forest
  - slash and burn
- Transportation
  - land; woods
  - rivers

Economics
- Farming
  - Slash and Burn
- Trade
- Monetary System

Art
- Architecture
- Beauty
- Artifacts
- Writing

Religion
- View of the universe
- War
- Calendars
- Hierarchy
- Gods
- Rites/Traditions

FIGURE 5.6. Continued

Subject Area: Social Studies - Lesson Plan
Conceptual Lens: System/Interdependence
Unit Theme: Independence Within the Mayan Culture
Grade Level: 6

Enduring Understanding:

Cultures reflect perspectives of beauty in their arts, dress, and decoration of the human body.

Guiding Questions:

What did Mayans consider beautiful?

How did they express beauty in their culture?

How do you perceive the Mayan concept of beauty?

How did the Mayans reflect their environment in their arts?

How does Mayan art compare and contrast with other ancient cultures and our modern culture?

Critical Content:	**Skills:**
• Mayan culture	• Interpretation of graphics
• Art	• Active listening
• Artifacts	• Notetaking
• Components of	• Summarizing, synthesizing
civilization	• Giving feedback to others
• Careers	• Working effectively on a team

Instructional Activities:

- Read article "What Price Beauty?" and explain in writing which modern beauty practices could be seen as bizarre in the future.
- Read article "The Maya Look," and design the Mayan version of a "mail-order catalogue" and present your design to the class.
- Use book/resources/ Internet to find examples of different forms of Mayan beautification practices.

(continued)

FIGURE 5.6. Continued

Subject Area: Social Studies - Lesson Plan
Conceptual Lens: System/Interdependence
Unit Theme: Independence Within the Mayan Culture
Grade Level: 6

Enduring Understanding:

Societies structure political systems to meet their needs.

Guiding Questions:

What were the needs of Mayans? Economic? Social? Basic?

How did the Mayan political system meet the needs of its people?

Compare the political system of the Mayans to the Egyptians.

What happens if political systems don't address the needs of the people?

Describe what occurred when the Mayan political structure did not meet the needs of the Mayan people.

Critical Content:	**Skills:**
• Mayan culture	• Using technology to access information
• Government	• Summarizing
• Components of civilization	• Notetaking
	• Interviewing
• Career information	• Respecting differences

Instructional Activities:

- Read "A Complex Social Structure." Outline, web, or take notes

- Create imaginary interviews with different people in the social structure

- Create a T-chart or modified Venn diagram comparing the political systems of the Mayans and Egyptians.

- Brainstorm basic needs of the Mayans and the ways those needs might have been met.

- Read the sections in the social studies book about Athens and Sparta government. Compare/contrast to the Mayan city-state structure. Hypothesize how the Mayan government did not meet needs, and the reaction of the Mayan people.

FIGURE 5.6. Continued

Formative Assessments:

Individual Learning Logs

Taskmaster's sheet on daily participation

Assessment of questions and notes from guest presentation

Scoring Guide Assessment of writing:

"Modern Beauty Seen as Bizarre"

Scoring Guide assessment of "Mail-Order Catalogue" presentation

Peer review of class notes

Culminating Performance Assessment:

What: Investigate the interdependence of systems within Ancient Mayan Culture

Why: ... in order to understand that social, economic, and political systems within a culture are interdependent.

How: As a cultural anthropologist/archaeologist just returned from a "dig," develop a museum piece representing a Mayan site which synthesizes information learned during the unit.
Create artifacts which reflect the components of civilization.
Develop supporting visuals using technology when available.
Select a presentation method to show the interdependence of the economic, and political or social system in the Mayan culture.

SOURCE: Sherry Alimi, Holmes Middle School, Wheeling Community Schools, Wheeling, Illinois. Used with permission.

FIGURE 5.7. My Family Unit Web

Unit Planner

Critical Content/Concept Web

Grade Level: First

Interdependence
(Conceptual Lens)

Unit Theme

My Family

Culture
• Education
• Entertainment and influence on family
• Holiday traditions
• Families working together
• Values and beliefs

Economics
• Budget/allowances
• Jobs
• Needs versus wants
  - shelter, clothing, food
  - goods families consume (consumption)
• Money
• Goods and services

Government
• Types of governments
• Regulations
  - influence on family life/structure
• Rights/responsibilities
• Family rules

History
• Families past and present
  - ancestors;
  How did families work together?
• Changing roles over time: mother, father, children

Geography
• Where families live
  - migration
  - influence of jobs on living location
  - living locations of extended family
  - effect of distance on family relationships :
  transportation;
  communication

* (concepts underlined)

Unit Overview

Some families are large; some are small. But your family is very important to you. Your family takes care of you and helps you meet your needs and wants. Have you ever wondered...
• Why families live in different cities?
• Why some of your relatives live in different locations?
• Why you have to follow rules?
• Why people use money?
• Why family members have to work together?
• What childhood was like for your parents and grandparents?

Let's find out!

FIGURE 5.7. Continued

Enduring Understandings (generalizations)		Guiding Questions
Culture		
1. Values and beliefs guide the decisions in a family.	1.	What is a belief? What is a value? Is there a difference? What is a decision? How are your decisions influenced by your families beliefs/values?
Economics		
2. Family members work to meet needs and wants.	2.	What are needs? What are wants? What needs do you have in your family? How does your family meet their needs? Wants? What can you do to meet your wants?
3. Families work together to make choices depending on their needs and wants.	3.	What is a choice? What is a compromise? How do families work together to make choices for the good of the family? Why is money sometimes coins and sometimes paper?
4. Families use money to purchase goods and services.	4.	What are goods? Services? Why must families pay money for goods and services?
Geography		
5. Occupations often determine the living location of a family.	5.	What is a living location? What is an occupation? What occupations are in your family? Why did your family move to your present living location?
6. Distance influences family communications.	6.	Do some of your family members live in different locations? How often do you see these family members? How do you communicate with them? How does distance affect the way you communicate with family members?

(continued)

119

FIGURE 5.7. Continued

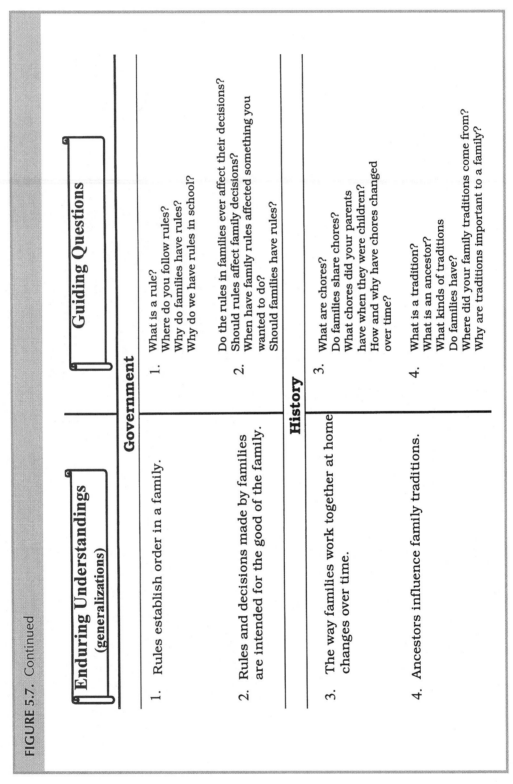

Enduring Understandings (generalizations)	**Guiding Questions**
Government	
1. Rules establish order in a family.	1. What is a rule? Where do you follow rules? Why do families have rules? Why do we have rules in school?
2. Rules and decisions made by families are intended for the good of the family.	2. Do the rules in families ever affect their decisions? Should rules affect family decisions? When have family rules affected something you wanted to do? Should families have rules?
History	
3. The way families work together at home changes over time.	3. What are chores? Do families share chores? What chores did your parents have when they were children? How and why have chores changed over time?
4. Ancestors influence family traditions.	4. What is a tradition? What is an ancestor? What kinds of traditions Do families have? Where did your family traditions come from? Why are traditions important to a family?

FIGURE 5.7. Continued

AC = Assessment Code:

Q - Quizzes	P - Prompts
T - Tests	O - Observations
WS - Work Samples	D - Dialogues
SA - Student Self-Assessment	

Critical Content and Skills:

Students will know...

	AC
1. The characteristics Of a family.	SA
2. The meaning of key concepts: role, money, goods, services...	D
3.	
4.	
5.	

Students will be able to do...

	AC
A. Express own ideas	D
B. Express ideas through different forms: writing, speaking and visual art.	WS
C. Listen for specific information.	Q
D. Adjust behavior appropriately in cooperative work group.	O
E.	

SOURCE: Social Studies Committee, Meridian Joint School District No. 2, Meridian, Idaho. Used with permission.

FIGURE 5.8. Idaho Unit Web

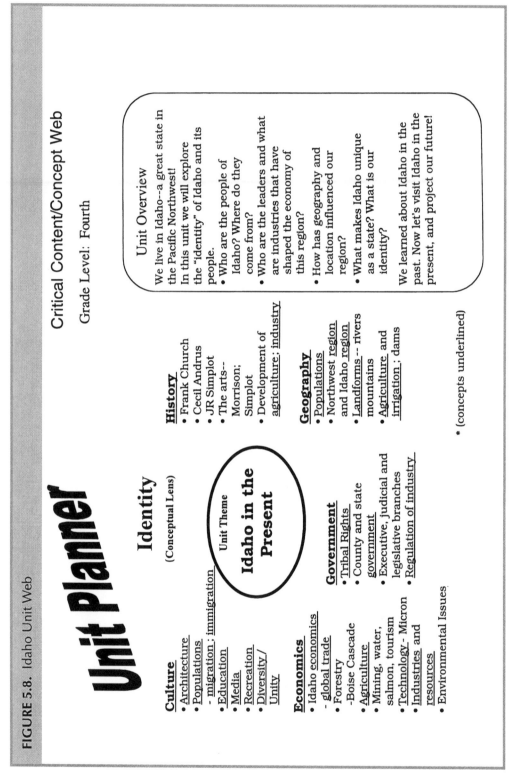

Unit Planner

Identity
(Conceptual Lens)

Unit Theme

Idaho in the Present

Culture
- Architecture
- Populations
- migration ; immigration
- Education
- Media
- Recreation
- Diversity/ Unity

Economics
- Idaho economics - global trade
- Forestry -Boise Cascade
- Agriculture
- Mining, water, salmon, tourism
- Technology - Micron
- Industries and resources
- Environmental Issues

Government
- Tribal Rights
- County and state government
- Executive, judicial and legislative branches
- Regulation of industry

Critical Content/Concept Web

Grade Level: Fourth

Unit Overview
We live in Idaho--a great state in the Pacific Northwest!
In this unit we will explore the "identity" of Idaho and its people.
- Who are the people of Idaho? Where do they come from?
- Who are the leaders and what are industries that have shaped the economy of this region?
- How has geography and location influenced our region?
- What makes Idaho unique as a state? What is our identity?

We learned about Idaho in the past. Now let's visit Idaho in the present, and project our future!

History
- Frank Church
- Cecil Andrus
- JR Simplot
- The arts-- Morrison; Simplot
- Development of agriculture; industry

Geography
- Populations
- Northwest region and Idaho region
- Landforms -- rivers mountains
- Agriculture and irrigation ; dams

* (concepts underlined)

FIGURE 5.8. Continued

Enduring Understandings (generalizations)

Culture

Guiding Questions

1. Differing values and economic concerns and/or interests can create tension and conflict between individuals, groups, or nations.

1. Why are Idaho loggers and environmentalists in conflict? What interest do biologists, farmers, sportsmen, developers, and hydroelectric companies each have in Idaho's river systems? Why may differing interests create conflict among individuals and groups?

2. Cultural, state, and regional celebrations express the identity of a people.

2. What celebrations do we have in Idaho that express the diversity, unity, and identity of our people?

Economics

3. Economic systems are complex institutions that include families, workers, large and small businesses, and governments.

3. What businesses and industries are important to the economy of Idaho? What factors have helped to develop these Idaho businesses? What is Idaho's role in the economy of the Pacific Northwest? What is an economic system? What makes an economic system strong?

4. Incentives, values, traditions, and habits influence economic decisions.

4. How are values formed? What are incentives? Does advertising suggest incentives for purchasing products? Are some products purchased through habit? Give examples of family economic decisions or purchases based on values? ...through habit?

5. The cost of goods and services relates to the supply and the demand.

5. Why is it possible to produce certain goods at a reasonable cost in Idaho? What determines the cost of a good or service?

(continued)

FIGURE 5.8. Continued

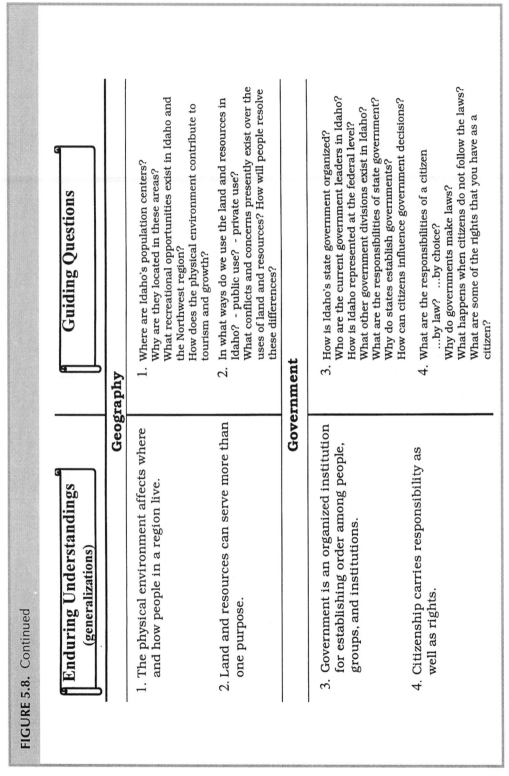

Enduring Understandings (generalizations)	Guiding Questions
Geography	
1. The physical environment affects where and how people in a region live.	1. Where are Idaho's population centers? Why are they located in these areas? What recreational opportunities exist in Idaho and the Northwest region? How does the physical environment contribute to tourism and growth?
2. Land and resources can serve more than one purpose.	2. In what ways do we use the land and resources in Idaho? - public use? - private use? What conflicts and concerns presently exist over the uses of land and resources? How will people resolve these differences?
Government	
3. Government is an organized institution for establishing order among people, groups, and institutions.	3. How is Idaho's state government organized? Who are the current government leaders in Idaho? How is Idaho represented at the federal level? What other government divisions exist in Idaho? What are the responsibilities of state government? Why do states establish governments? How can citizens influence government decisions?
4. Citizenship carries responsibility as well as rights.	4. What are the responsibilities of a citizen ...by law? ...by choice? Why do governments make laws? What happens when citizens do not follow the laws? What are some of the rights that you have as a citizen?

FIGURE 5.8. Continued

Critical Content and Skills:

AC = Assessment Code:
Q - Quizzes   P - Prompts
T - Tests   O - Observations
WS - Work Samples   D - Dialogues
SA - Student Self-Assessment

Students will know…	AC
1. Current environmental Issues in Idaho	WS
2. Important celebrations in Idaho and what they represent	
3. Information on Idaho businesses and industries	WS
4. Different cultural groups and populations in Idaho and their contributions	
5. The structure and function of Idaho government; current leaders	T
6. Factors that shape Idaho's identity	P

Students will be able to do…	AC
A. Identify fact and opinion	AC
B. Recognize point of view	SA
C. Write a persuasive essay	P
D. Locate current information from a variety of sources: Newspaper, Internet, pamphlets, brochures	
E. Conduct interviews	D
F. Read and interpret graphs and charts	T
G. Express personal convictions	T

SOURCE: Social Studies Committee, Meridian Joint School District No. 2, Meridian, Idaho. Used with permission.

FIGURE 5.9. High School Photography

CONCEPTUAL LENS: COMMUNICATION/CONTROL

Subconcepts:

Expression	Detail	Appropriation
Focus	Ethics	Culture
Contrast	Symbolism	Multiplicity
Light quality	Abstraction	Intent
Perspective	Integration	Limitation

Generalizations:

- ▶ Art communicates a perspective.
- ▶ Words and images combined, create powerful communications.
- ▶ Light quality affects image.
- ▶ Color and black-and-white imagery convey contrasting meanings.
- ▶ Detail can inform or obstruct meaning.
- ▶ Symbolism and abstraction can effectively evoke reality.
- ▶ A visual communication can convey multiple messages.
- ▶ Artists interpret and reflect the complexity of culture.
- ▶ Art combined with technology can shape and reflect culture.

Guiding Questions:

How does a visual communication evolve?

What makes a visual communication work?

How does an artist evoke reality without re-creating it?

Are visual communications ever "neutral"?

Why do both color and black-and-white images make sense to the viewer?

How does human vision work?

How do artists respond to technical limitations?

How does the artist decide on the amount of detail to incorporate in the work?

How does the quality of light affect the viewer's feelings toward an image?

What techniques can the artist use to convey multiple, conflicting messages in an image?

What is the relationship between art and culture?

How can words be used to enhance a visual image?

What role does ethics play in art?

How do art and technology interact to shape culture?

Processes/Skills:

Apply technical knowledge to creative problem solving:
    Manipulate camera controls of a manual camera for special effects.
    Use graphics software for photo-based communications.
    Use photographic chemicals to create color images.

FIGURE 5.9. Continued

Apply theory to technique:
 Manipulate film development for special effects.
 Integrate computer and camera technologies to create images.
 Use studio and natural lighting for special effects.

Activities (examples):

▶ Create a visual communication with a manual camera.

▶ Create photographs that have a controlled depth of field to direct the viewer's attention to a specific area.

▶ Create photographs that have controlled blur to create visual metaphors.

▶ Manipulate and enhance photographs with graphics software.

▶ Create color photographs using photographic chemicals.

▶ Experiment with studio and natural lighting to create a special photographic effect.

▶ Use creative darkroom techniques to communicate mood.

▶ Create extreme "candid" photographs using pushed film to communicate hidden truths.

▶ Read and discuss the ethics of "candid" photography and "paparazzi" versus photojournalism to realize the sociological impact of the camera.

▶ Create color negatives and prints to communicate using the full spectrum of color.

▶ Tone black-and-white prints (blue, sepia) to communicate using a limited color palette.

▶ Integrate words into a photograph using transparent overlays to explore the use of photography in graphic design.

▶ Use appropriated images creatively to create an image with complex meaning.

CULMINATING PERFORMANCE TASK

Analyze and evaluate your own photographs to understand that a body of work in art communicates a clear style, message, or both. Create and present in a portfolio eight mounted 8 × 10 prints that communicate your style, message, or both. The prints are to be made from your own negatives and must be well printed and well composed, with the style or intent clearly communicated.

As an art jurist, draw another artist's (student's) name and present a 3-minute summary and critique of the message and style.

Teacher note: As the designer of this unit, I worked from the activities to the concepts, generalizations, and essential questions. They evolved from an analysis of the activities' meanings, purposes, and intended learnings. This helped me organize the unit and integrate deeper levels of understanding into the material and instruction.

SOURCE: Rosamond Hyde, Gloucester High School, Gloucester, Massachusetts. Used with permission.

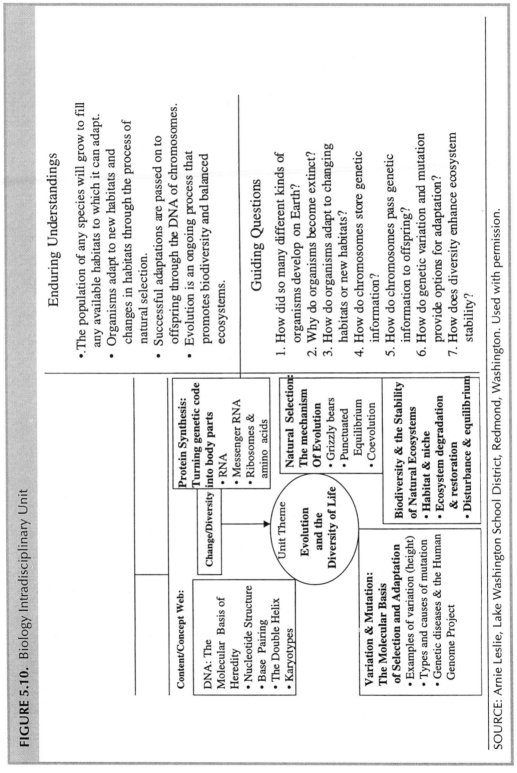

FIGURE 5.10. Biology Intradisciplinary Unit

Enduring Understandings

• The population of any species will grow to fill any available habitats to which it can adapt.
• Organisms adapt to new habitats and changes in habitats through the process of natural selection.
• Successful adaptations are passed on to offspring through the DNA of chromosomes.
• Evolution is an ongoing process that promotes biodiversity and balanced ecosystems.

Guiding Questions

1. How did so many different kinds of organisms develop on Earth?
2. Why do organisms become extinct?
3. How do organisms adapt to changing habitats or new habitats?
4. How do chromosomes store genetic information?
5. How do chromosomes pass genetic information to offspring?
6. How do genetic variation and mutation provide options for adaptation?
7. How does diversity enhance ecosystem stability?

Content/Concept Web:

Change/Diversity

DNA: The Molecular Basis of Heredity
• Nucleotide Structure
• Base Pairing
• The Double Helix
• Karyotypes

Protein Synthesis: Turning genetic code into body parts
• RNA
• Messenger RNA
• Ribosomes & amino acids

Unit Theme
Evolution and the Diversity of Life

Variation & Mutation: The Molecular Basis of Selection and Adaptation
• Examples of variation (height)
• Types and causes of mutation
• Genetic diseases & the Human Genome Project

Natural Selection: The mechanism Of Evolution
• Grizzly bears
• Punctuated Equilibrium
• Coevolution

Biodiversity & the Stability of Natural Ecosystems
• Habitat & niche
• Ecosystem degradation & restoration
• Disturbance & equilibrium

SOURCE: Arnie Leslie, Lake Washington School District, Redmond, Washington. Used with permission.

FIGURE 5.11. Chemistry Unit

System/Interaction

(Conceptual Lens)

Electronegativity
- periodic table trend
- ionic/covalent continuum

Bond Types
- covalent, ionic, metallic
- polar covalent
- orbital hybridization
- sigma and pi bonds

Molecular Shape
- VSEPR Theory
- Valence-bond theory
- polarity

Atomic Structures
- valence electrons
- formation of ions
- electronegativity

Unit Theme
Chemical Bonding

Intermolecular Forces
- London dispersion
- dipole-dipole
- hydrogen bonding

Bond Energy
- potential energy
- bond strength
- exothermic and endothermic bonds

Modern Materials
- liquid crystals
- polymers
- ceramics

Compounds & Properties
- amorphous solid
- crystalline solid
  - moelcular, ionic, atomic
- liquids
  - molecules with strong intermolecular forces
- gases
  - molecules with weak intermolecular forces

(continued)

FIGURE 5.11. Continued

Course: Chemistry
Unit Theme: Chemical Bonding
Conceptual Lens: System/Interaction

Instructor: _____
Length of Unit _____

Key Topics/ Concepts Subconcepts	Enduring Understandings (Generalizations)	Guiding Questions	Critical Content/ Key Facts (Know)	Instructional Activities/ Resources	Skill Objectives (Do)	Assessments
Bond Energy	Each chemical bond stores an amount of potential energy dependent on the atoms involved.	• How is potential energy stored in a chemical bond? • Does every bond have the same amount of energy? • What happens when the bond breaks? • How is the energy transferred to new bonds?	Potential Energy; Endothermic Reactions Exothermic Reactions		• Research the values of bond energy. • Describe the law of conservation of energy with respect to chemistry.	
Molecular Shape	The shape of molecules is determined by the repulsion of electrons in the chemical bonds and pairs of valence electrons.	• Why do electrons repel each other? • Why is the shape of a water molecule bent?	Electron repulse PR Theory		Predict bond Angles Describe the impact of different molecular geometries Determine polarity of molecules	

FIGURE 5.11. Continued

Course: Chemistry
Unit Theme: Chemical Bonding
Conceptual Lens: System/Interaction

Instructor: _____
Length of Unit _____

Key Topics/ Concepts Subconcepts	Enduring Understandings (Generalizations)	Guiding Questions	Critical Content/ Key Facts (Know)	Instructional Activities/ Resources	Skill Objectives (Do)	Assessments
Electro-negativity	The electro-negativity of an atom determines the type of chemical bond that is formed in a chemical reaction.	• How is electro-negativity related to the periodic table? • How can you predict the type of bond using the electro-negativity? • What are the types of bonds dependent on electro-negativity? • What types of compounds are produced from these bonds?	Concepts: - electro-negativity - ionic bond - covalent bonds - polar covalent bond - periodic trend	• 3D Periodic Table Lab • Calculate the difference in electro-negativity	Predict the bond type Analyze the continuum between ionic and covalent bonds to determine the degree of bond character. Describe the periodic trend. Predict if bonding will occur. Predict if bonding will not Occur.	Investigate chemical bonding in order to understand that the electro-negativity of an atom determines the type of chemical bond that is formed in a chemical reaction. Analyze bonds in an organic compound, inorganic compound, and water to determine the bond type using electro-negativy values. Plot the differences in electro-negativity on a bond character curve.
Atomic Structure	The increased stability of a completed outer atomic energy level drives chemical bonding.	• How does the element's electron configuration affect bonding? • Why is a completed outer energy level more stable? • Do all atoms need to form a completed outer energy level?	Electron configuration Atomic energy levels			

SOURCE: Jean Lummis, Washington Township High School, Washington Township School District, Sewell, New Jersey. Used with permission.

FIGURE 5.12. Physics Unit

Course: Chemistry
Unit Theme: __Chemical Bonding__
Conceptual Lens: __System/Interaction__

Instructor: _____
Length of Unit _____

Key Topics/ Concepts Subconcepts	Enduring Understandings (Generalizations)	Guiding Questions	Critical Content (Know)	Skill Objectives (Do)	Resources/ Materials	Assessments
Electro-magnetic force • Electric • Magnetic	Electricity and magnetism are two aspects of a single electromagnetic force. Charge 1 bodies can attract or repel with a force that depends on the nature and distance between them. Between any two charged particles The electro-magnetic force is vastly greater than the gravitational force.	• What happens when like charges are brought together? • How does the distance between two charges affect the force they exert on each other? • How is the EM force similar to the gravitational force? • Which force, EM or gravitational, is greater when objects are closer together? When they are far apart? • How do you produce a magnetic force? • How are the electric and magnetic forces related? • Why is the EM force considered a fundamental force?	How a magnetic force is produced. The criteria for a fundamental force, and why the E-M force fits the criteria.	Predict the repulsion and/or attraction of two particles. Calculate the E-M force using Coulomb's Law. Use Newton's Law of Universal Gravitation to compare the E-M force to the gravitational Force. Describe the production of the magnetic force. Calculate the magnetic force.	Demonstration Equipment: - glass/plastic rods - silk/fur - ring stand - pith ball - electroscope Text resource Instructor notes • Demonstrate the transfer of energy	Quiz Lab Report Outside Assignments Performance Task

SOURCE: Amy Carpinelli, Washington Township School District, Sewell, New Jersey. Used with permission.

cultural regions of the world. Three social studies integrated units were developed for each grade level with a conceptual focus that was developed through the grades.

Figure 5.13 shows in Unit I how the conceptual lens of Diversity/Commonality is developed through different topical themes at each grade level. Examples of such themes are "Diversity/Commonality in Self and Family" in kindergarten and "Diversity/Commonality in Family and Neighborhood" and "Neighborhood and Community" in Grades 1 and 2. This model allows for developing sophistication in conceptual understanding as students progress from thinking about content framed by enduring understandings related to "Diversity/Commonality in Families" in kindergarten through "Diversity/Commonality in Our World" at Grade 6. It is easy to see how the attachment of a conceptual focus to the traditional content takes thinking and learning to a higher level. The students participate in many activities to experience the concept and theme.

Unit II used the conceptual lens of Interdependence for the same grade-level themes (Unit III used the lens of Change/Continuity). Changing the lens essentially changes the units because understanding Diversity/Commonality is different from understanding the lessons to be learned about Interdependence. Some of the enduring understandings that guided the learning activities for the conceptual lens of interdependence through the grades included the following:

♦ Families work together to provide for needs and wants (K-1 grade levels).

♦ Nations work together to solve common problems (Grade 5).

♦ Advances in transportation and technology provide opportunities for developing nations to gain economic power (Grade 8).

Another interesting aspect of the Washington model is the use of geographical "biomes" (world geographic regions with similar climate and vegetation) to identify other cultures for study. Each grade level chooses cultures within a particular biome for in-depth study. The teachers reasoned that selecting cultures from different biomes allows students to learn how cultural groups interact with and use diverse environments for living. It also provides a representative sampling of cultures from around the world.

This social studies format allows for easy integration of curriculum as literature, art, music, drama, or other related subject topics are brought into the design. The move toward integrated curriculum is progressing slowly as teachers and administrators learn as they go. It is important to move forward at a pace that allows for cognitive processing of what works and what doesn't. One approach that does not work is to jump too quickly from single-subject area curriculum designs into seamless, integrated curriculum. If we lose the structure of the separate disciplines, we run the risk of losing many critical concepts and skills and of destroying a coherent educational plan. We first need to start with the articulation of the

(text continues on page 136)

FIGURE 5.13. Social Studies Excerpt

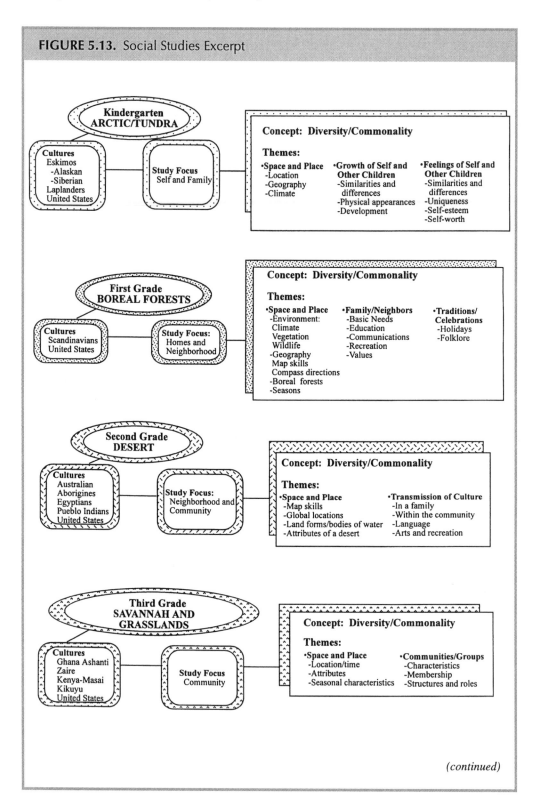

(continued)

FIGURE 5.13. Continued

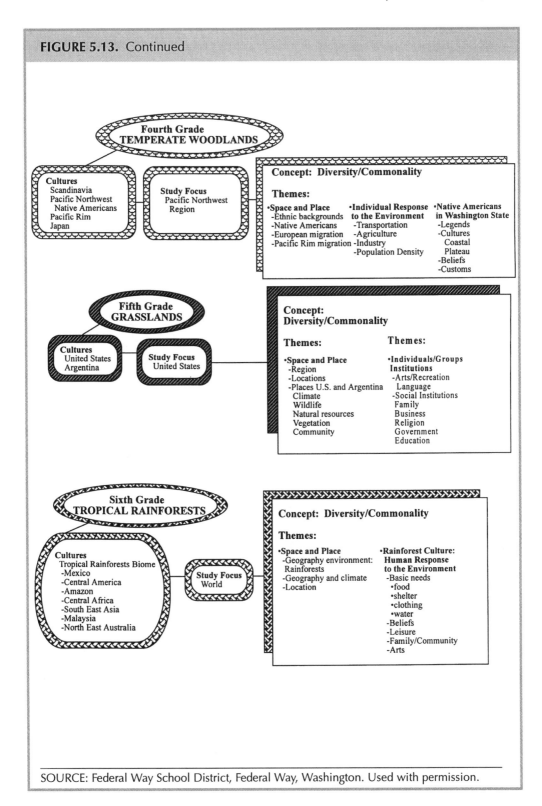

Fourth Grade
TEMPERATE WOODLANDS

Cultures
Scandinavia
Pacific Northwest
Native Americans
Pacific Rim
Japan

Study Focus
Pacific Northwest
Region

Concept: Diversity/Commonality

Themes:

•**Space and Place**
-Ethnic backgrounds
-Native Americans
-European migration
-Pacific Rim migration

•**Individual Response
to the Environment**
-Transportation
-Agriculture
-Industry
-Population Density

•**Native Americans
in Washington State**
-Legends
-Cultures
  Coastal
  Plateau
-Beliefs
-Customs

**Fifth Grade
GRASSLANDS**

Cultures
United States
Argentina

Study Focus
United States

**Concept:
Diversity/Commonality**

Themes:

•**Space and Place**
-Region
-Locations
-Places U.S. and Argentina
  Climate
  Wildlife
  Natural resources
  Vegetation
  Community

Themes:

•**Individuals/Groups
Institutions**
-Arts/Recreation
  Language
-Social Institutions
  Family
  Business
  Religion
  Government
  Education

**Sixth Grade
TROPICAL RAINFORESTS**

Cultures
Tropical Rainforests Biome
-Mexico
-Central America
-Amazon
-Central Africa
-South East Asia
-Malaysia
-North East Australia

Study Focus
World

Concept: Diversity/Commonality

Themes:

•**Space and Place**
-Geography environment:
  Rainforests
-Geography and climate
-Location

•**Rainforest Culture:
Human Response
to the Environment**
-Basic needs
  •food
  •shelter
  •clothing
  •water
-Beliefs
-Leisure
-Family/Community
-Arts

SOURCE: Federal Way School District, Federal Way, Washington. Used with permission.

critical concepts, content, and skills for each discipline and then work toward logically articulated, integrated curricula.

QUESTIONS AND RESPONSES: ELEMENTARY SCHOOLS

1. **Why should interdisciplinary units have both a concept and a theme?**

   Response: A concept by itself does not provide enough focus to the study across disciplines. A theme carries the idea of the concept into a form that is understandable and approachable for students and sets the parameters for the content study. Example:

   Conceptual lens: Culture

   Theme: "African and Japanese Art as Expressions of Culture"

   The theme brings focus and direction to the study of culture. The theme also can be stated as a question to engage students in their search for knowledge: "In what ways are African and Japanese art expressive of culture?"

2. **How does the concept-based unit design compare with the project approach and inquiry unit designs?**

   Response: Both the project approach and inquiry design models are open-ended frameworks that allow the student to go on the search for knowledge and construct personal meaning. The emphasis is on investigation and collaborative inquiry around a major topic of interest to the students. Sometimes, the inquiry may be around a concept alone such as "Change." Harste and Burke (1993) stress the importance of teacher planning in helping students define the inquiry questions related to the topic under study. They suggest using the disciplines as a viewing lens: "What generalizations, principles, or conclusions would a scientist want us to learn? . . . a psychologist? . . . an artist?" (p. 3).

   ♦ Because the project approach and inquiry models value the process of open-ended knowledge construction emanating from the interests of children, they do not address the issue of K-12 curriculum articulation.

   ♦ The concept-based unit design presented in this chapter also sends students on a search for knowledge and a personal construction of meaning, but the search is focused beyond the facts to higher-level enduring understandings related to the concept and theme, as opposed to purely open-ended inquiry. This structure has two benefits:

   − It facilitates the instruction of students' thinking so they can analyze, synthesize, and summarize factual information.

– It allows for an articulation of concepts and themes through the grades and protects a balance of process and content. The integrity of student construction of knowledge and responsibility for learning is still protected.

3. Can I use open-ended as well as structured unit designs in my classroom?

Response: Certainly. Both forms have unique benefits in the learning environment. The task will be twofold:

♦ To lay out the units of instruction so that the standards for content and process development are met

♦ To provide opportunities for open-ended, experiential learning

4. How can I engage students in the planning of the units?

Response: Once you are comfortable with the components of unit design, you can ask students to plan the unit overview with you. Find out what students know about the concept and theme. They can help define topics to be studied related to the concept and theme and can assist in developing the guiding questions. Remember, though, that you need to make certain there are open-ended guiding questions that will cause students to arrive at enduring understandings—those transferable lessons of life that help students make conceptual and real sense of their world.

5. How long should units last?

Response: The time varies. A kindergarten or first-grade unit may last only a few days to a week; a secondary unit developed by an interdisciplinary team may last 4 to 6 weeks.

6. How should I begin moving toward integrated instruction?

Response: Begin with a single unit. Learn from the steps for designing integrated units and then develop a second unit.

7. How many units might I introduce in a year?

Response: For a district core curriculum, there are usually three to four social studies–based units and three to four science-based units per grade level in a year. Other subjects, such as art or mathematics, also have their respective curriculum documents, but they integrate concepts and skills into social studies or science core units when it is reasonable to do so. Content that will not integrate is taught within its discipline. We do not want to "force-fit" content and concepts just for the sake of "integration."

8. How can I structure my day for direct and integrated instruction?

Response: Teacher preference plays heavily into this question, but I prefer direct instruction of skills in the morning and integrated unit work in the afternoon. Teachers may use learning centers and flexible skill groups in the morning as an alternative. Teachers design the learning experience in different ways, but they ensure that skills receive direct instruction as well as application in integrated units or other contexts.

Direct instruction means teacher presentation of skills to develop reading, writing, and speaking abilities or teacher presentation of content critical to the unit work. It is important to select carefully the content information presented in direct instruction, as opposed to content searched out by the student. The direct instruction of content is often for a motivational purpose or establishes the foundation for the student search.

9. I have difficulty finding a theme that lends itself well to the study of integrated science and social studies.

Response: Because social studies is oriented toward culture and humanity, it is sometimes difficult to bridge to the physical and nonhuman branches of science. You will find that environmental themes, such as pollution as a threat to humanity, lend themselves well to social studies as well as science because they have strong ramifications for both domains. We should not "stretch" to try and make a subject fit into a theme. This dilutes the integrity of the study as a whole. As Hayes-Jacobs (1989) states, "Validity within the disciplines requires . . . that concepts identified are not merely related to their subjects but are important to them" (p. 27). You will find that units with a science theme incorporate mathematics, health, vocations, and technology quite easily. Units with a social studies theme readily incorporate the arts, music, literature, and media. The thematic focus of units can be alternated throughout a year. Mathematics and language process skills apply across all curricular areas, however.

10. Is it always necessary to design integrated units that relate to the content of the district curriculum frameworks?

Response: Teachers need the latitude to design some units of interest and relevance to students that may not fall within the mandated frameworks. Some of the unit overview webs provided in this book are examples of teachers choosing to design a unit that deviated (e.g., "Escalation of Violence in America"). Teachers balance the professional responsibility to address the content mandated in curricular frameworks with the need to explore issues of critical and meaningful social significance. Realize that discipline-based concepts can be taught through any number of themes, so we can meet the mandates for teaching some of the required concepts through themes of choice.

QUESTIONS AND RESPONSES: SECONDARY SCHOOLS

1. **Some of our teachers do not see any need to change from the traditional approaches to curriculum and instruction. How can we bring them on board?**

   Response: The first step in encouraging change is education. Share and discuss articles as a staff that address current and critical issues in education from leading journals and newspapers such as *Phi Delta Kappan, Educational Leadership,* and *Education Week.*

   Teachers should also subscribe to field-specific journals, such as *Social Education,* the excellent publication from the National Council of Social Studies. Books and articles that share current information on economic, social, and political trends provide additional insight into change. Curriculum is largely shaped by these trends, and teachers need to be aware of the issues so that special interest groups do not take advantage of an awareness vacuum to install narrow interpretations into curricular materials.

   Chapter 1 addressed the issues of staff change. It can take 3 or 4 years to change a person's mental paradigm. Teachers are more receptive to new ideas when they see that their content and skills will not be lost in the change. Time spent in staff meetings discussing educational trends and the need for change are an invaluable first step. It also helps to begin the move toward concept-based curriculum with one concept-based, intradisciplinary unit so that teachers learn the rationale and process of unit design in their own subject before they move to the interdisciplinary format.

2. **How do we organize as a staff for interdisciplinary teaching?**

   Response: There are many different models—from a looser, multidisciplinary format with two teachers in different fields coordinating topics they are teaching, such as a literature and history teacher dealing with the Renaissance period at the same time in the year, to broader interdisciplinary teaching teams organized under theme-based (e.g., global business and marketing) and concept-based curriculum models.

   There are many examples of schools around the United States that have altered their class schedules to facilitate interdisciplinary teaching. Two examples are block scheduling of two or three subjects and the "school within a school" concept that sets up interdisciplinary teams of teachers with a set number of students who design the mini-school schedule according to the curricular and instructional plan. The degree to which a school decides to transform its curricular and instructional program is determined by the school and parent community. District-level support is crucial.

3. **What issues should we consider in determining our readiness to transform our curricular and instructional program?**

    Response:

    ♦ How committed is the staff to making change? Do you need to start with education and discussion as first steps?

    ♦ What leadership resources do you have? How knowledgeable are leaders in
      – Current trends
      – Articulating the horizontal and vertical curriculum through curriculum mapping
      – Concept-based curriculum and instruction
      – Integrating curriculum
      – Teaching to standards
      – Scheduling
      – Teaming
      – Consensus building
      – Conflict resolution

    The issues listed above will unfold as teachers learn by doing, but leaders need to have baseline knowledge or know where to find the resource help so that valuable time is not wasted in committees.

4. **I am a mathematics teacher. I don't have time for participating in an integrated curriculum because I have to prepare my students for the next level of mathematics, and it takes a full year.**

    Response: The revised national Mathematics Standards, published by the National Council of Teachers of Mathematics (2000), stress the importance of mathematical reasoning and problem solving, as well as communicating and using mathematics in real-world applications. Because integrated units revolve around life problems, issues, and concepts, they provide a fertile context for the relevant application of mathematics.

    Teachers are realizing that their job is not just to prepare students for the next level of mathematics but to prepare them for a life that makes use of mathematics. Because of the heavy emphasis in traditional instruction on the isolated drill and practice with algorithms, students often fail to see the relevance of their learning. Perhaps if students become personally engaged with the applications of the algorithm, they will need less drill and practice to gain understanding.

    Mathematics teachers in the changing paradigm realize that their job is not just to prepare students to follow and solve equations perfunctorily. Their job is to provide students with the process tools of mathematics and to see that those tools are used to solve real-world problems. Progressive teachers of mathematics extend understanding of topics across subject areas. They help students reason mathematically. Mathematics is a process tool just as language is a process tool. And like language arts, mathematics is a form of both thought and communication.

5. What is the role of mathematics in the integration process?

Response: Mathematics serves as a process tool in integrated units. Integrated units show students how mathematics is applied in real-world contexts to explain phenomena and solve problems. Mathematics resembles the language arts in integrated units. It is applied across the disciplines as a thinking and process tool. For too long, we have allowed mathematics to work in a box—isolated from the rest of the curriculum. We would never think of working with the language arts areas of reading and writing without a context, yet we have been doing so for a hundred years with mathematics instruction. It is true that mathematics must have a time for direct skill instruction. But the application of those skills flows naturally into integrated units of study. Where else can we find a context that brings so many different disciplines together to investigate an important problem, topic, or issue? Mathematics teachers should be overjoyed to have an opportunity to show how important mathematics is to the other disciplines. What a forum for demonstrating the power of mathematics in our everyday lives! And just as we say, "All teachers are language arts teachers," we should be saying, "All teachers are mathematics teachers" because both are process tools for thinking about content across the disciplines.

6. What is the role of the mathematics teacher on an interdisciplinary team?

Response: Because mathematics teachers have to teach a sequence of skills and concepts, they may not spend 3 weeks doing mathematics around the unit theme. But they should work in two ways on the team:

♦ Provide suggestions to other subject area teachers for mathematics applications that they could use when studying particular topics in those subjects (history, science, or art).

♦ Use topics from other subject areas to teach current skills being taught in the mathematics class.

The mathematics teacher is an invaluable team member and should plan the unit with the interdisciplinary team and identify his or her own concepts, generalizations, guiding questions, and skills to teach toward as the unit is implemented.

7. How do I identify the topics for the mathematics category on the web?

Response: Mathematics is the last subject to be webbed. Once the other disciplines have defined their topics for study, take mathematics out of the box and ask the question, "How can mathematics be applied to extend understanding of the topics listed under history, economics, geography, music, art, media, science, and so on?" Brainstorm all of the possible applications of mathematics related to the different subject area topics. Do not list mathematics activities on the web (e.g., "Estimate the dimensions of colonial ships"); just identify the mathematics processes and concepts at this time (estimation, percentage, etc.). The determination of specific activities comes later in the planning process.

8. How should our interdisciplinary team decide on a theme for our unit?

Response: As stated earlier, curriculum mapping is a useful tool for identifying critical content topics prior to designing integrated units. Social studies, as representative of culture and people, and science, as representative of the natural and physical world, often provide the base for identifying unit themes. The humanities—art, philosophy, music, literature, drama, and dance—usually fit well into culture-based themes. Technology, mathematics, and health work well in the physical and natural world themes. So themes can be drawn from the sociocultural world and the science world, or they may be drawn from contemporary or persistent issues in society.

9. How are concepts used in integrated units?

Response: There are one and sometimes two broader concepts (no more than two) that serve as a conceptual lens for a unit. The conceptual lens integrates and focuses the study beyond the facts. But realize that many other subconcepts are listed as content to study under each subject around the web. Concepts are used in three ways in units:

♦ To draw thinking to the level of knowledge transfer

♦ To help students understand the attributes of concepts by experiencing a myriad of concrete examples

♦ To help students learn how to identify and understand the "enduring ideas" (generalizations and principles) that emerge out of the unit study

To maintain the integrity of the different disciplines, some interdisciplinary teams choose a focus concept and then let each team "do their own thing" in their curriculum as long as the content ties to the focus concept. This approach may help students understand the attributes of a concept across a variety of examples, but it does nothing to help students integrate their thinking around a common theme, problem, issue, or question by drawing on the offerings of each discipline. Without discipline coherence—all subjects focusing on the conceptual lens and unit theme—there would be no interdisciplinarity. The disciplines would not be working together to facilitate the bigger idea that transcends the unit theme.

10. **How do we maintain the integrity of disciplines in interdisciplinary units?**

   Response: Many secondary teachers express concern that their discipline is merely a "handmaiden" to either social studies or science because integrated unit themes often come from these areas. *The key to maintaining the integrity of different disciplines in the integration process is for each subject area to identify and teach to its own discipline-based concepts.* The identification of subject area concepts is accomplished during the webbing process. Figure 5.14 shows a secondary web for a unit on the Revolutionary period in American history that illustrates how subtopics should be identified for each subject. Sometimes, the topic listed for a subject will actually be a general concept, such as "independence," but at other times the topic will be very specific, such as a book title (e.g., *The American Revolution,* by Edward Dolan). In the case of specific topics, it is helpful to list the related concepts to the right of the topic on the web. For Dolan's book, the related concepts might be "heroes, ideals, characterization." Please note that even though you are teaching the concepts of each discipline, your unit remains integrated and interdisciplinary because of the focus on the common unit theme and, directly or indirectly, on the conceptual lens.

11. **Why is discipline integrity important?**

   Response: If we cannot maintain the integrity of disciplines (i.e., conceptual integrity), then we should not design interdisciplinary units. Disregarding the conceptual base of the different disciplines leads to the "handmaiden" phenomenon. In a handmaiden design, all of the enduring understandings from the unit of study relate to the unit theme, which is usually based in the social or physical world (social studies or science). In a concept-based model, the enduring understandings for each discipline show a balance—some understandings relate to the unit theme, and some understandings express the enduring understandings of the different disciplines. Figure 5.15 shows enduring understandings that represent different subject areas and the guiding questions that tie the ideas to the unit theme.

12. **Will my subject area (physical education, health, anatomy/physiology, mathematics) get to be the main focus of an integrated unit? Do I always have to work under a social studies or science theme?**

   Response: There are times when a strong unit can be designed around a physical education or health concept. An example would be a unit based on the concept of fitness. As a content field, health has many concepts that would serve to organize a relevant interdisciplinary study: disease, organism, cycle, fitness, and so on. Because social studies and science are broader fields, however, they contain a greater range of concepts and themes. It is easier for the elective subjects to fit into the broader frames than the converse. Elective subjects do need

FIGURE 5.14. Revolutionary Period Web

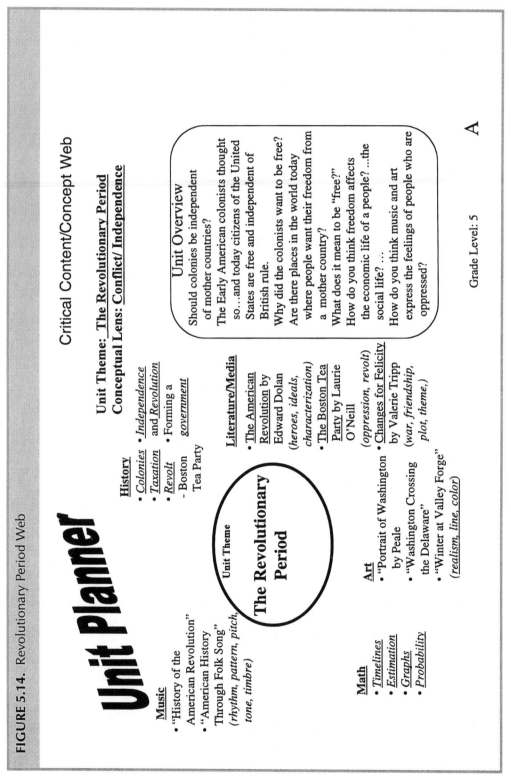

Unit Planner

Critical Content/Concept Web

Unit Theme: The Revolutionary Period
Conceptual Lens: Conflict/ Independence

Unit Theme
The Revolutionary Period

Unit Overview
Should colonies be independent of mother countries?

The Early American colonists thought so…and today citizens of the United States are free and independent of British rule.

Why did the colonists want to be free? Are there places in the world today where people want their freedom from a mother country?

What does it mean to be "free?"

How do you think freedom affects the economic life of a people? …the social life? …

How do you think music and art express the feelings of people who are oppressed?

Music
• "History of the American Revolution"
• "American History Through Folk Song"
  (*rhythm, pattern, pitch, tone, timbre*)

History
• *Colonies*
• *Taxation*
• *Revolt*
  - Boston Tea Party

• *Independence* and *Revolution*
• Forming a *government*

Literature/Media
• The American Revolution by Edward Dolan
  (*heroes, ideals, characterization*)
• The Boston Tea Party by Laurie O'Neill
  (*oppression, revolt*)
• Changes for Felicity by Valerie Tripp
  (*war, friendship, plot, theme,*)

Art
• "Portrait of Washington by Peale
• "Washington Crossing the Delaware"
• "Winter at Valley Forge"
  (*realism, line, color*)

Math
• *Timelines*
• *Estimation*
• *Graphs*
• *Probability*

Grade Level: 5

A

FIGURE 5.15. The Revolutionary Period Generalizations/Questions

Enduring Understandings (Generalizations)	*Guiding Questions*
1. Social, political, or economic oppression can lead to revolution.	1. Why did the colonists in early America resist British control? What is economic oppression? How do people react to oppression?
2. Music and art express the mood of a culture.	2. How did the music of the Revolutionary era convey the mood of the people? How does the timbre in music convey mood?
3. Realistic art conveys a sense of authenticity.	3. How did the artist use line and color to convey authenticity in "Winter at Valley Forge"?
4. Timelines can be used to track the sequence of events for determining causes and effects.	4. Why would historians want to use timelines in the analysis of historical events?
5. Political power can be a positive or corrupting influence.	5. In the story The American Revolution, how did _____ use his political power? What was the effect?

to design their own articulated curriculums prior to interdisciplinary integration. They can then select appropriate content and concepts for interdisciplinary units. The remainder would be taught within their own subject.

Physical education, health, and consumer science teachers can team to design powerfully relevant units for students based on personal, family, and community issues. It is effective to have flexible team structures. It doesn't work to force physical education into a science-based unit, for example, if the theme and concept are not appropriate. It is better to form the interdisciplinary team with members who can contribute increased perspective to the question under study.

13. I teach world languages. How does that fit in?

Response: World languages are based in culture and will fit into any social studies unit that organizes around a culture-based concept. They will also fit into science themes. The language, people, and land of the culture under study will provide the setting. World language teachers by necessity have a strong emphasis on skill development in their courses, as do English and language arts teachers.

14. How about technology? How does that fit in?

Response: Technology is a tool to access, ponder, and portray information. Like mathematics, it is applied across the fields of study to access information, extend understanding, and display learning. The uses of technology in society often fit into both social studies and science-based units. And certainly, with the increasing importance of technology in science and society, it is a key player in many units.

15. If I take time for integrated units, I won't be able to cover the material in my textbook.

Response: If you compare the thickness and size of a textbook today with a textbook from 1980, you will likely see a significant increase in size. One publisher is now sending out two volumes of world history for one course. If you look at the depth of treatment related to critical issues in history, you will find abbreviated summaries of key events compared to a 1980 text. If you feel compelled to "cover the book," you are essentially skimming over surface data, losing many students along the way, and sacrificing the development of intellectual sophistication and deeper understanding.

Belief in the new paradigm that "less is more" challenges you to focus curriculum and instruction around significant concepts and themes. Your textbook will be one of many resources that students will use as they search for knowledge. The classroom is characterized by small group and individual activity and process activities such as drama, debates, dialogues, artistic renderings, and music. Students will have greater retention of the key concepts and critical issues because of their personal involvement in learning. By participating in integrated, interdisciplinary units, the students will have the benefit of multiple perspectives and greater depth of understanding.

16. Does interdisciplinary integration require that all subjects be included in the study?

Response: No. The key to higher-level integration is the conceptual lens that takes thinking beyond the study of facts related to a topic. You should bring only those disciplines into the study that deepen understanding of the unit theme in relation to the conceptual lens. The following are two considerations as to how subjects and their topics of study should be selected to complete the webbing:

❖ You should not force both social studies and science into every unit. Although the conceptual lens can be treated by topics in both disciplines, the content may be so disparate that students would experience cognitive dissonance. I would not want to deal with cycles of human history in the same unit that I am dealing with cycles in the animal world. This unit would lack coherence and could not be considered interdisciplinary even though the conceptual lens of cycles is shared in common. This topic dissonance is a common error in unit development today. On the flip side, however, science and social studies do fit well together in some units. If the theme has both physical world and social world implications, then science and social studies can work together; otherwise, they should remain independent. Environmental issues or technology and society themes work well with the duality of subjects.

❖ When you are deciding on topics for each of the discipline categories, ask the following question: "Which topics would best develop understanding of this theme with this conceptual lens?" Remember that different conceptual lenses affect the choice of topics under the discipline headings.

SCHOOL-TO-WORK PROGRAMS

We cannot leave this chapter on integrated curricula without looking at some of the secondary school models that integrate academic and vocational programming. One example of this form is the "career path" model.

It is important to study the school-to-work models because they provide a relevant context for learning and problem solving. Just as concepts and interesting unit themes provide a rich context for focused, higher-level learning in the classrooms, an organizing theme such as "Production and Technology" provides focus and relevancy for an articulated and coordinated educational program. School-to-work models, such as the career path, provide a meaningful, future-oriented framework for learning. Content is applied in a purposeful context, and the relevancy question, "So what?" has an answer.

As you read about the designs that follow, think of the questions that need to be addressed by teachers, administrators, and parents as they articulate critical concepts, content, and processes under the organizing theme. Work still needs to be done in the area of articulating critical concepts and content to design relevant and meaningful integrated units within the career strands.

David Douglas High School, Portland, Oregon

David Douglas High School (2000) has developed a career path model of curriculum called "Project Stars" that allows students to select into a 4-year academic/career plan framed by one of the following career fields:

♦ Social and human services

♦ Health sciences

♦ Industrial and engineering systems

- Natural sciences

- Hospitality, tourism, and recreation

- Business and management

- Arts and communication

- Education and human development

Teachers, counselors, administrators, and three to five business partners are formed into interdisciplinary teams within each career constellation. The team establishes curriculum, sets policy, and determines how to provide the best program for students. They design curriculum and lessons to have students apply the concepts, principles, and processes of the academic curriculum in a career-related context. Besides the application of learning in classroom simulations of career tasks, students have opportunities to take part in internships, in-class projects, and student-led enterprises.

The Oregon Education Act (House Bill 3565) contains the legislation establishing educational performance standards for all students to be attained by the 10th grade (Certificate of Initial Mastery). This act further provides the opportunity for students to earn a Certificate of Advanced Mastery (CAM) by the end of 12th grade. This advanced certificate requires that students

- Earn passing grades in a total of six courses in a CAM program

- Complete a CAM portfolio showing proficiency in the required content areas, demonstrating specific knowledge and skills in the CAM specialty area, and documenting career-based learning experiences

- Complete a senior project/internship documented with journal entries covering 12 to 15 hours of work

Although the CAM is not required for graduation, the students who complete the requirements receive an additional endorsement on their diploma. Experiences for students in the various CAM constellations are relevant and engaging as they look to their futures. For example, one group of students in the natural sciences CAM established a hydroponics system and is harvesting organically grown lettuce. Another group has been working to hatch and raise quail with a generous donation of eggs from a local game farm. The industrial and engineering CAM built a light rail system for the school campus. This ambitious project included the construction of a terminal where the train is stored.

Legislation dealing with school-to-work transition is available in state governments and Departments of Education across the country. The federal government also has legislation to further the state efforts, but many school-to-work advocates feel that the emphasis on standards in core curricular areas has weakened vocational support over the past few years.

The Arizona Model for Vocational Technological Education

Since 1988, the Arizona Department of Education (1992) has been working on the restructuring of vocational technological education. This effort has involved the three state universities, many local school districts, and business and industry partners. Arizona vocational technological education is continually evolving toward a vision of high technical and academic competence.

The Arizona model provides four levels of instruction that begin in the seventh grade with a broad overview of occupations and development of core technical skills. The learning continues through postsecondary programs with increasing occupational specialization of knowledge and skills.

The four levels of sequenced instruction are integrated through six strands of developmental outcomes. The outcome-based strands in the Arizona model (Arizona Department of Education, 1992) are the following:

◆ Thinking skills—including decision making, problem solving, creativity, and dealing with change

◆ Career development skills—including career exploration, career decision making, and job acquisition skills

◆ Applied academic skills—including communications, mathematics, and science related to technical areas

◆ Life management skills—including interpersonal relationships, wellness, group processes, health and safety

◆ Business, economic, and leadership skills—including business economics, entrepreneurship, marketing procedures, and continuous improvement processes

◆ Technology skills—including computer skills and applications of new and advanced technologies

Each strand is defined by developmental outcomes, as shown in Figure 5.16.

The Arizona model is depicted in Figure 5.17. As students progress from Level 1 to Level 4, they move from the exploratory study of occupations and the development of basic work skills to specific occupational skill development and experience with advanced technologies. The outcome strands are woven throughout the academic and career curriculum and develop increasing sophistication as students progress through the grades.

The curriculum framework for Level 1 was developed by the staff of Arizona State University for predominantly junior high and middle schools. The framework identifies skills and concepts that cut across occupations and organizes content according to the following themes:

Communicating information

Explaining energy, matter, and machines

FIGURE 5.16. Arizona Model: Preliminary Strand Outcomes

LEVEL 1—TECHNOLOGICAL EXPLORATION AND FOUNDATIONS

Thinking Skills

- ▶ Describe the processes of decision making and problem solving
- ▶ Compare and contrast different decision-making and problem-solving skills
- ▶ Define and demonstrate how one acquires information
- ▶ Define a variety of creative thinking skills
- ▶ Describe the effects of change

Career Development Skills

- ▶ Describe and demonstrate school and work ethics
- ▶ Identify and explore areas of career interest
- ▶ Experience meaningful and relevant activities related to areas of interest
- ▶ Explore occupational cluster choices

Applied Academic Skills

- ▶ Identify and demonstrate basic academic skills
- ▶ Describe the relationship between academic skills and occupational skills
- ▶ Identify careers that capitalize on specific academic strengths and interests

Life Management Skills

- ▶ Identify characteristics of effective interpersonal relationships
- ▶ Identify wellness, health, and safety concepts
- ▶ Identify personal, economic, and environmental resources
- ▶ Define self-concept and identify self-esteem issues
- ▶ Identify and explore group processes
- ▶ Perform effectively as an individual and member of a team

Business, Economic, and Leadership Skills

- ▶ Describe basic economic concepts and systems
- ▶ Describe the characteristics of a successful business
- ▶ Describe the value of work to the individual, community, and nation
- ▶ Identify qualities and types of leaders
- ▶ Define and describe cultural diversity
- ▶ Explain the value of continually improving the work process

Technology Skills

- ▶ Describe and demonstrate basic technological principles and processes
- ▶ Demonstrate basic computer skills

SOURCE: Interim Design Report, July 1992. Arizona Department of Education. Used by permission.

FIGURE 5.17. Arizona Model for Vocational Technological Education

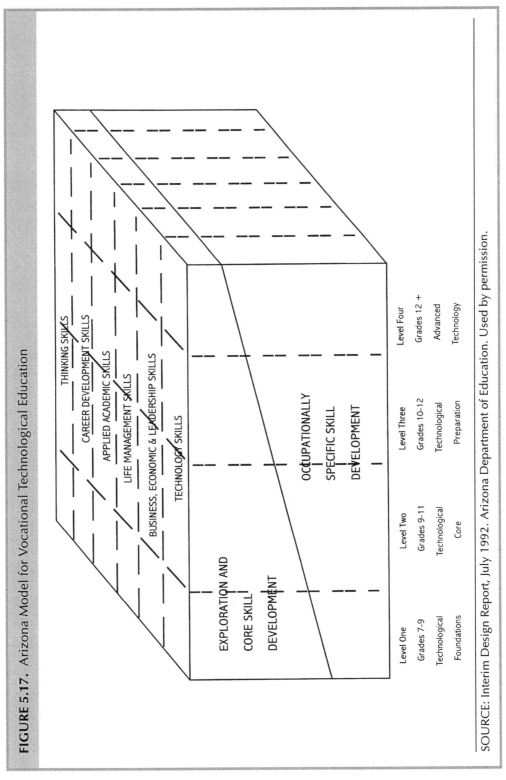

SOURCE: Interim Design Report, July 1992. Arizona Department of Education. Used by permission.

FIGURE 5.18. Arizona Model: Level 1 Competencies and Competency (Sample) Indicators

THEME A—COMMUNICATING INFORMATION

1.0. Students will gather, interpret, and evaluate information
1.1. Apply a decision-making/problem-solving strategy
1.2. Practice working in groups
1.3. Locate information sources
1.4. Match personal aptitudes and interests to courses of study
1.5. Explore careers in communication
1.6. Develop an awareness of career information resources
1.7. Verify the reliability and accuracy of information
1.8. Apply comprehensive strategies
1.9. Apply ethics in reporting and using information
1.10. Discuss similarities between class/school rules and work rules

THEME B—EXPLAINING ENERGY/MATTER AND MACHINES

1.0. Students will identify types of energy and their physical properties
1.1. Explain potential energy
1.2. Discuss the role of motion in kinetic energy
1.3. Identify the properties and uses of magnetism
1.4. Demonstrate the effect of friction on machines
1.5. Use temperature to control matter
1.6. Use light and color to alter matter

2.0. Students will understand the transfer of energy to power
2.1. Explain the use of air, fluid, and electricity in a power system
2.2. Use standard measurement abbreviations and equivalents
2.3. Use measuring and timing devices
2.4. Evaluate ethical implications of decisions about energy

SOURCE: Interim Design Report, July 1992. Arizona Department of Education. Used by permission.

Relating technology and science

Producing and processing

The themes are delineated further by specific competencies and competency-based indicators (see Figure 5.18).

Career Path Curriculum Design

The blending of a traditional liberal arts college preparation program in high schools and a career path model presents major curricular design questions:

♦ How can we preserve the integrity of a liberal arts philosophy and at the same time provide a school program that prepares students for work as well as for further education?

♦ How can we develop the high-level performance skills outlined in the Secretary's Commission on Achieving Necessary Skills (SCANS) report through an integrated academic and vocational curriculum?

Although I usually advocate making change in incremental steps, beginning with what is and moving forward as people appear ready in knowledge and desire, I hold a different view for high school restructuring. We have become complacently inured with the two-track model of vocational and college preparation programs in our high schools. We have been squeezing too many students through the cookie tube who are ill prepared for either work or college.

Our traditional high school curriculum is delivered as if all students, except those we funnel into vocational education, will graduate from a 4-year college. And unlike countries such as Germany or Japan, we have denigrated vocational education as less worthy than the college preparatory program. Yet the statistics show that even though 60% to 70% of students may begin university programs, only about 30% complete the 4 years. And will there be jobs in the designated fields for those graduates? Most students have traditionally had little experience with the kinds of skills outlined in SCANS. Yet the continuing health of our economic system depends on these skills and abilities.

We will never break down these barriers between the perceived academic and vocational tracks with minor tinkering. We need to design entirely new models for high schools, such as the career path models, that design integrated curricular programs to meet outcomes drawn from at least three sources:

♦ SCANS, to meet the needs of a quality workforce

♦ The aims of liberal arts curricula, to preserve the lessons of discourse, culture, and humanity

♦ Life skill curricula, to be prepared for daily living

A danger with career path models is that the liberal arts and life skill curricula will be lost in the preparation of future workers. But despite this possibility, we must alter the traditional program to bring contemporary relevance and meaning to each student's education. I believe the dangers can be avoided with thoughtful curricular planning and multiple-source outcomes, as stated previously.

Once the multiple-source outcomes and performance indicators are defined for the school program, two different approaches to curriculum design seem appropriate.

Key concepts related to the subject areas that support the particular career path are identified. In a career path titled "Environmental, Physical, and Health Sciences," examples of key concepts might be sustainability, deforestation, or pollution for the environment; force, cause and effect, or quantification for physical science; or model, disease, or organism for health sciences. With this approach, the content can be defined as topics related to the different concepts through the grade levels. Concepts can be repeated through the grades with developing sophistication of the related topical themes. New concepts can also be added as the curriculum becomes more complex.

For interdisciplinary units, what might be a narrow topic within a subject area study (e.g., machines and energy in physical science) is developed into a broader unit theme that draws from the different disciplines. An example of a broader, interdisciplinary theme linked to the concept of energy might be, "How is energy related to work in different occupations: oceanographer, forester, chemist, radiology technician, or recycler?"

The theme is viewed through a conceptual lens so that learning moves beyond low-level fact study. Remember that it is the conceptual lens that draws thinking to the analysis and synthesis levels. It is also helpful to phrase the topical theme in the form of a question, problem, or issue to send the students on a quest for knowledge and to motivate curiosity.

As process subjects, English and mathematics are applied across the interdisciplinary fields of study. All teachers are teachers of language, and mathematics extends understanding across disciplines. Both subjects communicate meaning. The skills of English and mathematics can be taught in single-subject study, but they gain meaning and practicality in authentic life contexts.

The second method for designing curriculum for career paths maintains the traditional subjects and encourages teachers to make connections to the vocations and vocational content of the career path. I would call this a coordinated curriculum approach rather than an integrated one because the curriculum depends on connections to vocations rather than integration of academic and vocational under common concepts and themes.

Significant high school change will require extensive dialogue between academic and vocational teachers, administrators, parents, and the business community. It will be important for all parties to see the perceived need and to agree that things must change. How that change occurs will require teamwork, the ability to leave the familiar in curriculum and instruction, and the willingness to take some risks. Teachers will need to feel that the risks are supported by administrators and parents. The business community must take a partnership role in helping to suggest and design "authentic" experiences or simulations for students. Schools can gain suggestions for classroom simulations by surveying local businesses for a list of employee activities that require the use of the various SCANS competencies. The survey describes the competencies and leaves room for the employer (or employees) to fill in related job responsibilities and tasks. These can then be transformed into classroom simulations by the teachers.

The current political pressure to meet the standards of traditional content areas makes progress more difficult for the school-to-work programs. I hope we don't jettison this valuable movement and the standards it offers for our country.

Florida's School-to-Work Continuum

For more than a decade, the state of Florida has been operating from its *Blueprint for Career Preparation* (Florida Department of Education, 1989) to provide a quality workforce. Vocational programs are being developed and refined according to the SCANS, which were outlined in Chapter 2. A variety of programs and incentives make up the school-to-work continuum from elementary through postsecondary school.

One example, the Quad County Tech Prep Program (St. Lucie, Okeechobee, Martin, and Indian River counties), is a cooperative partnership between the community college, the school districts, and local business leaders. At the high school level, the academic core uses applied academics and develops technical skills in six curriculum clusters: agriscience, business and office, medical, sales and marketing, trade and technical, or a public service–related career.

Educational summits are held yearly to provide feedback and suggestions from the 200-plus businesses in the county. Business leaders are included in the design and delivery of curriculum and staff development training as well. Students can earn college credits in high school through the tech prep program, and the Indian River Community College is developing applied academic programs to extend the training for students after high school.

It is critical that our traditional high school structure, organization, and pedagogical practices are rapidly changed. Involving students in meaningful, applied curriculum that develops their life skills, motivates their minds, and engages their spirits will brighten a fading light. All students deserve a quality education. We must fix the problems of slip in, slide through, or shoved out.

The programs that effectively blend vocational and academic curriculum when reasonable and structure learning toward high-level outcomes, such as those outlined in the SCANS report, offer promising models for secondary schools.

At the same time, we have to balance a curriculum that prepares students for work, citizenship, and family life, with a curriculum that

♦ Ensures success in further schooling

♦ Develops aesthetic knowledge and appreciation

♦ Develops healthy self-esteem, values, and ethics

It is for this reason that I advocate defining the major concepts and critical content that underlie the separate academic and vocational subject areas prior to integrating content. Concepts that cut across disciplines can then serve to integrate the content. The focus of content can be defined through the unit themes. Themes should be centered on significant issues, problems, or questions related to humanity and our world in all of its complexity. Themes are drawn from all contexts of life such as work, family, aesthetics, sport, health and well-being, and political, economic, and sociocultural issues. Even if a school has a career path focus, the themes of study need to include the range of life issues to develop a balanced foundation of knowledge, skills, attitudes, and values.

SUMMARY

Transforming instructional units from topic based to concept based is a relatively easy process when teachers use a conceptual lens to integrate students' thinking. This chapter looks at different examples of concept-based units from interdisciplinary to intradisciplinary and reinforces the idea that both forms can be concept based and integrated if a conceptual lens is used to focus the thinking to the integration level. Questions and answers related to the design and implementation of concept-based, integrated units help teachers with their planning.

Finally, the issue of school-to-work curricula and academic and vocational integration is discussed briefly. I strongly support the school-to-work movement not only because it provides a relevant context for academic applications and provides future work skills but because it also provides a powerful platform for engaging the hearts and minds of young people. School-to-work programs are active and require more student self-direction. When each student can "take charge," his or her intellect and emotions are tapped.

EXTENDING THOUGHT

1. What value does concept-based curriculum design have over topically based curriculum design in terms of the following?

   ♦ Reducing the overloaded content curriculum

   ♦ Focusing instruction to develop higher-level thinking

   ♦ Integrating content curriculum

   ♦ Facilitating the transfer of knowledge

   ♦ Sharing the commonality as well as the diversity of culture and humanity

   ♦ Highlighting the "lessons of history" through time

2. How can teachers transform a topic-based unit into a concept-based unit?

3. How can teachers involve students in the design of integrated units?

4. React to this statement: "Teachers do not need to know all of the specific content information of a unit prior to student engagement. They learn along with the students who search out and construct knowledge. Teachers do, however, need to think through the anticipated interplay of theme, concept, and topics to

determine some of the key generalizations or transferable learnings that they expect students to derive."

5. Discuss the dilemma at the high school level between providing a traditional college preparatory curriculum and a work preparatory curriculum. How can both aims be accommodated through an integrated curricular program that will alleviate the traditional view of academics versus vocational?

6 Assessing and Reporting Student Progress

Assessment experts and teachers work furiously to design performance assessments aimed at improving learning and reporting progress at the classroom level. Subject area committees at the national and state levels have outlined content and performance standards. In some cases, the standards are helpful because they are broad frameworks showing the critical concepts, key content, and desired performances for a discipline. In other cases, the standards are a rewrite of specific content objectives from the early 1980s, with the add-ons of expected performance outcomes. In most cases, the standards are being implemented with "high-stakes" legislation. Students will be denied a high school diploma if the standards are not demonstrated in the complex tests.

Policymakers appear in each generation with the persuasive argument that if we just test for what we want, the product will emerge. The testing machine will magically transform instruction to the identified ends. It is true that defining the targets for curriculum and instruction in the assessment instruments will assist in making changes in the classroom. But to assume that an instructional change to meet higher standards will occur without systematic staff development is short-circuit thinking.

We can and should set performance standards, as well as monitor and adjust curriculum and instruction, from elementary through secondary school to ensure that each child reaches appropriate graduating standards. But we are in a race with irrational expectations in many states—high-stakes cognitive and performance standards applied to bulging curricula, with inadequate attention to the need for teacher and administrator training, professional dialogue, and student support. Without this focus at the teaching level, the testing mandates are going to swing around and knock the policymakers off their feet.

Parents will not stand for their students being held back from graduation. The resulting dialogue will highlight the conditions of inequity and the needs for instructional and student support. Why wait for this hailstorm to occur? Why not develop a reasonable "systems" approach for addressing the desired student standards? Rather than a simplistic, top-down "test is best" mentality, we should evaluate the foundation for learning at the classroom level and weigh instructional practices and student needs against the desired graduation standards.

Each component of the school system—curriculum, instruction, evaluation and assessment, decision making, leadership, roles, communication, human resource development, parents, and community—should be evaluated and aligned toward the achievement of success for all students as defined by desired standards. Although some school districts are taking such a systems approach to restructuring, too many districts are simply doing what we have always done—writing low-level content objectives at the district level that match the topics of state standards. But little changes in the classroom because the curriculum design reinforces coverage rather than deeper, intellectual engagement. And the design problem is inherent in the way objectives are written—tacking a verb onto a topic with an assumption that a deeper understanding will be reached.

In this chapter, we will focus on the component of evaluation and assessment, beginning with a brief comparison of standardized, criterion-referenced, and performance-based measures. Then we will take a closer look at process and performance assessments by studying specific classroom examples. Key to the discussion will be the critical importance of student self-assessment. The value of "authentic" assessment as a means of relating learning to real-life contexts and situations will be displayed through selected examples. Steps for designing performance assessments to evaluate what students know, understand, and can do will lead into a summary discussion on the value of performance-based measurement.

A BRIEF REVIEW: FORM AND FUNCTION

Normative-Referenced Tests

Normative-referenced tests are designed to assess and compare mass populations on specific items of knowledge or skill. They can be multiple-choice and machine-scored instruments. When these tests are used to place a student or a group of students in rank order compared with other test takers in the same grade or age population, the test is normatively referenced. Normative-referenced, standardized tests were influenced heavily by the use of a multiple-choice format on the Army Alpha examination during World War I. The Alpha format efficiently and effectively sorted nearly 2 million military personnel to determine aptitude for officer status (Popham, 1993).

Criterion-Referenced Tests

Criterion-referenced tests became especially popular in the late 1970s and 1980s as an attempt to identify clearly and specifically what knowledge and skills students are to master. Criterion-referenced tests measure the objectives taught in the classroom. They intend to highlight a student's strengths and weaknesses. Because of their close alignment to the curriculum, it has been traditionally assumed that remediating the test areas would achieve student success.

According to James Popham (1993), however, weak test design—focused too often on "skill and drill" instruction—has impeded the potential of quality criterion-referenced tests. Popham states that we need to promote "generalizable" mastery of critical knowledge and skills. This can be accomplished through criterion-referenced tests that focus on the intellectual skills required by the testing task and that provide a variety of assessment tactics. We will return to the issue of generalizability of assessment results later in this chapter.

Alternative Assessments

Alternative assessments is a catchphrase for forms of assessment that depart from the traditional multiple-choice, normatively referenced tests. The late 1980s raised questions with the testing establishment concerning the usefulness of standardized tests in sharing information on what students are actually capable of "doing." In response to the many questions and to meet the changing emphases in assessment, alternative forms of assessment have been designed. Each form emphasizes a specific focus for assessment:

♦ *Standards-based assessment* is concerned with measuring the progress toward graduating student standards identified by states and school districts.

♦ *Performance assessments* combine content and process into a format that shows what students know—and what they can do with what they know. Performance assessments take knowledge to the doing level. The assessments may be authentic, as defined below, but are not always so. Performance assessments often take traditional content, such as information on the Civil War, and engage students in a performance task calling on knowledge and skills. The performance might be an essay, a play, a debate, or a visual representation related to an aspect or issue of the Civil War.

♦ *Portfolio assessment* emphasizes student self-assessment. A portfolio is a collection of student work that tells a story through time. It shows growth and development related to established criteria. The purpose of a portfolio is to facilitate classroom learning and instruction.

♦ *Authentic assessment* is based on meaningful performances that are drawn from real-world contexts. The assessments are simulations of problems, issues, or challenges that a professional worker or adult might face in his or her life.

Alternative assessments support the recognized need to develop the internal process or lifelong learning skills of each child.

Developmental Process Assessments

The alternative assessments discussed in the preceding section measure both process and content. But they are only "snapshots" of a student's performance in time.

To effectively monitor a student's continuous development within each process area from primary grades through high school, we need to identify the developmental characteristics or indicators for each developmental stage. The developmental stages may be defined by grade bands, such as kindergarten through Grade 2, Grades 3 to 4, and Grades 5 to 6, or by individual grade designations with a range of indicators. The developmental indicators are grouped under organizing categories. For example, the process area of writing can be defined by the categories of organization, mechanics, style, and development.

Specific indicators for beginning, intermediate, and advanced performance provide teachers with a developmental road map for helping students celebrate how far they have come and for showing the next steps. Figure 6.1 provides an example of writing indicators from the fourth-grade level in a K-12 sequence of developmental indicators from the Federal Way, Washington School District. These indicators are used by teachers in an ongoing assessment of student writing collected in progress portfolios.

Many school districts have developed indicators for writing, reading, and speaking. The best indicators are those that are drawn from the actual performance of students in the district. In Federal Way, the writing indicators were developed by a large teacher committee that examined hundreds of samples of student writing, K-12, to identify the salient indicators for each category.

It is important to develop a folio of exemplar papers for each grade band. These papers provide teachers with concrete examples of beginning, intermediate, and advanced work in each category. Critical to quality assessment is teacher training on how to assess papers according to the identified criteria and standards.

THE IMPLICATIONS OF PROCESS ASSESSMENT

Process and content are two different entities. Process is developed internally within each child; content is inert and exists outside of the child. Because of these differences, we should teach and assess process and content in different ways. But traditionally, we have treated them alike. We have called the processes of reading and writing "subjects." We have graded students in these "subjects" using a deficit model—emphasizing what they cannot yet do, rather than celebrating accomplishments, and encouraging them along the path to the next stage of development. I believe this deficit approach to process development is one reason why so many children feel defeated by third grade.

Two examples illustrate the deficit model for grading process development. The first example is from the Federal Way, Washington School District. When the

FIGURE 6.1. Federal Way Writing Indicators

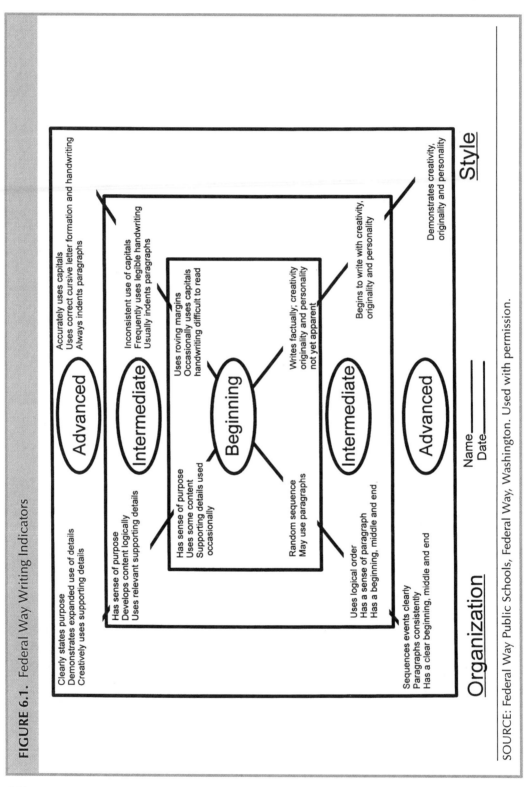

SOURCE: Federal Way Public Schools, Federal Way, Washington. Used with permission.

teachers in Federal Way reviewed their first draft of the writing indicators K-12, they realized that the writing indicators for the advanced-level students were all affirmative statements: "Clearly states purpose," "Creatively uses supporting details," "Demonstrates personality," and so on. The beginning level, however, used overwhelmingly negative statements: "No purpose shown," "Lacks supporting details," "Lacks personality," and so on.

The teachers recognized that this approach to writing assessment, which rightfully measures a student against a set standard, broke down at the beginning levels. A deficit model took over at this level, defining what students could not do rather than showing the developmental capabilities that were demonstrated in the beginning stages of writing for their age range. Teachers realized how defeating the negative assessments were to a child. How many of us would want to go to work and be told, day in and day out, what we cannot do in our performance? Wouldn't we achieve greater growth by knowing how much positive gain we were making toward the standard?

The teachers took the first draft and reframed the question for students in the beginning developmental levels of writing: "What abilities *are* demonstrated at each developmental stage as they work toward the standard?" This was difficult because it meant task analyzing to find the indicators of success at the beginning developmental levels of the writing process. The discussion among the teachers was invaluable, however, as they began to look at their students as developing rather than as deficit learners. Conceptually, they started to view each learner as being on a positive learning curve rather than being a plus or minus point on a bell-shaped curve.

The second example of a deficit assessment mode relates to the measurement of graduation standards. Some districts have developed qualitative scales to assess individual performance for outcomes such as "collaborative contributor." The highest level of the scale describes the collaborative contributor with positive indicators such as "task oriented," "monitors own behavior to facilitate the work of the group," "contributes ideas thoughtfully," and so on. The lowest level of the scale describes the student's performance in deficit terms: "off-task," "does not monitor behavior to support group," and "disrupts group process."

If we believe that the ability to collaborate is a developmental process, then we have to wonder why we assess the student's progress as if he or she should have already arrived—no matter what the age or developmental level. Would we use such a deficit model to encourage a 1-year-old to walk or a 2-year-old to talk? Teaching for process development in the school-age child requires the same kind of praise, encouragement, and support that we provide the preschool child who is learning to talk, walk, think, and speak. Assessment scales need to be supportive of learning at all levels rather than negatively evaluative of students at the beginning levels.

The deficit model of assessment is apparent in most performance-based rubrics even today. Are we really measuring "progress" toward a standard if we give no credit at the beginning levels for what students can do in relation to the standard? What effect does negative feedback have on the developing processes that are so sensitively related to the child's ego and personal being? Highly successful coaches set and clarify the standard for athletes—but they positively celebrate small advancements toward the goal. Corrections are made, but expressed belief in the individual and support through the different levels of development are the main strategies for training.

REPORTING PROCESS DEVELOPMENT

As a result of the renewed perspective that language is a developing process, many schools have revised their elementary report card. Student progress in writing is placed along a developmental continuum at the beginning, intermediate, or advanced level in kindergarten through sixth grade. The goal is to place all language skills on a developmental continuum on the report card and remove the meaningless letter grades. Each parent receives a booklet showing all of the writing indicators, K-12, when a child enters school. Parents are encouraged to follow and assist their children's progress.

Report cards that give a letter grade for reading, writing, oral communication, or any other developing process skill do not provide a helpful profile for what the child has actually accomplished. Narrative reports that detail the child's progress through descriptive indicators of actual performance are far more meaningful to both parents and children. These reports become even more valuable when the child has self-assessed his or her own work according to defined performance indicators. Figure 6.2 from Southwood Elementary School in Orlando, Florida shows excerpts from a Grade 1 report card based on descriptive indicators.

In many other districts around the country, teachers are providing students with developmental writing indicators such as those shown in Figure 6.1. They ask the students to self-assess their writing and provide written reactions before turning their work in to the teacher. Peer assessment is often a step in the writing process. There has been a great deal written in the literature concerning the benefits of both peer assessment and student self-assessment and critique. I believe self-assessment, especially, is a critical practice to help students take more responsibility for their learning and to encourage a high standard of high-quality work.

Wang, Haertel, and Walberg (1993), in a *Review of Educational Research* article titled "Toward a Knowledge Base for School Learning," present the results of a comprehensive meta-analysis of factors influencing the teaching and learning process as drawn from quantitative research syntheses, summaries by educational experts, and narrative reviews representing thousands of statistical relations. Although the journal also contains review articles that question the feasibility of generalizing the conditions for teaching and learning from rules formed by researchers who are removed from the context of the classroom (Kleibard, 1993), I feel the results deserve consideration.

According to Wang et al. (1993), the categories having the most influence on student learning, as shown through the meta-analysis, were the following:

- ◆ Classroom management
- ◆ Metacognitive (the student's ability to self-assess)

FIGURE 6.2. Southwood Elementary Report Card

	Quarter			
	1	2	3	4
Reading/language				
Recognizes high-frequency words				
Identifies and uses letters and sounds in reading				
Can retell, discuss, summarize, and supply information from stories				
Identifies main ideas from text				
Identifies supporting information				
Uses strategies to identify words and construct meaning				
Selects appropriate materials to read				
Recognizes rhyme, rhythm, and patterned structures				
Distinguishes between fiction and nonfiction				
Can formulate questions				
Recognizes standard language patterns (questions, statements)				
Writing				
Composes simple sentences and stories				
Develops a purpose and plan for writing				
Uses basic sentence structure with punctuation				
Uses correct spacing between words				
Writes legibly				
Applies simple editing skills				

Mastery	+	Applies knowledge/skill in different ways; transfers and extends knowledge
Developing	✔	Has made some progress toward mastery; applies knowledge/skills in a limited way
Needs Improvement	–	Seldom applies knowledge/skills; seldom works independently and requires additional support
Introduced	I	Introduced but not assessed at this time
Not Yet Introduced		

(continued)

FIGURE 6.2. Continued

Reading Development

 Emergent reader—The child is not yet reading but is developing concepts of print. This reader may know several high-frequency words and pretend to read familiar texts. Occurs at approximately ages 5 to 6.

 Early reader—The child is in the stage when true reading is beginning to occur. This reader is developing strategies for reading and self-correction. Occurs at approximately ages 6 to 8.

 Fluent reader—The child is gaining control of reading so that self-correction is becoming automatic. Silent reading is becoming part of the child's behavior. Occurs at approximately ages 7 to 10.

Writing Development

 Emergent writer—The child uses scribbling and letter-like approximations to convey meaning. Many words are represented by the first letter sound of the word. Occurs at approximately ages 5 to 6.

 Early writer—The child uses beginning sounds, ending sounds, and vowels. More words are spelled correctly than approximated. Occurs at approximately ages 6 to 8.

☐ Fluent writer—The child is expressing more complex ideas with greater ease. These writers are using some editing and proofreading skills to improve the message. Occurs at approximately ages 7 to 10.

SOURCE: Southwood Elementary School, Orange County School District, Orlando, Florida. Used with permission.

♦ Cognitive (general intelligence, prior knowledge, specific content knowledge, as well as motivational and affective attributes such as perseverance and enthusiasm for learning)

♦ Home environment and parental support

♦ Student and teacher social interactions

The findings show that *proximal* variables—those close to the student such as psychological, home environment, and instructional variables—have strong influence on school learning. *Distal* variables, or variables that are farther removed from the student, such as state and district policies or student demographic characteristics, have less of an impact on learning (Wang et al., 1993).

This analysis is an alignment with current beliefs and trends in education. Although we have always been concerned with classroom management as an issue, the question today is how to manage a classroom so that the cognitive and metacognitive structures are facilitated to maximize learning. Thinking students and thinking teachers take greater responsibility for their work and function at increasingly sophisticated levels of performance.

Schools are vitally concerned with bringing parents in as partners in the educational process. This concern coincides with the findings by Wang et al. (1993) that home environment and parental support are critical to the educational success of children. All of the performance assessments in the world will not bring success to a suicidal child who is verbally or physically abused.

Finally, teachers have always known that the interpersonal interaction with each of their students has a significant impact on their students' success. Students look to their teacher for acceptance and support. We need to value all children, talk and connect with them, and show interest in their growth and development.

ASSESSING CRITICAL THINKING DEVELOPMENTALLY

Critical thinking is one of the most challenging areas that needs to be assessed as a developmental process. It is challenging because there are few, if any, models that define indicators of developing sophistication for this area. There have been some benchmark "snapshots" that describe critical thinking in a general way as applied to a specific task, but we need a more complete picture to assist teachers.

There is no question that the development of sophisticated thinking abilities is required for individual success in the 21st century. National, state, and district learning standards specify the ability to think critically, problem solve, and reason as key goals for education. But teachers have had little training in how to teach for and assess thinking abilities. This is a more serious problem than most policymakers recognize. Teachers know that this is a critical area of need for staff development.

In addition to the limited emphasis on this area in teacher training programs, our traditional curriculum fosters the antithesis of higher-order thinking. A primary focus on kings, queens, dates, isolated mathematical algorithms, grammar drills, and the memorization of isolated fact after fact hinders the pursuit of higher-order understandings. Lower-order memory work should not be the end of instruction. It should be viewed as a necessary tool for effective higher-order thinking.

Today, the trend is away from isolated thinking skill instruction to embedded thinking as a natural part of the teaching and learning process. So the question remains, "How can we identify the developmental indicators of critical thinking to facilitate the progress of each child as he or she moves through the grades?"

STANDARDS FOR THINKING

We can find help in answering the question by starting with the standards for critical thinking that have been identified by Richard Paul at the Center for Critical Thinking, Sonoma State University. Paul (1993a) states, and rightly so, that it is not enough only to analyze or evaluate material. We also must apply a set of standards to specify the quality of analysis or evaluation that is performed.

Eight of the 14 intellectual standards identified by Paul (1993a) are as follows:

- ◆ Clarity
- ◆ Depth
- ◆ Accuracy
- ◆ Breadth
- ◆ Precision
- ◆ Significance
- ◆ Relevance
- ◆ Logic

To maintain coherence with the terminology used in this chapter, we will substitute the word *traits* for Paul's *standards* because we define a trait as a characteristic or quality to be evaluated and the standard as the set point for quality performance.

To help students learn how to think critically, we need to define the indicators for each of these traits. What does clarity "look like" at Grades K to 2, 3 to 5, 6 to 8, and 9 to 12? We might say that "clarity is clarity" no matter what the grade level. This is true. Clarity is a concept with the attributes of clearness and lucidity, no matter what the grade level. So when we begin to assess what the critical thinking standards look like at each grade band, we have to go beyond the simple, generalizable attributes.

We need to consider how clarity will be expressed as applied to particular content. The expression of clarity as a developmental performance is dependent on a number of factors:

- ◆ The sophistication of the content in terms of depth and complexity of ideas
- ◆ The cognitive processing of the students—their ability to analyze, synthesize, and organize content and ideas
- ◆ The communication ability of the students—their skill in conveying ideas so that others clearly understand the message

Let's examine a specific case in which increasing sophistication of content provides a framework for assessing developing sophistication in critical thinking processes.

In Chapter 5, I discussed the idea of organizing a social studies curriculum according to a limited number of organizing concepts that cut through Grades K to 6. The expanding themes at each grade level are considered in relation to the organizing concept of interdependence for the instructional unit. The theme of families and interdependence at Grades K to 1 leads to increasingly sophisticated themes: "Communities and Interdependence," "States and Interdependence," "Interdependence in Our Nation," and "Interdependence in Our World." Content is "nested" under these increasingly sophisticated conceptual themes.

As students participate in many activities related to the theme of study, they will develop increasingly sophisticated generalizations to parallel the depth of the content study. Remember that a universal generalization is two or more concepts stated in a relationship. So a child arrives inductively at increasingly sophisticated generalizations related to the concept of interdependence at the various grade levels:

Grade 1: A family cares for its members.

Grade 3: A community provides for needs and wants.

Grade 5: A society is socially and economically interdependent.

Grade 6: Nations vary in their economic dependence on trade.

A teacher might provide students with one or more generalizations at the end of a learning unit and ask the students to give examples and defend or refute the generalization based on the unit study and additional student-generated examples. The teacher states that "clarity" will be one of the traits by which the presentation is judged. The product can be oral, written, or visual, but all of the expected traits and criteria for assessment are made clear to the student at the beginning of the unit work.

How will we let first graders know what "clear examples" look like? How about clarity for our fifth or sixth graders? Students can be invited to participate in developing the indicators for a trait. Along with a discussion of the trait, students need to see and discuss actual examples of clear examples and presentations. They need to self-assess their own work for clarity.

As learners progress through the grades, the standard for clarity challenges the student because they have to organize and express increasingly sophisticated content. They also have to explain in a self-assessment why their work has met or is developing toward the standard performance.

Helping students to define the meaning and standard expectations for a trait and challenging the students to reach the standard with increasingly complex material will be a big step forward for education.

The Elements of Reasoning

Paul (1993b) discusses the importance of considering the elements of reasoning when evaluating students' critical thinking processes. Paul defines the elements of reasoning as "the basic conditions implicit whenever we gather, conceptualize, apply, analyze, synthesize, or evaluate information" (p. 154). We must evaluate whether the student is using the elements of reasoning and apply the intellectual standards (traits) to his or her thought process. Paul's elements of reasoning are summarized briefly:

1. Purpose, goal, or end in view: To what end goal or purpose is the reasoning focused?

2. Question at issue or problem to be solved: Has the question at issue or the problem been clearly formulated?

3. Point of view or frame of reference: The student's point of view should adhere to the relevant intellectual standards. It may be broad, flexible, fair, and clearly stated, for example.

4. The empirical dimension of reasoning: Students receive feedback on their ability to give evidence that is gathered and reported clearly, fairly, and accurately. The empirical data are measured against the standards.

5. The conceptual dimension of reasoning: Any defect in the concepts or ideas of the reasoning is a possible source of problems in student reasoning. Are concepts and ideas clear and relevant to the issue?

6. Assumptions: The students' assumptions are measured against the standards. Are the assumptions justifiable? Clear? Crucial or extraneous?

7. Implications and consequences: Students need help in internalizing both the relevant standards for reasoning out implication (and consequences) and the degree to which their own reasoning meets those standards.

8. Inferences: Assessment would evaluate a student's ability to make sound inferences in his or her reasoning. When is an inference sound? Are the inferences clear? Justifiable? Do they draw deep conclusions, or do they stick to the trivial and superficial?

Generalizability

An issue of concern in performance assessment relates to the generalizability of test results related to the content under scrutiny. Just because a student demonstrates content knowledge related to the Westward Movement, for example, does not ensure that the student will demonstrate content knowledge related to any other topic in American history. Generalizability of knowledge is not guaranteed.

Because of this problem, some assessment specialists (Baker, 1994; Popham, 1993) recommend that the assessment focus be placed on the generalizable process skill. Their reasoning is that assessment results of specific content knowledge are not generalizable, but process abilities do generalize. We apply common process skills across content fields. Therefore, the results of process skill assessments are generalizable. Critical thinking is an example of a generalizable process skill.

This approach acknowledges the importance of assessing process skills, but it still leaves two questions:

♦ Can we assume that process performance is generalizable? Process performance—how well a student reads, writes, speaks, thinks, or performs—is directly correlated to the degree of conceptual difficulty presented by the assessment task. The process performance is only generalizable to tasks of comparable conceptual difficulty.

♦ Is it possible to generalize content knowledge and understanding beyond the given assessment task? I believe we have a problem with generalizability of content because we focus our assessment on the lower-level topic. We would find assessment results related to content to be far more reliable in relation to generalizability if we assessed for the students' understanding of the generalizations arising out of the concepts. The generalizations must be supported by specific fact-based examples, which allow us to assess conceptual understanding, specific supporting content, and sophistication in the use of the process skills involved in the task. We assess, therefore, the three components of the tripartite curriculum model described in Chapter 3 (see Figure 3.1).

As an example, if we use the generalization related to the concept of interdependence—"Trade is dependent on supply and demand"—secondary school students could be required to do the following:

♦ Analyze and support the generalization, "Trade is dependent on supply and demand," using specific examples from in-class learning and other current world examples.

♦ Relate the concepts of dependence and interdependence to the concepts of trade and supply and demand.

This assessment places the focus on "generalizable" knowledge and skills—the process skill of "analysis" and understanding of a generalization that encompasses many examples across cultures and through time. The generalizability of the content holds to other examples of the stated generalization.

The generalizability of the process of analysis is dependent on the conceptual ability (concepts), prior knowledge (critical content), and process skill (application). We can generalize a student's ability to use a process skill, such as critical thinking, when the performance tasks are matched to the student's developmental level. We can generalize performance to the point that the variables of a task (conceptual, prior knowledge, and process applications) are congruent with other tasks.

DESIGNING PERFORMANCE ASSESSMENTS FOR INTEGRATED TEACHING UNITS

Chapter 4 outlined a formula for writing a culminating performance task for integrated units of instruction. The culminating task provides a high-level performance showing what the student knows, understands, and can do as a result of the unit study. Although units will use a variety of assessment formats, the performance task(s) will carry significant weight in assessment. For this reason, it is important to design a quality scoring guide (rubric) or set of criteria and standards to direct, define, and assess the quality of work.

Scoring Guides—General Development

There are four common elements included in a rubric:

1. One or more *traits* that serve as a basis for judging:

   Traits can be identified as the broad categories to be assessed, such as content knowledge or oral presentation.

   Traits can also be presented as a set of criteria that the student is expected to fulfill. For example, assessment criteria for a unit on "Media as a Persuasive Force in American Society" might be the following:

   - Evaluate the forms and techniques of media in American society.

   - Analyze the characteristics of persuasion as a force.

   - Design a persuasive advertisement (oral or written) for your new product. Incorporate at least three elements of persuasive advertising.

2. A definition and examples to clarify the meaning of each trait:

   The definition and examples answer the question, "What are the attributes of the trait to be assessed? How do we define *oral presentation,* for example? Attributes might include the following:

   - Clarity—A clear and lucid message

   - Voice—Tone, volume, projection, confidence, feeling tone appropriate

   - Stance—Shoulders back, head up, relaxed posture, avoidance of distracting mannerisms, and speech habits

   - Audience awareness—Monitors and adjusts presentation according to audience reactions

When criteria are set for a culminating performance, they need to be explained clearly to students:

- What are the expectations for evaluation, analysis, and design in the unit on media as a persuasive force in American society?

3. A scale of value (or counting system) on which to rate each trait (examples):

Qualitative scale: Excellent Highly Competent Competent Developing

Numerical scale: 4 (*high quality*) to 1 (*developing*)

The qualitative and numerical scales are often combined in performance scoring guides.

4. Standards of excellence for performance levels with models or examples for each:

4 = *Excellent*—The oral presentation is well organized and focused. The presenter makes eye contact with the audience and speaks clearly without distracting mannerisms. The audience is engaged with an appropriate feeling tone. Audience reaction is monitored as the presentation proceeds, and appropriate adjustments are made to reengage the audience when necessary.

3 = *Highly competent*

2 = *Competent*

1 = *Developing*—The oral presentation has a topic focus. Eye contact is made twice with an audience member. Voice tone is audible, but variability in feeling tone is yet to be developed. Presentation stance is appropriate.

I have taken the liberty of using the term *developing* at the base level in the previous scoring guide to support the philosophy of developing growth toward a standard and to avoid a deficit model of viewing progress. Students should view assessments as evidence of their "progress" toward the standard. They should also be counseled as to the next stages of development and shown models of the standard work.

Scoring Guide Examples

Figure 6.3 provides a typical scoring guide model for teachers to use in constructing a task, trait, or generic scoring tool.

Table 6.1 shares a scoring guide by Jacqueline Kapp, a visual arts teacher in Gloucester, Massachusetts—a pen-and-ink line collage composition creating movement with a curvilinear, organic line.

FIGURE 6.3. Typical Scoring Guide Model

Typical Rubric Model

Rubric For: _____

Attribute of the Expected Outcome and its Characteristics _____

>>Developmental or Skill Continuum>>

Level

4 — Expert Characteristic _____

3 — Proficient Characteristic _____

Standard

2 — Beginner Characteristic _____

1 — Novice Characteristic _____

NS — Nonscorable Characteristic _____

Decide if the rubric is task-specific, or generic. Make it as authentic and generalizable beyond the classroom as possible. Use an odd number of levels to judge balance of a skill or an attitude; use an even number of levels to mark the point where a skill must be consistently shown to be judged adequate. Use more levels for finer differentations, especially in high-stakes situations. The standard is the expected target behavior. Have at least one level above the standard and two below it to show students what is next in the skills/attitude beyond basic competency. State rubric in both teacher and student ("I...") Language.

SOURCE: Steve Schuman, Federal Way Public Schools. Federal Way, Washington. Used by permission.

TABLE 6.1 Pen-and-Ink Scoring Guide

Criteria	Apprentice	Practitioner	Expert
Variety of line	Variety of three to five different organic lines in a variety of thickness	Variety of more than five distinct organic lines of various lengths and thickness	Neat and deliberate execution of organic lines of multiple variety, length, and thickness
Quality of line	Occasional line control	Control of line apparent; neat work	Professional-quality line; consistent, deliberate start and stop; flawless, neat work
Use of materials	Uses two different pen nibs to create line variety; uses the pen in a proper upright position	Uses two different pen nibs to create line variety; uses pen in upright and upside down position for line variety	Uses several different pen nibs to create line variety; uses the pen in proper positions for predetermined effect; does not spill ink
Craftsmanship	Lines vary between clear and messy; collage not yet well constructed	Lines are neat and collage is constructed well	Lines are crisp and clean; collage is professionally constructed and presented
Demonstrates understanding of the concept of movement	Movement can be weakly detected	Movement is clearly created by the placement of the lines	Movement is clearly accomplished by the placement of the squares in the composition; secondary movement is also created to present an exciting presentation

SOURCE: Jacqueline Kapp, Gloucester Public Schools, Gloucester, Massachusetts. Used with permission.

TABLE 6.2 Prejudice Unit Rubric

Excellent	Highly Competent	Competent
The presentation is characterized by	The presentation is characterized by	The presentation is characterized by
• Unusually effective and clear diction	• Clear and effective diction	• Clear diction
• Impeccable grammar	• Appropriate grammar	• Acceptable grammar
• Strict adherence to rules of debate	• Adherence to key rules of debate	• Adherence to general rules of debate
• Well-thought-out, insightful arguments with strong, relevant, and specific supporting evidence; historical and contemporary examples, along with reasoned historical and contemporary workable solutions	• Well-thought-out arguments with supporting evidence; adequate historical and contemporary examples along with historical and contemporary workable solutions	• arguments with some supporting evidence; a few historical and contemporary examples, along with historical and contemporary workable solutions
• Absence of contradictions and fallacies of logic	• Absence of contractions	• No major contradictions

SOURCE: Bimey Middle School, Charleston, South Carolina. Used by permission.

Table 6.2 provides another example of a scoring guide for a unit on prejudice. The guiding questions that frame the study are included to illustrate the path of study that leads to the culminating performance.

Criteria for Quality Scoring Guides

Grant Wiggins (1998, pp. 184-185) sums up the criteria for evaluating rubric design in *Educative Assessment*. Figures 6.4 and 6.5 share Wiggins's insightful and helpful points.

FIGURE 6.4. Quality Rubrics

1. Are sufficiently generic to relate to general goals beyond an individual performance task but specific enough to enable useful and sound inferences about the task.

2. Discriminate among performances validly, not arbitrarily, by assessing the central features of performance, not those that are easiest to see, count, or score.

3. Do not combine independent criteria in one rubric.

4. Are based on analysis of many work samples and on the widest possible range of work samples, including valid exemplars.

5. Rely on descriptive language (what quality or its absence looks like) as opposed to merely comparative or evaluative language, such as "not as thorough as" or "excellent product" to make a discrimination.

6. Provide useful and apt discrimination that enables sufficiently fine judgments but do not use so many points on the scale (typically more than 6) that reliability is threatened.

7. Use descriptors that are sufficiently rich to enable student performers to verify their scores, accurately self-assess, and self-correct. (Use of indicators makes description less ambiguous and hence more reliable by providing examples of what to recognize in each level of performance. However, even though indicators are useful, concrete signs of criteria being met, specific indicators may not be reliable or appropriate in every context.)

8. Highlight judging the impact of performance (the effect, given the purpose) rather than overreward processes, formats, content, or the good-faith effort made.

SOURCE: Wiggins, G. (1998). *Educative Assessment: Designing Assessments to Inform and Improve Student Performance.* Copyright © 1998. Reprinted by permission of Jossey-Bass, Inc., a subsidiary of John Wiley & Sons, Inc.

PORTFOLIOS

How do we define a portfolio? In a draft paper prepared for the Institute on Assessment Alternatives, Paulson and Paulson (1994) provided an adaptation of a definition from the Northwest Evaluation Association:

A portfolio addresses the question "who am I" and tells a coherent story of the student as learner. It is a purposeful, integrated collection of student work that shows student effort, progress, or achievement in one or more areas. The collection includes evidence of student self-reflection and stu-

FIGURE 6.5. Technical Requirement for Rubrics

1. *Continuous.* The change in quality from score point to score point is equal: The degree of difference between 5 and 4 is the same as between 2 and 1. The descriptors reflect this continuity.

2. *Parallel.* Each descriptor parallels all the others in terms of the criteria language used in each sentence.

3. *Coherent.* The rubric focuses on the same criteria throughout. Although the descriptor for each scale point is different from the ones before and after, the changes concern variance of quality for the (fixed) criteria, not language that explicitly or implicitly introduces new criteria or shifts the importance of the various criteria.

4. *Aptly weighted.* When multiple rubrics are used to assess one event, there is an apt, not arbitrary, weighting of each criterion in reference to the others.

5. *Valid.* The rubric permits valid inferences about performance to the degree that what is scored is what is central to performance, not what is merely easy to see and score. The proposed differences in quality should reflect task analysis and be based on samples of work across the full range of performance; describe qualitative, not quantitative, differences in performance, and do not confuse merely correlative behaviors with actual authentic criteria.

6. *Reliable.* The rubric enables consistent scoring across judges and time. Rubrics allow reliable scoring to the degree that evaluative language (*excellent, poor*) and comparative language (*better than, worse than*) is transformed into highly descriptive language that helps judges to recognize the salient and distinctive features of each level of performance.

SOURCE: Wiggins, G. (1998). *Educative Assessment: Designing Assessments to Inform and Improve Student Performance.* Copyright © 1998. Reprinted by permission of Jossey-Bass, Inc., a subsidiary of John Wiley & Sons, Inc.

dent participation in setting the focus, establishing the standards, selecting contents, and judging merit. A portfolio tells the student's own story of what is learned and why it is important. (p. 4)

Paulson and Paulson (1994) also present an interesting summary of a rubric for judging portfolios that outlines four stages of student growth as shown through their portfolios. This draft summary is presented in Figure 6.6.

When educators and assessment experts started to look for ways to document and define what students can do, in addition to what they have learned, the portfolio was a natural answer. After all, artists and writers have used portfolios for years to document their work and growing talent.

There were questions that needed to be answered, however.

FIGURE 6.6. The Four Stages of Portfolio Growth: A Summary of the Rubric for Judging Portfolios

An Off-Track Portfolio

An off-track portfolio is simply a container of student work or assessments, without an attempt on the part of the learner to provide organization. There is no attempt by the learner to make a coherent statement about what learning has taken place. The child's understanding of the task is minimal—the portfolio is about "collecting what the teacher asks for." For the student, the portfolio was built by following instructions. Self-reflective statements, if present, add little to clarify organization or explain learning.

An Emerging Portfolio

In an emerging portfolio, there is a sense of intentionality controlling some of the student's choices. Students may not be able to verbalize the reasons, even as they reflect on their choices, but the reviewer may be able to recognize a relationship between some exhibits or infer the reasons. Or there may be evidence that the student had some insight into the teacher's purposes. Although evidence of self-reflection adds information to the presentation, at this point in the development of the portfolio, there is insufficient information or organization to characterize the portfolio as either a story or learning or a portrait of the learner.

An On-Track Portfolio

An on-track portfolio is in the process of becoming a story of the student as an independent learner. There are relationships between one part of the portfolio and another. There is evidence of student ownership. The learner has a personal investment in selecting and explaining the content. It is possible to distinguish other stakeholders' goals from the student's or to recognize instances when they overlap. The portfolio may be created for others to assess, but there is also evidence of self-assessment. The student's voice is always audible.

An Outstanding Portfolio

An outstanding portfolio is a coherent story of the student as a reflective learner in which all the parts of the portfolio bear a clear relationship to each other and to a central purpose. There is an awareness of the perspectives of other stakeholders, and the student's self-assessment has been enhanced by this knowledge. A reviewer can look at the portfolio and easily understand how the judgments about the learner came to be made and the degree to which different stakeholders would agree. When reviewing the portfolio, outsiders get the feeling they really know the person whose achievement is depicted there and have a fair understanding of how the learning came about.

SOURCE: Paulson and Paulson (1994). Multnomah E. S. D. 11611 N.E. Ainsworth Circle, Portland, Oregon, 97220. Used by permission.

- How can we measure the contents of a portfolio with valid and reliable results? Are the results generalizable?

- Who selects the items that go into a portfolio?

- Is it possible to develop and measure cross-domain work in a single portfolio? Can the portfolio contain writing samples, mathematics problem solving, art, or even a video presentation?

Many questions have circulated around the use of portfolios over the past 5 years. Sheila Valencia (1991), in a chapter titled "Portfolios: Panacea or Pandora's Box?" provides a balanced review of current thinking related to the perceived benefits and concerns related to the use of portfolios. Generally, states Valencia, portfolios have such appeal today because they are *authentic* in terms of the types of activities, the setting for the task, the alignment with the classroom curriculum, and the correlation to current views on learning and cognition.

Other benefits cited in Valencia's (1991) summary include using portfolios to monitor and celebrate a student's skill and knowledge *growth* over time and to *empower* teachers, students, and parents. The teacher's professional judgment is valued and is critical to the developmental growth of each child. The child is empowered by engaging in self-reflection and self-evaluation. And finally, the portfolio empowers the parents because it provides empirical evidence of what their children know and can do. Parents can help guide educational progress and will have a tool to facilitate communication with their children, teachers, and other parents.

On the caution side of the portfolio issue, Valencia (1991) raises questions related to the "purpose, standards, quality, feasibility, and [need for] staff development" (p. 39).

As with most innovations, I see the need for a balanced perspective in regard to the use of portfolios. Three facets of portfolio use that are especially valuable are the following:

- The focus on student self-selection, reflection, and evaluation of portfolio contents: This engenders student responsibility for learning and develops the thinking student.

- The focus on assessing each student's developmental growth over time through exhibits of work: This is a positive approach to developmental learning. It is based on a value and belief in individual growth rather than on a comparative judgment of worth.

- The view of teacher and student as collaborators in the assessment of growth over time: The teacher learns valuable skills for monitoring and assessing developmental learning. This requires critical thinking, analysis, and problem solving. The student and teacher share information and views, and the student feels supported and encouraged.

Although portfolios offer us one of the best tools for authentic assessment, I agree with Valencia and many other leaders in education today that they will not provide all of the answers. They deal more effectively with the process side of development. Until we figure out a better way to show conceptual development related to content and comparative student data, we will continue to be faced with normative, standardized tests. We must continue to search for a better alternative to address the content side of learning. Perhaps what we learn from portfolios and other forms of performance assessment will lead us to a number-one alternative for the number-two bubble sheet dilemma.

QUESTIONS AND ANSWERS

1. What is a scoring guide (rubric)?

Answer: A set of criteria and a scale of value to assess work or performance. The scoring guide specifies the criteria for judging, traits and indicators of developmental performance, and a standard of excellence.

2. What is a standard?

Answer: A set point for quality (not minimal) performance against which student growth can be measured developmentally and over time.

3. How should teachers view standards?

Answer: Teachers should view a standard as a goal for each student. This means developing and implementing support strategies to help each child move along the continuum of progress. It also means refusing to accept work that has shown no effort. It means expecting the best effort and providing support to ensure success.

4. How do we grade learning disability or slower achieving students?

Answer: I would rather we "assess" than "grade." The assessment should be based on how much growth the student has made over time, toward the standard, if we are measuring developmental process skills such as writing or speaking. Conveying this growth to the child and parent through the use of work samples, scales of growth, or developmental indicators is preferable to a letter grade. If required to give letter grades, then the grade should be based on the evident growth, but there also needs to be a narrative description or method for showing the developmental level (beginning, intermediate, advanced).

5. How do we grade mastery of content?

Answer: Because content is not a personal, developmental process, you can grade the student's mastery differently. Letter grades are more appropriate for evaluating mastery of content. How much content a student has learned is a quantitative matter, but if you are assessing the student's personal thinking ability in relation to the understanding of content, then you are back into a developmental growth assessment. In any case, however, letter grades are a weak form for conveying depth of knowledge and ability to perform.

6. Why is there so much emphasis today on the design of performance rubrics?

Answer: There is increasing emphasis on rubrics because they help clarify our teaching outcomes for students. Teachers often find, as they design the rubrics, that their assessment activity does not really address the critical outcomes they wish to measure. Quality rubrics clarify the assessment criteria and standards for process performance and content knowledge. Teachers often adjust their assessment activity after developing the rubric. They strive to align the task with the expected outcomes as defined by rubric criteria and standards.

SUMMARY

In the frenzy to meet the economic, social, and political demands of an interdependent world, government and business have teamed to set an agenda for schools. National and state governmental bodies legislate academic standards, and subject area committees work to define what students must know and be able to do by high school graduation.

This movement can be helpful to schools if the issues of time and funding for training and technology are addressed. If the assessments that accompany the national and state standards are high stakes, and issues such as training and inequitability of resources and opportunity have not been addressed, the plans will fail. States that address the classroom issues related to the attainment of standards will have the greatest chance of success.

Demands for higher levels of performance in what students know and can do are causing a tidal wave in the testing community. Old paradigms of bell-shaped curves; normative, standardized testing; and reliability, validity, and generalizability are all shaken up.

States now purchase or develop "standards-based" assessments to measure how well students are meeting expectations. Some states have embraced the notion that assessments must reflect conceptual understanding as well as core knowledge and skills. This is a positive step on the assessment end—it is just that these state leaders usually fail to realize that the teachers have not been trained on how to teach for conceptual understanding or even to differentiate between standards that are factual, conceptual, or skill driven. This is no small matter when it comes to raising standards.

Other states have fallen back on the traditional standardized tests from publishers. In some cases, these standardized purchases have poor alignment with the state standards. You can imagine the frustration of teachers and students at test time! And even if there is alignment, we are reinforcing a factory mentality for an intellectual age.

Despite the political heat from standards, alternative assessments are claiming their "authentic" role in meeting the new educational demands. Teachers attend workshops and conferences, feeling the pressure to understand the talk of portfolios and performance assessments. Performance assessments are carried out in classrooms. They measure what students know and can do through complex tasks that combine content and process skills. A rubric sets the criteria and standard for the performance. What used to be a letter grade with a few subjective comments now appears as a numeric or qualitative scale of performance descriptors or indicators.

Portfolios tell a story of the student's growth in knowledge and skill over time. The student self-evaluates his or her work according to defined criteria and a standard. The goals are student responsibility and increased learning.

New forms of assessment squeeze in beside the old. At times, they bump against each other. The fit is not comfortable. Teachers prefer the newer forms, and the public prefers the old. But the two must share space until educators develop the newer forms to a level that satisfies public questions and concerns.

EXTENDING THOUGHT

1. How do traditional report cards need to change to reflect process development and content knowledge?

2. If you were the public relations director for your school, how would you help parents see the value of performance assessment? How would you address their concerns with standardized test scores?

3. What is a performance assessment?

4. How can performance assessment assist you in meeting the educational needs of your students?

5. How does self-assessment contribute to the development of independent learners?

6. What is the teacher's responsibility in teaching to a standard for each child? What happens in schools when the standard is only assumed to be for the top 30% of the student population?

7 Concept-Based Instruction

There are three basic components in transitioning to a concept-based model of curriculum and instruction. The first is understanding how concept/process curriculum design differs from the traditional fact-based model. The second is the actual design of a concept/process curriculum design and assessments. This chapter looks at the third component—concept-based instruction.

Concept-based instruction differs from fact-based instruction in a significant way:

Fact-based instruction places the instructional emphasis on learning the facts related to specific topics. Knowledge related to the facts is the end goal.

Concept-based instruction places the instructional emphasis on understanding the concepts, principles, and transferable ideas that arise from the study of significant topics and facts. Deeper conceptual understanding supported by specific facts is the end goal.

Because the instructional emphasis shifts to the understanding of ideas, the student and teacher are required to use higher levels of thinking. Students and teachers consider and apply facts in the context of the related concepts and generalizations. This ability to think beyond the facts and link specific information to abstract ideas is a skill that must and can be taught. Previous chapters in this book outlined the theory and practice of designing concept-based curriculum; this chapter suggests some instructional strategies and activities to help students "bridge" from facts to concepts and "big ideas."

SUGGESTED ACTIVITIES

Concept Maps

The *Mind Map Book* by Tony Buzan (1996) explains clearly the strategy of concept/content mapping. This strategy is useful in helping students understand the idea of related concepts and ideas. Buzan recommends that mind maps use color and pictorial images in addition to words to engage personal creativity and emotions. These personal mind maps help students make a greater number of connections between related concepts and topics.

Figure 7.1 shares the mind map of Ron Raddock, a teacher and educational consultant, as he listened to a presentation on concept-based curriculum design.

Try creating a word mind map for one of the concepts below. The idea is to help students see how specific concepts and topics "nest" under broader concepts as you move away from the central core. Notice also that the concepts become more specific (microconcepts) as you move outward.

How is *depth of understanding* developed for a core concept based on your mind map?

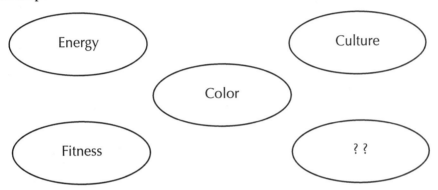

Students in Mrs. Vrchota's fifth-grade class at Southwood Elementary School in Orlando, Florida, read *The Missing Gator of Gumbo Limbo* by Jean Craighead George. Mrs. Vrchota used a variety of strategies to help students think about their learning. Students created concept maps such as the one shown in Figure 7.2, by Cristina Oliveras.

When students mind-map a concept or topic before and after a unit of study, they can see their personal growth in the depth and breadth of knowledge and understanding.

Other strategies used by Mrs. Vrchota included Venn diagrams comparing *The Missing Gator of Gumbo Limbo* with another piece of literature, as well as a prediction chart, which asked students to predict the events of each chapter, then write whether their prediction was accurate following reading. Another strategy, called *multiple effects,* asked students to take an event in the story and predict the various effects that the event might produce. All of these strategies force students to become intellectually engaged with the study and reinforce deep understanding and retention of knowledge.

Students must also be able to relate the facts they are studying to the enduring ideas—the generalizations—that will transfer to new specific examples. Below are suggested activities to help students "bridge" their thinking from factual examples to the big, enduring ideas.

FIGURE 7.1. Mind Map

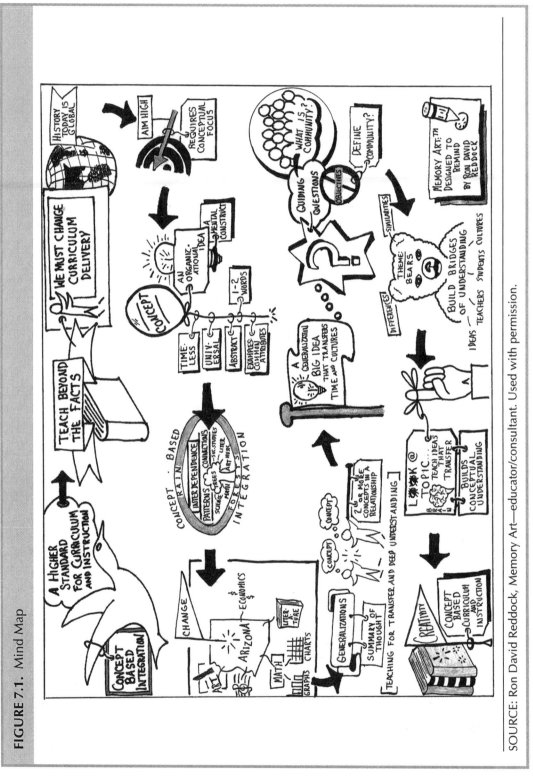

SOURCE: Ron David Reddock, Memory Art—educator/consultant. Used with permission.

FIGURE 7.2. Dajun Concept Map

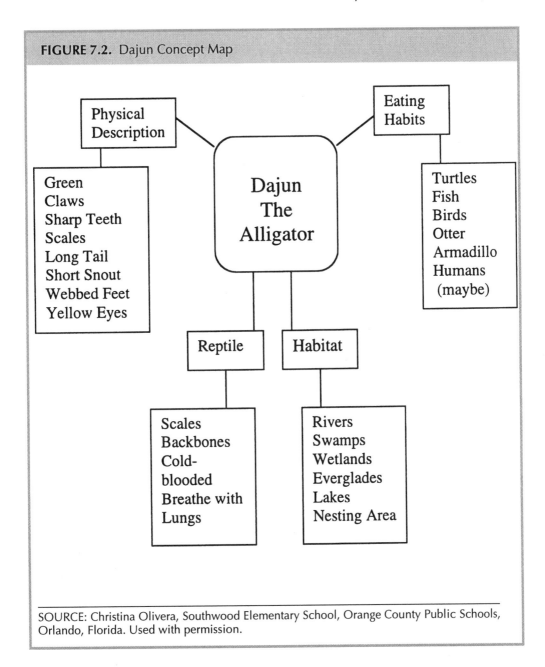

SOURCE: Christina Olivera, Southwood Elementary School, Orange County Public Schools, Orlando, Florida. Used with permission.

Visual Metaphors

Students draw a visual representation of a generalization. They are given the "enduring understanding" and decide on a specific example that can be drawn to represent the idea. They must understand the conceptual idea to convert it into a specific representation.

Generalizations	Possible Examples
Science	
Organisms adapt to changing environments.	Animal that changes color to match the environment (e.g., snowshoe rabbit, chameleon)
Fine arts	
A visual communication can convey multiple messages.	An advertisement that conveys a mood and a message, a dance that tells a story and demonstrates artistic interpretation, and a painting that conveys conflicting emotions (e.g., joy and sadness)
Social studies	
Community members have roles.	(Pictures showing various community members in their different roles)

Card Games

Instead of having students draw a visual representation of the unit, the teacher can make a set of cards to have students play a matching game. The cards are composed of "pairs"—a generalization with its matching example, which can be in the form of a picture or a set of written examples. The student who gets the most pairs in each group is the winner of the game. Three to four students per group with six to eight generalizations and their matches is workable. There will be 12 to 16 cards total in a deck.

Big Ideas Through Time

Another technique to help students understand the enduring quality of generalizations is to have them find different historical examples of a significant enduring idea, such as "Revolutions create social, economic, and political change." Students can make a booklet comparing the social, economic, and political changes driven by three historical revolutions. They summarize the comparison by addressing a series of guiding questions such as the following:

◆ What is a revolution?

◆ Why do people reach the point of revolution?

◆ What kinds of changes occur in society as a result of political revolutions?

◆ Do all revolutions lead to social, economic, and political change?

♦ Are the changes identical in every revolution?

♦ What factors influence the kinds of changes that occur?

♦ Are revolutionary changes always positive for a society?

♦ Do revolutions affect other nations? How?

♦ Are there other kinds of revolutions?

♦ What do they have in common with political revolutions?

♦ What role do leaders play in revolutions?

♦ How did the American Revolution shape the political, social, and economic directions of our country?

Reflecting

Vaughn and Estes (1986) developed a comprehension strategy called *insert,* which asked students to use a marking system in the margins to react to text. Marianne Kroll and Ann Paziotopoulos, two outstanding teachers from Palos Park, Illinois, adapted the comprehension strategy and called it *reflecting.*

Reflecting is a coding technique that allows students to identify their thoughts and feelings as they react to different pages of text. Kroll and Paziotopoulos (1995) developed two rubber stamps with coded reactions to use on 2″ × 1½ ″ sticky notes. The stamped sticky notes require students to reflect and consciously interact with text. Students circle their reactions to specific pages of text as they read the following:

SHARP	**LEARN**
S = Makes me Sad	L = Learned new/important information
H = Makes me Happy	
A = Anticipate something	E = Explored the cause/effect
R = Reminds me of something	A = Arrived at a conclusion
P = See a problem	R = Recognized different perspectives
©1995 Kroll and Paziotopoulos	N = Noticed character traits
	©1995 Kroll and Paziotopoulus

The reflection notes focus students on the meaning of text and invite their reactions. Students are free to use blank notes to record additional or different reactions. Reflection notes also mark locations so that students can refer to specific pages in discussions or written analyses. The notes also allow the students to support their thoughts and feelings with specific references from the text.

Modeling is a critical instructional strategy when students are learning the reflecting procedure. Using an overhead projector or a big book, the teacher reads a page of text and then self-reflects aloud, "What thoughts or feelings cross my mind when I read this page?" The teacher talks through the critical text on the page to model the thinking process for students and then circles a letter or letters that reflect his or her thoughts and feelings.

When modeling, the teacher is careful to identify metacognitively the various steps for thinking about the relationship between specific text and the selections on the reflection notes and to share those connections with students. For example, on the SHARP note, if the teacher circled *A = Anticipates something,* she or he would think aloud and share the text clues that created the feeling of anticipation. After the coding lesson and student practice, the teacher models the use of reflection notes as a way to keep track of thoughts and feelings in reading a book. The teacher helps students understand that thoughts and feelings are reinforced or may change as new information comes into the story.

Reflection notes can be used at all grade levels across different types of reading material, from content specific to literature based. Reflection notes can be used by individual students to record their reactions to text and can then be used in cooperative groups to stimulate discussion and raise awareness of different perspectives on issues. Students develop a deeper understanding when they are required to defend, explain, or elaborate on a position.

Reflection notes allow students at different reading levels to read suitable books on a common theme. They can share their thoughts and feelings on the theme, in cooperative groups or literature circles, by referring to their particular book selection and notes. Reflection notes help differentiate curriculum and instruction without isolating students.

Reflection notes can be used at home as an enjoyable sharing activity between parent and child. The student takes home a book and 10 prestamped sticky notes. Five sticky notes are in one color for the student; the other five notes are in a different color for the parent. As the parent and child read the book together, they each ask, "What am I thinking about on this page?" They circle their codes independently and compare and discuss their reflections at the end of the book.

One third-grade student shares her reflections on *The Enormous Crocodile* based on her sticky note thoughts:

The Enormous Crocodile

There are many ideas to think about from the book, *The Enormous Crocodile.* First I was sad on page 7 when the crocodile said he was going to eat the children because I wouldn't want to get eaten by a crocodile.

Next I was sad again on page 8 when the crocodile bit Trunky the Elephant because Trunky was a nice elephant and there was no reason for the crocodile to bite him.

Then I anticipated something on page 18. I anticipated that the crocodile was going to eat the children because the children wanted to collect coconuts and the crocodile had coconuts on him.

Finally, I anticipated something on page 39. I anticipated that the elephant would let go of the crocodile and the crocodile would go flying into space.

SOURCE: Lauren Nelson, third-grade student, Palos Park School District, Palos Park, Illinois. Used with permission.

Teachers do not assume that students know how to recognize or evaluate their own thinking. Students are taught specific procedures for thinking about text—and the reflection notes provide critical support. Students are responsible for identifying and supporting their own reactions to text material.

Reflection notes can be adapted to help students bridge their thinking from facts to the conceptual, enduring understandings. Teachers may give students reflection notes containing several of the enduring understandings that were developed throughout a unit of study. Students are asked to find specific factual examples from a variety of resources and communicate why they think the examples support the deeper understanding. When students can support an idea with more than one specific example, they demonstrate a more sophisticated grasp of the idea.

Brownies for Sale

Two other teachers from Palos Park School District—Deanna Jackson and Deborah Pope, who also have an excellent grasp of concept-based curriculum—developed an economics unit for Grade 4, titled "Brownies for Sale." This unit teaches the students valuable lessons and concepts in economics. They requested parents' help in a letter explaining that students were going to hold a bake sale to learn about economics concepts such as consumers, producers, supply and demand, and profit. Parent and student decided on the item they would make, purchased the ingredients to allow 12 individually wrapped items, and recorded the cost. They prepared the baked good and noted the time required for preparation. Then they set the price (no more than 50 cents) so that the student could make a profit.

Students made advertisements to be placed around the school, and the sale was on. The day after the bake sale, the students figured out the profit they made by completing this form:

Bake Sale Cost and Profit Worksheet

Kind of baked good _____

List of materials and ingredients purchased _____

Total cost of materials _____

Total amount of time for preparation and packaging _____
Price per bag _____

12 – _____ number of bags left = _____ number of bags sold

_____ number of bags sold × _____ price per bag

= _____ gross profit – _____ total cost

= _____ net profit

The students used an economics vocabulary sheet and this economics study guide to answer to prepare for a test:

Economics Study Guide

1. Review the definitions of the economic words. Use your economic vocabulary sheet or your social studies book.

2. Be able to answer the following questions about the bake sale:
   ▶ Who were the producers?
   ▶ Who were the consumers?
   ▶ What was the profit?
   ▶ Why did you need to know the total cost of your materials?
   ▶ How did supply and demand affect the amount of baked goods that were sold at different times during the day?
   ▶ Even though each person made their own baked good, were they really self-sufficient? Why or why not?
   ▶ From the video, we learned the term *opportunity costs*.
   ▶ How does this idea relate to the bake sale?
   ▶ How did the bake sale demonstrate interdependence?
   ▶ What factors helped the consumers decide what to buy?
   ▶ What would you do differently for the next bake sale to increase profits?

Students discussed the successes and failures of the sale. For example, did some baked goods sell better than others? Was it price, advertising, or appearance? Then the students decided how to use all the money earned from the bake sale to benefit the students of the school.

Adapting Activities

I highly recommend *Active Learning: 101 Strategies to Teach Any Subject* by Mel Silberman (1996). Besides offering excellent tips for teachers on how to actively engage students in learning generally, the 101 activities can be adapted to help students bridge from facts to concepts and big ideas. I will provide just a few examples showing how teachers can adapt the following activities.

Trading Places (p. 35)

This activity helps students understand that concepts can be categorized and ordered from broader to more specific.

Procedure:

1. Divide class into three teams.

2. Give three students on each team a blue sticky note naming a macroconcept under study (e.g., migration, government, energy).

3. Give the other students on each team a yellow sticky note with a related "subconcept" for one of the blue concepts on their team (e.g., "rules" or "roles" for government).

4. Students with yellow notes gravitate to their macroconcept.

5. Then each group organizes its concepts from the blue macroconcept (broadest concept) to the microconcept (most specific). The first group to line up its concepts correctly from macro to micro provides the rationale for their ordering of concepts and is applauded.

Rotating Trio Exchange (p. 59)

This is a way to allow students to share what they know and understand based on a unit of study. It could be used at the end of a unit to summarize learning. The questions you pose will become more complex as the rounds proceed. Your goal is to engage the mind of each student as they share the depth of their knowledge.

Procedure:

1. Develop a set of questions for your students representing the factual, conceptual, and philosophical levels. For example, with a unit on the American Revolution, the following questions could be included:

   ■ Factual: What were some of the causes of the American Revolution?

   ■ Conceptual: How do revolutions create change in a society?

   ■ Philosophical: Should governments support revolutions in foreign countries?

2. Divide the students into trios. Arrange the trios in a circular pattern.

3. Give each trio the same opening question. Select the least challenging question for this round. Have students share their answers within their trio.

4. After a suitable period of discussion, ask the trio to assign a number—0, 1, or 2—to each member. For the next question, direct students with number 1 to rotate one trio clockwise. Ask the students with number 2 to rotate two trios clockwise. Students with the number 0 remain seated at the trio site and raise their hands so they can be located by rotaters.

5. Start a new round of trio exchange with a more difficult question.

6. You can rotate trios as many times as you wish.

Lecture Bingo (p. 75)

There are times when a lecture on content is in order as the most efficient way to impart critical information to students. The following adapted activity will help keep students "minds-on."

Procedure:

1. Create a lecture-based lesson with up to nine key points.

2. Develop a bingo card that contains these key points in a 3 × 3 grid. Place a different point in each box.

3. Create several cards with the same points located in different boxes on the card.

4. Distribute a card to each student along with a strip of nine self-sticking colored dots.

5. Instruct students to place a dot on their cards for each point that you discuss.

6. Students call out "Bingo!" when they have three vertical, horizontal, or diagonal dots in a row.

7. As an advanced variation on this game, extend the card with three rows and print one enduring idea in each row. To call out "Bingo!" a student must also identify and place a dot beside the enduring understanding that best reflects the big idea for the lecture.

The Law and Society

Teachers at all levels are thoughtfully planning their lessons to engage the minds and hearts of their students. Greg Isaacson, an exemplary high school teacher in Orlando, Florida, teaches a comprehensive law class for 24 students in

Grades 10 to 12. He works in a school with a 4 × 4 schedule. Students take four classes each semester and attend four 110-minute classes each day.

Greg wrote his thoughts and reflections on his instructional plan and the students' grasp of key concepts. As you read the following excerpt, can you identify the teaching strategies that motivate and engage the interest of Greg's students and that facilitate deeper levels of understanding?

All of the students in my class are in the Law Magnet Program, an honor's-level program for college-bound students. The class is ethnically diverse. The majority of students have been in other classes with me in previous years. In the middle of our "Law and Society" unit, I was teaching to the broad generalization that "law can shape society's values." I also wanted them to understand that "tort laws can shape, reflect, and enforce society's values." More specifically, I wanted them to recognize and objectively analyze how product liability suits can regulate industries that the legislature cannot, to recognize and analyze how "unreasonably dangerous products" are eliminated from the marketplace through products liability lawsuits, and to recognize and analyze how class action suits can be an effective litigation tool against manufacturers of unreasonably dangerous products.

I asked students to write a paper explaining how law affects their lives on a daily basis in order to assess their prior knowledge and genuine understanding from previous classes and discussions. Then we examined in greater detail cases mentioned during a class discussion—specifically, the cigarette and gun manufacturing lawsuits. We then did two assignments applying concepts learned. The first was an interpretive prediction of the outcome of the cigarette and gun lawsuits in the future. The second was an analytical discussion presented as a persuasive memo following a small group project, which asked students to identify potential targets of litigation from the vast array of potentially dangerous consumer products on the market.

Because, in my experience, students respond better to specific details when they can approach them from a broader, more identifiable context, I began this lesson with an open discussion on socially related topics and gradually focused the discussion and their thought processes on increasingly specific legal concepts.

Going into the transition between general discussion and our focused discussion on cigarette manufacturers' liability, I anticipated that students would make the stock arguments against banning cigarettes. I had hoped to illustrate how litigation could accomplish the same goal through the product liability lawsuit. The key concept for them to grasp was the difference between some beneficial aspects of alcohol when used as intended, as voiced by one student, and no benefits with cigarettes when used as intended, which was noted by two other students. This discussion effectively illustrated the "unreasonably dangerous product" principle.

Besides using the "general to specific" approach whenever a new concept or topic was introduced, I also allowed students to discuss peripheral issues as a means of "fleshing out" a concept before adding depth to the idea. For example, when I moved from the general concept of liability to the more specific concept of tort law, I asked a student to explain the difference between civil and criminal trials, drawing on their prior knowledge and understanding. I also encouraged students to apply concepts under study to their own life experiences.

I modeled thinking strategies when appropriate. At one point in the lesson, I made the statement, "I know this because. . . ." when applying what I knew about black-market guns to a future of black-market cigarettes. This models the thinking strategy of conceptual transfer of knowledge.

The use of humor and current events engages student emotions and interest, which helps them retain knowledge. Political cartoons provide an effective springboard for discussions on perspective.

Students know that I expect them to explain and defend their thinking with supporting data and sources. I look for evidence in class discussions that students have an enduring understanding of the complex legal concepts. When Jerry was able to clearly and concisely articulate the difference between a criminal and a civil case, he made the transition between the general concept of liability and the more specific concept of tort law. When Sarah brought up the second-hand smoke argument as an additional way cigarettes were unreasonably dangerous, she also asked a particularly insightful question, "What is the intent of cigarettes?" She was aware that no logical benefits derive from cigarettes and therefore met the test of an unreasonably dangerous product.

Fairy Tales and Archetypes

Another outstanding middle school teacher, Louise Hamilton, from Greenville, North Carolina, developed a literature unit based on the play *Into the Woods* by Stephen Sondheim and James Lapine. *Into the Woods* weaves four well-known fairy tales into a coherent whole through the use of an original quest story in which Rapunzel's older brother, a baker, attempts to remove the witch's curse of barrenness by collecting for her a cow as white as milk (Jack in the Beanstalk), a cape as red as blood (Red Riding Hood's), hair as yellow as corn (Rapunzel's), and a slipper as pure as gold (Cinderella's in the Grimm version of her story).

Hamilton used the dual conceptual lens of "archetypes/conflict" for the unit to help students realize that stories can survive centuries of oral transmission into a variety of media formats because they portray conflicts that are timeless. The conflicts that develop the theme of *Into the Woods* are those of adolescents struggling to grow up. All of the main characters go "into the woods" and struggle to resolve conflicts before moving on to the next stage in their lives: Jack must make his way

---

TABLE 7.1 Conceptual Mind Map

Childhood Role	Changes From Childhood to Adulthood	Adult Role	Fairy-Tale Character
Economically dependent	Learn to earn your own way in the world using your talents	Wage earner who can support self and family	Jack
Vulnerable	Learn to protect yourself from the dangers of the world	World-wise and competent	Little Red Riding Hood

SOURCE: Louise Hamilton, Pitt County School District, Greenville, North Carolina. Used with permission.

---

in the world, although he seems ill equipped to do so even to his doting mother; Little Red Riding Hood must learn to take care of herself even in the presence of the wolf; Cinderella must find a husband who will accept her for what she truly is; Rapunzel must escape from the clutches of her overprotective "mother"; and the baker and his wife must learn to work together if they are to conceive, much less parent, a child. This initiation into maturity is one of the archetypal human experiences.

To help students abstract their thinking from the specifics of the play to the deeper significance, Mrs. Hamilton provided a number of activities, including the following:

♦ Complete the chart (see Table 7.1) comparing characteristics from your own childhood role to the expectations for an adult role. Identify what kind of changes you will need to make to meet your adult role. Identify a fairy-tale character with a similar challenge.

♦ Identify archetypal characters in the play such as the "good mother," the "terrible mother," the "good father," the "absent father," or the "kindly grandparent."

♦ Choose a character to follow through Act I. Note what the character is like at the beginning of the play, what happens to him or her during the first act as he or she goes into the woods, and any changes that take place in the character.

♦ Form cooperative groups around your particular character and discuss the character's family background and the conflict faced in the adolescent woods experience. Use a handout to record how your character's past prepared him or her to handle the communal and personal crisis that will be faced in ever after (in Act II).

Report and justify to the class your group's hypotheses on the future success of your character in handling his or her crisis.

♦ Synthesize what you have learned about archetypal conflicts, characters, and settings to create a fairy tale of your own that reflects your own life as an adolescent or another point of view (environmentalist, peace advocate, etc.). Take the part of the protagonist in your tale and represent the "real world" by identifying the conflict, describing the human emotions felt by the protagonist and antagonist, and using symbols to convey story concepts (e.g., giant [powerful], beans [poverty], gold hen [wealth]).

Technology and Concept-Based Instruction

Technology is an integral tool for instruction in today's classrooms because it engages the mind and motivates the student. Educational leadership was a theme issue on "Integrating Technology Into the Curriculum" for February 1999. Don Tapscott, president of New Paradigm Learning Corporation in "Educating the Net Generation," provides a snapshot of students using technology to study the topic of saltwater fish.

Students use the web and other resources to gather information on a saltwater fish of their choice. They research concepts such as breathing, propulsion, reproduction, diet, and predators.

As an example of the resulting fish presentations, one group created a shark home page complete with hotlinks to each of the researched concepts. In their oral presentations, students projected their information onto a screen, including video clips of sharks and a Jacques Cousteau discussion of sharks as an endangered species. Then students used the Web to visit and ask questions of the Aquarius staff—an underwater research site off the Florida coast. The class decided to hold an online forum on the dangers that sharks and humans pose to each other, with students from other countries (Tapscott, 1999, p. 11).

It is easy to see why students who use technology show greater interest and motivation in their learning. Technology allows students to become personally and intellectually engaged as they direct their learning. The teacher is a facilitator (and a learner along with the students). The concept-based teacher would identify key concepts and generalizations to guide learning, but students would search for knowledge and understanding and creatively share their insights.

For teachers implementing concept-based curriculum, please email me (hlynn@worldnet.att.net) and share your tips and instructional strategies for helping students bridge from facts to enduring understandings. Often, the strategies and activities being used to teach the fact base can be altered to teach students to think beyond the facts. I am compiling ideas to share with teachers as they continue the journey with concept-based curriculum and instruction.

FIGURE 7.3. "Hey, That's Not Concept Based!"

SOURCE: Cartoon by David Ford. david@twocrowcartoons.com

SUMMARY

Designing concept-based units is the first step as teachers learn what concept-based curriculum is—and how it changes classroom pedagogy. When the teacher implements a concept-based unit, the real challenge begins. Teaching concept-based curriculum is an intellectual model that takes the thinking of both students and teacher through the facts to the level of conceptual, transferable understanding. This chapter provides valuable insights into the thinking of teachers, such as Greg Isaacson, Louise Hamilton, and the Palos Park School District teachers as they plan for concept-based instruction.

When students become personally intellectually engaged in school, they experience a love of learning. In the final chapter, we continue to explore how teachers can stir the head, hearts, and souls of their students.

EXTENDING THOUGHT

1. What is your understanding of the difference between topic-based instruction and concept-based instruction?

2. Why is it difficult at first to shift to concept-based instruction?

3. Can you think of an instructional activity that could be adapted to develop conceptual understanding? What adaptation would you make?

4. If you were observing a teacher in a concept-based classroom, what would you see and hear?

5. Why is it important for principals to understand concept-based curriculum and instruction?

6. What do parents need to understand about concept-based classrooms?

Stirring the Head, Heart, and Soul

Creating a Love of Learning

The classroom buzzes with activity. Children work in small groups intent on discovering mysteries of life: How do birds fly? Just what is in those owl pellets? How do caterpillars change into butterflies? Why don't animals talk like humans? What would happen if the desert suddenly gained rivers? The teacher circulates from group to group—listening, asking probing questions, suggesting resources, and encouraging the efforts. Students express ideas; their friends question and extend the thinking. New ideas emerge.

The room is rich with material. Student work lines the walls, and books, art prints, science materials, and mathematics manipulatives are evident in the plentiful workspace. Students use desktop computers and build reports on their findings. They access databases to find relevant material to the theme under study and compare notes on global pollution with students around the world. They design Powerpoint programs to display their knowledge and scan in pictures to enhance the graphic appeal. These are the students of the computer age.

Down the hall, in another classroom, students sit in rows and stare at their social studies textbook while child after child reads a paragraph. The teacher perches on a stool in the front of the room and asks questions about the facts just read. Some posters hang on the wall, and books sit in tidy position on the shelves, sorted by size. The room is quiet except for the bored drone of the student reading and a bee that works furiously to escape through a window.

STIRRING THE HEAD

Brain-Based Learning

Teachers are the architects for learning. They design the environments for developing minds. Caine and Caine (1991), in a seminal book called *Teaching and the Human Brain,* differentiate between "surface knowledge" and "meaningful knowledge." Surface knowledge is referred to as the traditional memorization of facts and procedures. To be meaningful, however, students must be able to perceive relationships and patterns to make sense of information. Students make sense of information by relating it to their unique past experience and the current environmental context and interactions (Caine & Caine, 1991).

David Sousa (1995), in *How the Brain Learns,* differentiates between "rate of learning" and "rate of retrieval" (of information). He suggests that intelligence is the rate of learning something. He counters the notion that rate of retrieval is strongly related to intelligence, however, and states that it is a learned skill. Sousa offers teaching strategies for helping students efficiently retrieve information from long-term storage. One strategy is "chunking"—grouping smaller items to be remembered into meaningful clusters or assigning a memorable descriptor to the category of smaller items.

I believe that teaching to enduring understandings taps into the chunking strategy. If students have deep understanding of a conceptual relationship, such as "Organisms create niches in an ecosystem," then they can transfer the idea across examples. The idea serves as a placeholder for chunking like examples and helps students link new examples to previous examples.

Brain research further supports the thesis that meaningful education is based on complex and concrete activities that engage students' minds, hearts, and emotions. Caine and Caine (1991) state that "brain-based learning" involves the following:

♦ Designing and orchestrating lifelike, enriching, and appropriate experiences for learners

♦ Ensuring that students process experience in such a way as to increase the extraction of meaning

Brain-based learning supports the current movement to integrate curriculum as an effective way to facilitate the brain's search for patterns and connections. An integrated curriculum also develops depth of understanding by presenting a message through a variety of contexts and disciplines (Caine & Caine, 1991).

Sousa (1995) agrees with the value of integrated curriculum:

The more connections that students can make between past learning and new learning, the more likely they are to determine sense and meaning and thus retain new learning. Moreover, when these connections can be extended across curriculum areas, they establish a framework of associative networks that will be recalled for future problem solving. (p. 70)

A key point in the Caine and Caine (1991) text involves the ideas of *disequilibrium* and *self-reorganization.* Disequilibrium occurs "when the original state of equilibrium is disturbed." When a learner meets new information that is confusing or disturbing, he or she enters a mental state of disequilibrium. This state is reconciled when "the learner moves to a broader or more inclusive notion— a more sophisticated schema or [mental] map (Cowan, 1978; Doll, 1986)" (Caine & Caine, 1991, p. 129).

Caine and Caine (1991) also quote Doll (1989) on the use of the concept of disequilibrium through an experiment in teaching mathematics:

> The concept of self-organization through disequilibrium meant we had to organize the Friday curriculum and our presentation of it in such a manner that we had enough of a "burr" to stimulate the students into rethinking their habitual methods but not so much of a burr that reorganization would fall apart or not be attempted. Maintaining this dynamic tension between challenge and comfort was one of the skills we had to perfect. (pp. 67-68)

As architects for learning, teachers realize that a classroom built on traditional, control-oriented structures is antithetical to the engagement of reasoning, creative minds. As teachers move from old models of instruction, they develop new ways of viewing:

- ♦ Teachers need some wisdom, not all wisdom.
  - – In the newer models of instruction, teachers have enough wisdom to know key lessons to be learned from content instruction, but they look forward to learning more lessons along with their students as they discover and share new knowledge.
- ♦ The textbook is only one tool for gaining information.
  - – The learning environment is resource rich, with computers, magazines, videos, books, and dialogue corners for exploring ideas among friends. The community is an extension of the classroom, and students give service to learn social responsibility and the application of knowledge to life.
- ♦ Tight control is replaced by purposeful enthusiasm.
  - – The teacher recognizes that a purposeful, enthusiastic search for knowledge engages the student's self-direction; the teacher becomes a structural design engineer and "facilitator" rather than a maintenance engineer and "controller."

Thinking Teachers for Thinking Students

It is common talk today that students who take responsibility for their learning are more interested and engaged with the subject at hand. The same holds true for teachers. Teachers who take responsibility for the design, delivery, and assessment of curriculum and instruction show greater interest and engagement with the learning process. Districts that encourage teachers to design quality curricula to use in their classrooms stimulate higher levels of thoughtfulness in teaching.

Teachers who depend on textbooks or the nebulous *they* to tell them what and how to teach are not thinking. Thinking teachers work within the required curricular structure, but they personalize the design for student learning by thinking deeply and creatively about students, outcomes, and their plans for curriculum and instruction.

Teachers hold a clear vision of student success and challenge themselves to draw out the best efforts. They think on their feet and watch for opportunities to pop provocative questions. They listen for the students' thoughtful rationale.

Student Engagement and Constructivism

Although the *constructivist* terminology is popular today, the philosophical basis for the ideas has been around since the days of educators and philosophers such as Pestalozzi, Froebel, Herbart, Dewey, and James. As with most trends in education, the term *constructivist* has a continuum of interpretations.

Jacqueline Grennon Brooks and Martin Brooks (1993), in a booklet titled *The Case for Constructivist Classrooms,* provide a set of teaching behaviors that they believe can be used to frame the constructivist methodology. The first behavior is at the heart of a purist, constructivist philosophy, so I have provided a short extension of the thought. This is followed by the remaining teaching behaviors identified by the authors.

Constructivist teachers encourage and accept student autonomy.

Students take responsibility for learning by posing questions and issues and searching for answers, connections, and possible new problems. The teacher's frame for an assignment affects the degree of autonomy and student initiative for learning. Heavy lecture and overcontrol of student work rob students of opportunities to be self-reliant thinkers. According to Brooks and Brooks (1993), constructivist teachers

- ◆ Use raw data and primary sources, along with manipulative, interactive, and physical materials

- ◆ Use cognitive terminology such as *classify, analyze, predict,* and *create* when framing tasks

- ◆ Allow student responses to drive lessons, shift instructional strategies, and alter content

- ◆ Inquire about students' understandings of concepts before sharing their own understanding of those concepts

- Encourage students to engage in dialogue, both with the teacher and with one another

- Encourage student inquiry by asking thoughtful, open-ended questions and encouraging students to ask questions of each other

- Seek elaboration of students' initial responses

- Engage students in experiences that might engender contradictions to their initial hypotheses and then encourage discussion

- Allow wait time after posing questions

- Provide time for students to construct relationships and create metaphors

- Nurture students' natural curiosity through frequent use of the learning cycle model (pp. 103-118)

The authors end the discussion on teaching descriptors with the following statement: "These descriptors can serve as guides that may help other educators forge personal interpretations of what it means to become a constructivist teacher" (Brooks & Brooks, 1993, p. 118).

My personal interpretation of the constructivist ideas supports all of the teaching behaviors outlined in the Brooks's listing but deviates from a purist belief system on one significant point. I believe it is possible to have students initiate the search for knowledge, discover connections, and construct personal conceptual frameworks within the context of an articulated core content curriculum. The key, as the Brooks's booklet stated, is how the teacher frames the assignments. Is the area under study framed by open-ended "guiding questions" that engage the students' interest and intellect?

Students do not always need to decide on the problems for study, although they should have opportunities to do so. The currently popular "project approach" is an example of the purist constructivist philosophy in action. Students decide on or are given by the teacher a problem, issue, concept, or topic to pursue. The questions for study are open-ended and engage students in the search and construction of knowledge. My problem with using this open project-as-you-go approach is that it fails to address the need for a developmental core content curriculum. The articulation of a core content curriculum and expected learnings appears antithetical, in the purist perspective, to the processes of constructing and creating knowledge.

I believe, however, that students need to balance the acquisition of conceptually based content learnings and the development of lifelong processing skills. Teachers need to know some of the key generalizations that students will discover as they work with units of study. If teachers do not have these key learnings in mind as they facilitate the students' search for knowledge, then how can they know which questions to ask to stimulate deeper thought?

Suppose that Mr. Jackson has engaged his high school students in a unit on the concept of persuasion. The theme of the unit is "Media as a Persuasive Force in American Society." Students have brainstormed many questions to guide their search for knowledge: Is the media a positive or negative force in society? How do the media affect public opinion? How are the media controlled? What is the role of the media in a society?

Mr. Jackson begins the unit by finding out the student conceptions of persuasion. As they begin searching for answers and debating positions, Mr. Jackson uses effective questions to challenge the students to mentally rise above the many examples of media persuasion. He wants them to discover the deeper ideas or generalizations related to the concept of persuasion. If he has not taken his own thinking to this level, then students will end their learning with simplistic answers.

For example, a simple response to the question, "How does the media affect public opinion?" might be answered "by using propaganda techniques to sway thinking." The teacher continues to question, "How? Why? When? Is this good or bad?"

When students are given opportunities to deal with life-relevant questions, problems, and issues, they feel a need to know. They develop analytical and critical thinking skills as they research, probe, dialogue, and defend positions. A particularly effective strategy asks students to take one position on an issue and then defend the polar position to gain insight into varying perspectives.

One of the problems with traditional content curriculum is that it usually fails to make the significant connections to events and trends of the day. The textbook study is dry, dull, and lacks relevance for the student. The challenge for teachers is to help bring meaning to the students' learning.

One key to meaningfulness is to teach to the lessons that transfer through time, using events and content as examples rather than end products of the learnings. Another key is to help students find the connections between past and present events. A third suggestion is to apply the teaching behaviors of a constructivist philosophy. Students who are motivated to take responsibility in the search for knowledge will see greater relevance in the content under study.

If there were one single factor that would revolutionize education and bring success for all children, I believe it would be the constructivist notion that students who are motivated to take responsibility for their own learning will be successful learners. But to bring about this situation, we would need to change many traditional beliefs and practices in education:

- Teachers would need to forget the bell-shaped curve and believe that all children can and should be successful learners.

- The deficit model of grading developmental processes would have to go. The new paradigm would celebrate success as students move along the continuum in reading, writing, thinking, communicating, drawing, dramatizing, or any other developing process.

♦ The pursuit of trivia would be replaced by curricula that hold meaningfulness or importance for students.

♦ Teachers would need to continue the development of personal capacities in critical and creative thinking to challenge and motivate their students to even higher levels of knowing and performing.

♦ Curriculum and assessment would have to move from bits of study to coherent, in-depth, and integrated units of study. The big ideas would be the focus for content instruction because they force the intellect to integrate conceptual and concrete thoughts to deepen understanding.

♦ Teachers would know when to lead and when to follow in supporting each child's journey to self-responsibility.

♦ The current trend to have students (and teachers) self-reflect on their work according to defined criteria and standards would need to continue.

Excellence in the Basic Skills for All

I am going to say it. The most important job of the kindergarten, first-grade, and second-grade teachers is to ensure that every child can read, write, listen, speak, think, create, and compute. If the learning environment for these process skills is positive and supportive, then the students will be successful. Success will engender a healthy esteem. It does little good to spend half a day on self-esteem activities if the child feels like a failure every time he or she looks at a book. The time is better spent on building literacy and fostering individual creative expression. Self-esteem is nurtured at school through the ongoing positive interactions between the child and the teacher and between the child and classmates. Self-esteem building is not a 15-minute program four times a week.

Children who are not academically successful in the primary grades usually fall farther and farther behind as they proceed through the school. With a 30% drag at the primary level, it is no surprise that we have a 30% drop-out rate in high school.

Primary grade teachers, like their colleagues at the other levels, have been affected by increasing curricular and societal demands. They feel (and sometimes are) compelled to teach every topic and every special program, from tarantulas to teeth. But the reality is that these teachers will not be able to meet the needs of all of their developing learners if they aren't freed from the overdemands on their classroom time. Add to the heavy curriculum the interruptions caused by intercom announcements and assemblies (a schoolwide problem), and we have a serious time problem.

Students apply literacy skills in the context of content-based curricula. Teachers at the primary level should be allowed to teach to broad-based units of study in social studies and science and then apply the process skills within the integrated units. Art, music, and literature can fit into these units according to the concept and theme under study. Health can fit into integrated science-based units. Mathematics has application across all fields of study. By teaching to broad units of study, teachers will have more time to meet the needs of individual students and ensure their success.

At the primary level, the teachers must directly teach students the process skills of reading, writing, and so on. *Teach directly* means focused daily instruction and opportunities for application, with the critical skills necessary for successful performance. Critical skills in reading aren't the hundreds of microskills that used to fill up the front of teachers' manuals, but they are the essential components for being able to decode words, read fluently, gain meaning, and construct knowledge. This instruction is time-consuming and challenging because of the beginning development of our littlest learners.

STIRRING THE HEART AND SOUL

Joanna was in the 11th grade. Her grandparents were survivors of the Holocaust. She wanted to share their story with her classmates as her English project but knew that a simple retelling would not convey the depth of pain, degradation, and grief that spun their world in the concentration camps. Joanna spent hours talking with her grandparents, internalizing their thoughts, fears, anger, and hopes as they recounted the terrible years.

Joanna searched for the Holocaust videos that showed families being herded onto trains traveling to annihilation. She pieced film clips together to build a montage of images—fearful children clinging to mothers; husbands, wives, and babies crying as they were separated; faces of questioning, then pain; smoke paving a trail toward the heavens; and sunken eyes and gaunt bodies hanging onto fences like skeletons left behind.

On the day of the class presentation, Joanna portrayed her grandmother as a young teenage girl, reliving the Holocaust as she had experienced it. As the video silently rolled through the stirring scenes, Joanna sat beside the monitor and poured out the story of loss and grief, of pain and fear, of hatred and hope.

The students sat quietly, riveted on the emotional performance. Questions hung in the air waiting to be discussed: "How could humans treat other humans in this way?" "How do people find the strength to survive when their families are destroyed?" "Could this happen again?"

Joanna stirred her classmates. They felt personally involved in the human story. As a finale to the presentation, Joanna introduced her grandparents to the class. They shared how they had moved on to rebuild their lives and ended with a plea, "Never forget the lessons of the Holocaust. Be always on the lookout for man's inhumanity to man, whether it be on your street or in a far corner of the world."

Joanna's presentation stimulated a general discussion of contemporary examples of man's inhumanity to one another. Students looked to the deeper reasons underlying the acts of inhumanity, such as fear, ignorance, and prejudice. They talked of the ramifications of inhumane acts and considered the question, "How 'civilized' is man?"

Feeling Teachers for Feeling Students

Joanna's teacher encouraged his students to express their passion for the subject matter in their presentations. He modeled enthusiasm for thoughts, ideas, and knowledge. Whether the subject under discussion engendered empathy, anger, joy, or pride, the teacher demonstrated the role of emotion. Joanna could have told the students her grandparents' story as if she were reading an essay, but the students would not have experienced their pain. They soon would have forgotten the lessons. When feelings are tapped in a nonthreatening environment, learning can be enhanced.

Teachers as a group are caring individuals who reach out to each child, intent on fostering academic, social, and emotional development. They recognize that the child personality is a fragile work in progress. They manage their own emotional lives privately and focus in school on supporting each child in myriad ways:

- ◆ Modeling values and ethics—positive enthusiasm, empathy, reason, dialogue in conflict, honesty, and caring

- ◆ Knowing and connecting interpersonally with each child—asking each one about their thoughts, activities, and opinions

- ◆ Supporting risk taking—encouraging each child to try, even if they fail, and setting an environment of trust and belief in abilities

- ◆ Building on success—valuing quality effort and praising growth

- ◆ Providing clear directions and expectations—setting the stage for quality learning

- ◆ Allowing and planning for different patterns of learning—getting out the magnifying glass to read the work of the gifted writer who discovered that by writing microscopically, one could get more thoughts on a page

- ◆ Seeing the giftedness in the perceived problem children—the "verbal motormouth," the "graffiti artist," the "takeover leader," and the "social butterfly"

When teachers delight in the uniqueness of children, they come to know each child well. They take time to find out a child's likes and dislikes, their interests and questions. They look for the gift that each child brings and take opportunities to fan the ember into flame. They see in the shy boy a desire to lead and in the crude drawing of a little girl an unusual expression of deep emotion. They mention their observations and provide opportunities, guidance, and encouragement as the children realize they have gifts to develop.

In secondary schools—where students shuffle from class to class in 50-minute intervals, and bells fragment subjects, discussions, thinking, and learning—teachers have little time to discover the unique gifts of students. With up to 150 students per day flowing in and out, the first day's greeting, "I want to get to know you," becomes a major task.

Some secondary schools have restructured the use of time, personnel, and curriculum to solve the problems of too much to teach, too little time, and too many lost teenagers. Schools-within-a-school divide the student population and assign them to a multidisciplinary team of teachers. They plan a curriculum that can be offered in longer blocks of time so that students do not have to change classes every hour. Each teacher takes responsibility for personally connecting with an assigned group of students so that they have someone to turn to with questions or for help.

As teachers have more time with students in class, they are more aware of students who need help and draw on resources to assist. The school has open communication channels with community agencies and calls for their help when necessary. Parents are contacted when a child is having trouble in school, and joint efforts prevent growing despair.

In some schools, the same group of teachers keeps their assigned students for more than 1 year. This allows a greater bond of understanding and respect to develop between students and teachers. When they enter school in the fall, students pick up where they left off, and time is not lost while new teachers assess what the students know.

Many elementary schools are also keeping a group of students with one teacher for multiple years. This practice, called *looping,* provides greater security for the child and allows the teacher to know each child personally. A teacher may have first and second graders in his or her classroom. When the second graders move on after 2 years, the teacher "loops" back and picks up a new group of first graders to add to the returning second-year students.

Elementary teachers have always believed in nurturing the development of each child, but some feel that even a full year with a child does not provide enough time to find and foster his or her unique talents and abilities. These teachers also desire the extended years with a child to provide a smooth transition and ongoing development of their educational program.

Finally, keeping a group of students for multiple years allows students to know their teacher as a social being with dreams, interest, and talents. In a classroom that stirs the head, heart, and soul, the teacher interacts positively with students. This teacher is passionate about learning and conveys the excitement to students.

Stimulating the Creative Spirit

When we talk of a passion for learning that stirs the heart and soul, we talk of a creative spirit—minds that are eager to create deliver with enthusiasm. Just as we provide students with opportunities to dialogue to gain insight into the meaning of content, so must we provide opportunities for students to create and evaluate through various forms of artistic expression.

Eliott Eisner (1994), in *The Educational Imagination,* discusses the idea of connoisseurship in the arts as "knowledgeable perception" and appreciation. Eisner emphasizes that perception and appreciation for a work of art require a "sensory memory" (p. 215). The connoisseur must draw from memory the sensory comparisons made over a range of experiences in a particular mode of expression. Connoisseurship, says Eisner (1994), goes beyond mere recognition of artistic aspects to the perception of subtleties, complexities, and important aspects of a work.

The traditional educational emphases on linguistic and mathematical forms of representation and the generally weak teacher training in art instruction have shortchanged our students. How can we engender the developing qualities of a connoisseur in our children? How can we help them appreciate the subtle stories in their own work? How can we help them use the arts as a form of unique personal expression and as a way of viewing, representing, and thinking?

In *Frames of Mind,* Howard Gardner (1993) provides a valuable service to children in calling for educational valuing of multiple forms of intelligence. Spatial intelligence, expressed in part through the arts, is one form of intelligence described by Gardner. But simply providing more standardized "art activities"—colored cutout bunnies with cotton ball tails or copy paper snowflakes to frame the bulletin board—won't develop the arts intelligence to the level of subtle nuance and expression.

When students use the skills of connoisseurship to assess the work in their creative products, whether it be a piece of pottery, a dance, a visual display, or a musical presentation, they expand their intelligence by integrating technical, sensory, emotional, and interpretive ways of knowing. This unique and complex response values and supports the developing mind.

In his latest book, *The Disciplined Mind,* Gardner (1999) makes a powerful case for maintaining the integrity of the various subject area disciplines in education:

> Education cannot fit every student with a full set of lenses; indeed, we are doomed to fail if we aim to make each youngster into a historian, a biologist, or a composer of classical music. Our goal should not be to telescope graduate training but rather to give students access to the "intellectual heart" or "experiential soul" of a discipline. Education succeeds if it furnishes students with a sense of how the world appears to individuals sporting quite different kinds of glasses. (p. 157)

Students who learn how to express their unique thoughts and ideas through multiple modalities and disciplinary perspectives have broadened opportunities for taking personal responsibility in learning. They are not dependent on the linguistic road to independence.

LOVING TO LEARN

The Passionate Learner

Passion—boundless enthusiasm, zeal, interest, excitement . . . the antithesis of boredom. The passionate learner is every teacher's dream. But in a room of 30, we are likely to find a handful of these enthusiasts. What does the passionate learner look like? How can we help all children find interest and excitement in learning?

Passionate learners share their interest and enthusiasm in a variety of ways. You may see a beaming face and glistening eyes as the student proudly holds up his or her work to be admired. You notice intent concentration as a problem is solved, or a piece of work is crafted to quality. Excited talk fills the room as thoughts and ideas are shared between team members making new discoveries. Or you see the introspective child, off in a corner, engrossed in a book on rocks and minerals—a future geologist.

What do these students have in common that qualify them as passionate learners?

♦ *A love of learning*—a realization that information brings interesting ideas and that new information can be connected to prior information to solve problems and make discoveries

♦ *Inquisitive minds*—questioning attitudes that seek to know answers

♦ *Self-worth*—students who care about themselves and value their personal thoughts and ideas

How easy our job would be if all students maintained these qualities throughout their school years. But the reality is that many students fail to hold these attributes for a host of reasons. Perhaps their response to a threatening environment, at home or in school, is to shut down and withdraw. Perhaps they have never discovered the joy in learning.

Teaching is an art of individual prescription. Even though we may at times teach the group, we must know every child and his or her educational needs as an individual. We cannot assume that every child will naturally be a passionate learner, with an inquisitive mind and a healthy self-ethos.

We spend so much time in school focusing on the content we teach. A few students voraciously absorb the information. They have the attributes of the passionate learner. Some students dutifully memorize the required content and enter class with their pencils poised, ready to "go for the silver or bronze." And about a third of the class sit back in their chairs with a glazed look in their eyes, trying to figure

TABLE 8.1 The Passionate Learner Index Chart

Nurtures	*Hinders*
+ 60 Teacher as facilitator of learning	− 50 Occasional sarcasm to disruptive students
+ 50 Support for risk taking	− 80 Deficit model for assessing process development, as in writing
+ 70 Open dialogue; thinking focus	− 30 Too open—unclear structure for the constructivist philosophy
+ 80 Cooperative learning	− 20 Letter grade and time-driven evaluations
+ 90 Valuing of all students; interpersonal connecting	− 60 Performances usually written or spoken rather than allowing other modalities such as art, drama, or music
+350 Total	−240 Total

out the easiest way to pass the test with the least amount of effort. Finally, we have the bottom two seat-warmers, who find school so excruciatingly painful that they count the days to their 16th birthday.

Could we reach more of our children if we assessed the learning environment for its ability to nurture passionate learners? Are there things going on in classrooms that destroy the passion that young children bring to school? I will share some ideas in this regard, but I encourage every teacher to evaluate his or her own classroom and come up with a "Passion for Learning Index." First, list all of the attributes of the learning environment in your classroom that nurture the passionate learner. Then, in a second column, list all of the attributes that hinder the passionate learner.

For each item in the nurture column, assign plus points from 1 to 100, according to impact. Assign minus points to items in the hinder column. The points are your subjective judgment as to the negative or positive impact value of each item. The higher the point value, the greater the positive or negative impact. Total points should not exceed 350 in either column. Table 8.1 provides a sample listing to stimulate thought.

Once the points are assigned to the nurture/hinder items, the Passion for Learning Index can be determined by subtracting the negative points from the positive. In the example provided in Table 8.1, the index is +110. This result is your assessment of how well you nurture the critical qualities found in passionate learners. The higher your score and the closer you come to 350, the more enthusiasm you should see for learning. The teacher in Table 8.1 needs to address some critical aspects to raise the score. This Passion for Learning Index can also be determined for your school as a whole by doing the exercise as a total staff.

Now comes the important step. What are you going to do about your negative scores? Develop your action plan, implement your strategies for change, and monitor the results by watching those passionate learners come to life!

A Challenge to Teachers and Parents

Most children are naturally inquisitive. You can see it in their eyes at a year of age. They study their environment, and you notice the thoughtfulness as they see a live kitten for the first time. Their interest is sparked, and they toddle on chubby little legs after the vanishing ball of fur—eager to grab the strange little creature and examine it more closely.

The responsibility to nurture curiosity is a challenging task. It means being patient with the pesky questions that always seem too complicated to answer: "Where do babies come from?" "Why are leaves green?" "Where did my grandpa go?"

It means expanding the experience base of the child—reading books together, traveling, hiking the nature trails, talking, sharing, laughing, playing—using all of the senses to interact with the environment and to construct conceptual perspectives.

It means positively affirming children's ideas and efforts as they explore new territory. It means realizing that children are composed of many parts—minds, hearts, emotions, and bodies—all developing toward an integrated whole. It means continually stirring the head, heart, and soul and loving each child so that they love themselves.

SUMMARY

Teachers and parents are partners. They share the job of nurturing the head, heart, and soul of a child. In their own ways, they contribute to the development of self-esteem, confidence, and the important belief in self. They look for the child's strengths and gifts and build on each successful try. They ensure competence in the basic skills of schooling and provide experiences that continually expand what the child knows and can do.

Teachers design the environment for learning. Control-oriented structures are being replaced by busy, purposeful settings where students take increasing responsibility for constructing knowledge.

New skills beckon teachers to workshops and conferences. They realize that preparing students for the future is as complex as the future itself. Teachers of today must use higher-level thinking, processing vast amounts of information related to the students they teach, the abstract and essential learnings of content, and the most effective instructional strategies for each situation. A teacher's organized mind brings clarity to complexity and focus to an educational vision.

Children who love to learn do so with their head, hearts, and souls. Teachers who have a passion for teaching and learning and a keen interest in the development of each child engage students in wanting to know—to explore questions and issues that extend from their world.

Loving to learn is a gift. In some, it is a natural quest of an inquisitive mind. In others, it is an undiscovered well, covered over with untapped talent. Creating a love of learning means discovering a wellspring of talent, supporting the flow of energy, and celebrating success along the way.

I invite you to share the gift and the secret of loving to learn—stirring the head, heart, and soul.

Resource A

ALTERNATE UNIT FORMAT – A

Course: Unit Theme _____

Instructor _____

Length of Unit _____

Conceptual Lens:

Key Topics/ Concepts and Subconcepts	Enduring Understandings (Generalizations)	Guiding Questions	Critical Content/ Key Facts (Know)	Skills (Do)	Instructional Activities and Resources	Assessments

ALTERNATE UNIT FORMAT – B

Subject _____

Instructor _____

Length of Unit _____

Unit Theme:

Conceptual Lens:

Critical Content (key topics, concepts, facts):

Generalizations:

Guiding Questions:

Suggested Activities:

Skills:

Performance Task(s):

Other Assessments:

Resources/Tools:

Resource B

The Wisconsin *Guide to Curriculum Planning in Art Education* (Wisconsin Department of Public Education, 1995) presents a nice summary of key concepts in the visual arts. If we look at a concept as being timeless, universal, abstract, and represented by different examples sharing common attributes, then we can consider elements and principles of design and the elements and principles of artistic conception as being concepts representing the various levels of generality, abstractness, and complexity.

The macroconcepts of "artistic conception" provide a set of conceptual lenses for evaluating the quality of artistic content and form. The Wisconsin art guide suggests some of these broad concepts that are key characteristics of art evaluation in this culture:

♦ Authenticity—the degree to which the work of art is an authentic statement springing from the combined knowledge, skills, experiences, and attitudes of the artist

♦ Integrity—the internal consistency of the artwork that expresses the artist's recognized style or "voice"

♦ Innovation—in studio arts, the degree to which the work differs from work done by other artists or from earlier works by the same artist

♦ Insight—a quality in a work of art that causes people to realize something about the world or themselves that had previously gone unnoticed

The principles and elements of design are the perceptual tools shaping the visual forms of artistic expression (Wisconsin *Guide to Curriculum Planning in Art Education*, 1995, p. 95).

The Wisconsin guide shares some of the most common principles—the broader concepts associated with the form given to artistic content:

Unity	Variety
Balance	Harmony
Repetition	Contrast
Gradation	Dominance

The elements of design are the specific discipline-based concepts that provide the language for discussing art. The following are some of the most common elements:

Line	Shape
Form	Color
Pattern	Texture
Direction	Value

Christina Fitzgerald, a teacher from Palmdale School District in Palmdale, California, offers the macro- and microconcepts for drama shown in Table B.1. Each macroconcept can serve as an integrating or conceptual lens on the more specific microconcepts. The microconcepts provide the language and content for exploring and evaluating the macroconcepts.

Music also has macro- and microconcepts to structure the discipline. The set of concepts shown in Table B.2 was drawn from the music curriculum at Meridian School District, Meridian, Idaho. The microconcepts supply the language for experiencing and evaluating the macrolevel ideas.

The concepts shown in Table B.4 for physical education are a combination of suggestions from Elizabeth Shawver and Michelle Verdon from Davenport, Iowa, and the Physical Education Curriculum Committee from Meridian, Idaho. Can you reorganize these concepts under the appropriate macroconcept headings?

The National Research Council (1996) suggests 10 integrating or macro-concepts as conceptual lenses for the content of science (see Table B.5). These are called *integrating concepts* because they can be applied across the life, earth, and physical science disciplines and lead to the broadest conceptual ideas for explaining our lives and universe. In other words, the macroconcepts can be applied

TABLE B.1 Drama Concepts

Macroconcepts				
Character	*Movement*	*Voice*	*Theme*	*Design*
Microconcepts				
Physical	Body position	Tone	Culture	Style
Personality	Action/reaction	Pitch	Conflict	Meaning
Background	Purpose	Size	Time	Mood
Relationship	Order	Quality	Perspective	Structure
Conflict	Influence	Dialect	Beliefs/values	Function
Motivation	Angle	Patterns	Choices	Expression
Change/growth	Line	Expression	Influence	Feeling
Obstacle	Balance	Articulation	Diversity	Symbol
Wants/needs	Timing	Pronunciation	Identity	Realism
Habits	Space	Beat/pause	Power	Selective realism
Feeling/emotion	Logic	Breathing	Destruction	Setting
Type/role	Physical expression	Diction	Innocence	Costume
Purpose	Direction	Emphasis	Isolation	Lighting

SOURCE: Christina Fitzgerald, Antelope Valley Union High School District, Palmdale, California. Used with permission.

across all of the microconcepts. The microconcepts are a random set of concepts drawn from the national science standards (National Research Council, 1996). Notice that these microconcepts could be structured further according to their levels of generality, complexity, and abstractness.

The National Council for the Social Studies (1994) uses a set of eight conceptual "themes" that are actually a set of macroconcepts for the different disciplines of social studies (see Table B.6). Each set of macroconcepts emphasizes a different discipline of the social studies.

TABLE B.2 Music Concepts

Macroconcepts		
Aesthetics	Expression	Performance
Microconcepts		
Rhythm	Rhythm	Rhythm
Melody	Melody	Melody
Harmony	Harmony	Harmony
Timbre	Timbre	Timbre
Form	Form	Form
Dynamics	Dynamics	Dynamics
Articulation	Articulation	Articulation
Tempo	Tempo	Tempo
Text	Text	Text
Mood	Mood	Mood
Culture	Culture	Culture

SOURCE: Meridian Joint School District No. 2, Meridian, Idaho. Used with permission.

TABLE B.3 Health Concepts

Macroconcepts		
Physical wellness	Mental/emotional wellness	Social health
Microconcepts		
Disease/disorder	Relationships	Relationships
Nutrition	Feelings	Communication
Exercise	Behaviors	Family/community
Safety	Rights	Coping skills
Choices	Responsibilities	Needs
Responsibility	Stress	Interdependence
Abuse/neglect	Coping skills	Conflict resolution
Change/growth	Self-esteem	Rights/responsibilities
Sexuality	Anxiety	Support resources
Safety	Needs	Lifestyles
Life cycle	Conflict resolution	
	Choices	
	Symptoms/signs	
	Lifestyle	
	Anger management	

SOURCE: Adapted from Health Curriculum, Meridian Joint School District No. 2, Meridian, Idaho. Used with permission.

TABLE B.4 Physical Education Concepts

Space	Speed	Motion
Movement	Strength	Range
Angle	Endurance	Force/power
Action/reaction	Patterns	Behaviors
Energy	Cooperation	Weight transfer
Flexibility	Conflict	Growth/development
Physical fitness	Motor fitness	Locomotion
Balance	Teamwork	Cooperation

SOURCE: Elizabeth Shawver and Michelle Verdon, Davenport Public Schools, Davenport, Iowa, and the Meridian Public Schools, Physical Education Curriculum Committee, Meridian, Idaho. Used with permission.

TABLE B.5 Science Concepts

Macroconcepts				
Systems *Order*	*Evidence* *Models*	*Change* *Constancy*	*Evolution* *Equilibrium*	*Form* *Function*
Microconcepts				
Environment	Properties	Matter	Balance	Living things
Entropy	Conductivity	Energy	Heredity	Natural/ constructed
Relative distance	Similarities/ differences	Transfer	Ecosystem	Organism
Population	Fission/fusion	Waves	Habitat	Cells
Patterns	Cycles	Motion	Position	Organs
Behavior	Waves	Force/power	Regulation	Diversity
Transfer	Traits	Conservation	Survival	Density
Interaction	Erosion	Mutation	Behavior	Conduction
Reproduction	Weathering	Adaptation	Natural selection	Convection
Niche	Fossils	Disorder	Extinction	Bonding

SOURCE: National Research Council (1996). *National Science Education Standards*. Washington, DC: National Academy Press.

TABLE B.6 Social Studies Concepts

Macroconcepts

Culture	Time, Continuity, Change	People, Places, Environments	Individual Development and Identity
Individuals, Groups, Institutions	Power, Authority, Governance	Production, Distribution, Consumption	Civic Ideals

Microconcepts

Culture	Role/status	Leadership	Freedom
Similarities/differences	Patterns	Government	Equality
Perspective	Conflict/ cooperation	Limits	Citizenship
Behavior	Traditions	Transportation	Policy
Identity	Laws/rules	Communication	Supply/demand
Needs/wants	Interdependence	Groups/institutions	Incentives
Time	Common good	Origin	System
Change/continuity	Rights/ responsibilities	Ethics/values and beliefs	Barter
Location/place	Environment	Customs	Exchange
Space/regions	Power	Influence	Markets
Resources	Order	Justice	Consumption

SOURCE: National Council for the Social Studies (1994).

Acknowledgments

Joint School District No. 2
Meridian, Idaho
Director of Curriculum
Dr. Linda Clark

Joint School District Number 2
Meridian, Idaho
Physical Education Committee
Physical Education Concepts

David Moser—Coordinator

Jeanie Yancey, Mary McPherson Elementary

Dawnetta Earnest, Spalding Elementary

Danette Lansing, Eagle Hills Elementary

Kay Maffey, Andrus Elementary

Ann Pardew-Peck, Joplin Elementary

Diane Sanders, Ridgewood Elementary

Erin Mackay-Brown, Chaparral Elementary

Randy Thomas, Eagle Middle School

Winnie Morrison, Lowell Scott Middle School

Jennie Fowler, Eagle Middle School

Kip Crofts, Eagle High School

Joint School District Number 2
Meridian, Idaho
Health Education Committee
Health Education Concepts

Betty Tomtan—Coordinator

Gail Correia, Chief Joseph Elementary School

Mary Thomas, Joplin Elementary School

Carolyn Stoval, Eagle Elementary School

Cindy Hall, Spalding Elementary School

Kathy Fink, Lake Hazel Middle School

Khristie Bair, Eagle Middle School

Wendy Spiers, Eagle Middle School

Sandra Gauss, Eagle High School; Academy

Laura Joki, Crossroads Elementary

Lynn Fugar, Meridian High School

Helyn Haase, Eagle Academy

Joint School District Number 2
Music Education Committee
Music Curriculum Excerpt

Linda Berg—Coordinator

Trudi Cochrane, Joplin Elementary

Cynthia Cook, Frontier Elementary

Frank Eychaner, Centennial High School

Greg Felton, Lowell Scott Middle School

Carol Friedli, Frontier Elementary

Diane Johnson, Mary McPherson Elementary

Carole McFadden, Pioneer Elementary

Barb Oldenburg, Lake Hazel Middle School

Corlyss Peterson, M. McPherson Elementary

Billie Jo Premoe, Frontier Elementary

Janet Smith, Chief Joseph Elementary

Joint School District Number 2
Mathematics Education Committee
Mathematics Curriculum Excerpt

Cindy Sisson—Coordinator

Heather Borchert, Lake Hazel Middle School

Lynette Thueson, Lowell Scott Middle School

Lisa Colon, Eagle Middle School

Dave Warren, Meridian Middle School

Charrie McNelis, Meridian Middle School

Nick Johnson, Meridian Middle School

Linda Pence, Meridian Middle School

Theresa Tooman, Lowell Scottt Middle School

Bonnie McMoran, Lake Hazel Middle School

Bobbie Newbern, Eagle High School

Bob Rois, Meridian High School

Bob Baldwin, Eagle Academy

Bernadette Sexton, Eagle Academy

David Gural, Eagle High School

Julie Kelsen, Meridian High School

Lavon Sanders, Meridian High School

Sheri Brooks, Centennial High School

Tacoma Public Schools
Tacoma, Washington

Visual Arts Curriculum

Director, Curriculum Development
 and Implementation
  Hertica Martin—1998 to present
  Susan Burstad—prior to 1998

Arts Education Facilitator
  Jonathan Acker—1998 to present
  Diane Lister—prior to 1998

Arts Education Consultant for Lessons,
 Materials, and Resources
  Meredith Essex

Arts Education Consultant for
 Curriculum Writing
  Susy Watts

K-8 Visual Arts Education Committee—1998 to present
Anne Tsuneishi
Vicky Corley
Doris Jew
Jon Ketler
Monica Weidman

The Visual Arts Education Committee prior to 1998 laid the groundwork for the final document.

Secondary Visual Arts Education Committee prior to 1998

Gretchen Alden	Sue Kloeppel	Diane Pittman
Sandy DiLoreto	Linnea Knutson	Sondra Spark
Margaret Herd	Chuck Larsen	John Vick
Christine Hill	Kathy Menson	Miguel Villahermosa
Ken Hotsko	Gretchen Mottet	Monica Weidman
Mike James	P. Spencer Norby	Lee Whitehall

Elementary Visual Arts Education Curriculum Committees prior to 1998

Carolyn Barnes	Sue Keene	Pati Powers
Donna Basil	Elise Korsmo Michaels	Renee Rossman
Dick Brown	Gloria Lee	Jona Sasaki
Janice Brownlee	Rachel Lovejoy	Carolyn Shain
Roland Clark	Kathy Martin	Marilyn Thomas-Penney
Mary Dorgan	Mary Anne Mathern	Janet Wainright
Rebecca Herbers	Diane Perkins	Dennis Webster
Sally Jerome	Lyn Powers	Monica Weidman
		Jann Wetsch

Glossary

Benchmarks: Agreed-on developmental mileposts.

Block scheduling: Extended class periods at the secondary school level; intended to allow for curricular coordination or integration of compatible subject areas.

Career paths: Theme-based organizational structure for high schools that facilitates a school-to-work transition plan.

Concept: A mental construct that frames a set of examples sharing common attributes; concepts are timeless, universal, abstract, and broad. Examples: cycles, diversity, interdependence.

Conceptual theme: A unit title that includes a concept. Example: Interdependence in the Amazon rainforest.

Constructivist: A philosophy and methodology for teaching and learning that highlights the student construction of knowledge on a path to learner autonomy.

Cooperative learning: A teaching strategy that groups students in pairs or teams to problem solve, discover, and discuss ideas or investigate topics of interest.

Curriculum: The planned curriculum is an educational response to the needs of society and the individual and requires that the learner construct knowledge, attitudes, values, and skills through a complex interplay of mind, materials, and social interactions.

Curriculum framework: A planning guide for educators that states subject area content and process outcomes in general terms.

Developmentally appropriate: Refers to the match between the learning task and the student's cognitive, social, or physical ability to perform the task successfully.

Generalizations: Two or more concepts stated as a relationship. Enduring understandings; the "big ideas" related to the critical concepts and topics of a subject. Example: Freedom is the basis of democracy.

Indicators: Observable behaviors that reflect a point on a skill or knowledge continuum.

Integrated curriculum: The organization of interdisciplinary or intradisciplinary content under a common, abstract concept such as *interdependence* or *conflict*. Must have a conceptual focus to be integrated.

Interdisciplinary: A variety of disciplines sharing a common focus for study. Must be "integrated."

Intradisciplinary: A single discipline study. Must be "integrated."

Multidisciplinary: A variety of disciplines coordinated to a topic of study; lack a conceptual focus.

Objectives: Specific statements of what you want students to know; specific content or skill focus; measurable, usually by paper-and-pencil test.

Performance assessment: A complex demonstration of content knowledge and performance that is assessed according to a standard and a set of criteria; shows what students know and can do.

Portfolio: A decided collection of student work and self-assessment that is used to showcase excellence or to demonstrate progress on a developmental performance.

Process skills: Internal student abilities that develop in sophistication over time. Examples: Reading, writing, speaking, thinking, drawing, singing, and dramatizing.

Rubric: A multilevel set of criteria to show or measure development in assessing work or performance toward an instructional outcome.

Scoring guide: Another name for rubric.

Standard: An agreed-on definition of quality performance.

Systems thinking: A framework for looking at interrelationships and patterns of change over time (Senge, 1990, 1999); critical for successful school restructuring.

Topical theme: A unit title that does not include a concept. Example: Amazon rainforest.

Tripartite model of curriculum design: A balanced approach to concepts, critical content, and developmental process in teaching and assessment.

References

Arizona Department of Education. (1992). *The Arizona model for vocational/ technological education.* Phoenix, AZ: Author.

Baker, E. L. (1994, January). *The use of performance assessments.* Keynote presentation at the Fourth Annual International Conference on Restructuring Curriculum-Assessment-Teaching for the 21st Century, National School Conference Institute, Phoenix, AZ.

Banks, J. A. (1991). *Teaching strategies for ethnic studies.* Boston: Allyn & Bacon.

Berliner, D., & Biddle, B. (1997). *The manufactured crisis: Myths, fraud, and the attack on American public schools.* New York: Addison-Wesley.

Bloom, B. S., Engelhart, M. D., Furst, E. J., Hill, W. H., & Krathwohl, D. R. (Eds.). (1956). *Taxonomy of educational objectives: The classification of educational goals: Handbook I. Cognitive domain.* New York: David McKay.

Bracey, G. (1998). *The eighth Bracey report on the condition of public education.* Bloomington, IN: Phi Delta Kappan.

Brooks, J. G., & Brooks, M. G. (1993). *The case for constructivist classrooms.* Alexandria, VA: Association for Supervision and Curriculum Development.

Buzan, T. (1996). *Mind map book.* New York: Penguin.

Caine, R. N., & Caine, G. (1991). *Teaching and the human brain.* Alexandria, VA: Association for Supervision and Curriculum Development.

Coles, A. D. (1999). Gallup poll finds Americans committed to public schools. *Education Week, 19*(1), 12.

Cowan, P. A. (1978). *Piaget with feeling: Cognitive, social and emotional dimensions.* New York: Holt, Rinehart & Winston.

David Douglas High School. (2000). *Project stars.* Portland, OR: Portland School District.

Doll, W. E. J. (1986). *Curriculum beyond stability: Schon, Prigogine, Piaget.* Unpublished manuscript.

Doll, W. E. J. (1989). Complexity in the classroom. *Educational Leadership, 47*(1), 65-70.

Drake, S. M. (1998). *Creating integrated curriculum.* Thousand Oaks, CA: Corwin.

Eisner, E. W. (1994). *The educational imagination.* New York: Macmillan.

Erickson, H. L. (1998). *Concept-based curriculum and instruction: Teaching beyond the facts.* Thousand Oaks, CA: Sage.

Florida Department of Education. (1989). *Blueprint for career preparation.* Tallahassee, FL: Author.

Gardner, H. (1993). *Frames of mind: The theory of multiple intelligences.* New York: Basic Books.

Gardner, H. (1999). *The disciplined mind.* New York: Simon & Schuster.

Greider, W. (1997). *One world, ready or not: The manic logic of global capitalism.* New York: Simon & Schuster.

Harste, J. C., & Burke, C. L. (1993, March). *Planning to plan: Supporting inquiry in classrooms.* Paper presented at the Curriculum Planning Workshop on Whole Language, Tacoma, WA.

Hayes-Jacobs, H. (1989). *Interdisciplinary curriculum: Design and implementation.* Alexandria, VA: Association for Supervision and Curriculum Development.

Hayes-Jacobs, H. (1997). *Mapping the big picture: Integrating curriculum and assessment K-12.* Alexandria, VA: Association for Supervision and Curriculum Development.

Kleibard, H. M. (1993). What is a knowledge base, and who would use it if we had one? *Review of Educational Research, 63*(3), 295-303.

Kroll, M., & Paziotopoulos, A. (1995). *Literature circles: Practical strategies for responding to literature.* Darien, IL: Author.

Krueger, J. (1998, March). Reassessing the view that American schools are broken. *Economic Policy Review,* pp. 29-43.

National Council for the Social Studies (NCSS). (1994). *National standards for the social studies.* Washington, DC: Author.

National Council of Teachers of Mathematics. (2000). *Principles and standards for teaching mathematics.* Reston, VA: Author.

National Research Council. (1996). *National science education standards.* Washington, DC: National Academy Press.

Paul, R. W. (1993a). A model for the assessment of higher order thinking. In J. Willsen & A. J. A. Binker (Eds.), *Critical thinking: How to prepare students for a rapidly changing world* (pp. 103-151). Santa Rosa, CA: Foundation for Critical Thinking.

Paul, R. W. (1993b). Using intellectual standards to assess student reasoning. In J. Willsen & A. J. A. Binker (Eds.), *Critical thinking: How to prepare students for a rapidly changing world* (pp. 153-164). Santa Rosa, CA: Foundation for Critical Thinking.

Paulson, F. L., & Paulson, P. R. (1994). *A guide for judging portfolios.* Portland, OR: Multnomah Educational Service District.

Popham, J. (1993, January). *Educational testing in America: What's right, what's wrong?* Keynote presentation at the Third Annual International Conference on Restructuring Curriculum-Assessment-Teaching for the 21st Century, National School Conference Institute, Phoenix, AZ.

Reich, R. B. (1992). *The work of nations.* New York: Vintage.

Report card on for-profit industry still incomplete. (1999). *Education Week, 19*(16), 14-16.

Schmidt, W. H., McKnight, C. C., & Raizen, S. (1997). A splintered vision: An investigation of U.S. science and mathematics education. *U.S. National Research Center for the Third International Mathematics and Science Study (TIMSS)*. Dordrecht/Boston/London: Kluwer Academic Publishers.

Schrag, P. (1997, October). The near-myth of our failing schools. *Atlantic*, pp. 72-80.

Secretary's Commission on Achieving Necessary Skills (SCANS). (1991). *What work requires of schools: A SCANS report for America 2000*. Washington, DC: U.S. Department of Labor, Secretary's Commission on Achieving Necessary Skills.

Senge, P. M. (1990). *The fifth discipline*. New York: Doubleday.

Senge, P. M. (1999). *The dance of change: The challenge of sustaining momentum in learning organizations*. New York: Doubleday.

Silberman, M. (1996). *Active learning: 101 strategies to teach any subject*. Boston: Allyn & Bacon.

Sousa, D. A. (1995). *How the brain learns*. Reston, VA: National Association of Secondary School Principals.

Taba, H. (1966). *Teaching strategies and cognitive functioning in elementary school children* (Cooperative research project). Washington, DC: Office of Education, U.S. Department of Health, Education, and Welfare.

Tapscott, D. (1999, February). Educating the Net generation. *Educational Leadership, 56*(5), 7-11.

Thurow, L. (1993). *Head to head: The coming economic battle among Japan, Europe, and America*. New York: Warner.

Thurow, L. (1999). *Building wealth: New rules for individuals, companies and countries in a knowledge-based economy*. New York: HarperCollins.

United Nations International Children's Emergency Fund (UNICEF). (1993). *The progress of nations*. New York: Author.

United Nations International Children's Emergency Fund (UNICEF). (1999). *United Nations convention on the rights of children* [Online]. Available: www.unicef.org

Valencia, S. W. (1991). Portfolios: Panacea or Pandora's box? In F. L. Finch (Ed.), *Educational performance assessment* (pp. 33-46). Chicago: Riverside.

Vaughn, J. L., & Estes, T. H. (1986). *Reading and reasoning beyond the primary grades*. Boston: Allyn & Bacon.

Wang, M. C., Haertel, G. D., & Walberg, H. J. (1993). Toward a knowledge base for school learning. *Review of Educational Research, 63*(3), 249-294.

Wiggins, G. (1998). *Educative assessment: Designing assessments to inform and improve student performance*. San Francisco: Jossey-Bass.

Wiggins, G., & McTighe, J. (1998). *Understanding by design*. Alexandria, VA: Association for Supervision and Curriculum Development.

Wineburg, S. (1999). Historical thinking and other unnatural acts. *Phi Delta Kappan, 80*(7), 488-499.

Wisconsin Department of Public Education. (1995). *A guide to curriculum planning in art education* (2nd ed.). Milwaukee: Author.

Index

CORWIN
PRESS

The Corwin Press logo—a raven striding across an open book—represents the happy union of courage and learning. We are a professional-level publisher of books and journals for K–12 educators, and we are committed to creating and providing resources that embody these qualities. Corwin's motto is "Success for All Learners."

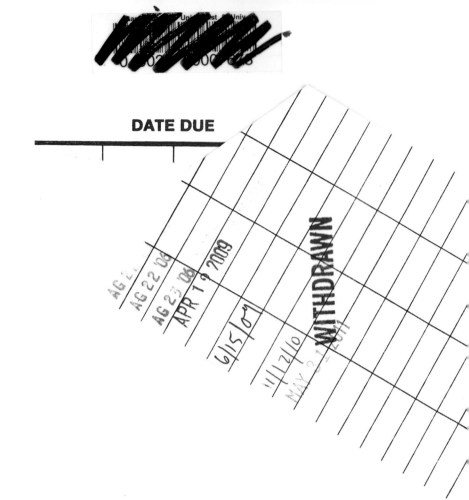